Institutions for the Common Good

The protection of domestic populations by international institutions is both an anomaly and an enduring practice in international relations. It is an anomaly because in a system of sovereign states the welfare of individuals and groups falls outside traditional definitions of state interest. Yet since the evolution of the nation-state system, collectivities of states have sought to protect religious minorities, dynastic families, national minorities, ethnic communities, individual citizens, and refugees. Cronin explains this phenomenon by developing a theory that links international stability with the progress of a cohesive international order. His book examines how states attempt to provide for international stability by creating International Protection Regimes – multilateral institutions designed to protect clearly defined classes of people within sovereign states. It argues that in the aftermath of major systemic changes states try to create international orders by regulating the relationship between governments and their populations, particularly in newly formed and reorganized states.

BRUCE CRONIN is an Assistant Professor of Political Science and Director of the Master's Program in International Relations at the City College of New York. He is the author of *Community under Anarchy: Transnational Identity and the Evolution of Cooperation* (1999), which was awarded the International Studies Association's 2000 Chadwick Alger Prize for the best book on international organization.

D0782705

CAMBRIDGE STUDIES IN INTERNATIONAL RELATIONS

Institutions for the Common Good

International protection regimes in international society

Bruce Cronin

City College of New York

CAMBRIDGE
UNIVERSITY PRESS

PUBLISHED BY THE PRESS SYNDICATE OF THE UNIVERSITY OF CAMBRIDGE
The Pitt Building, Trumpington Street, Cambridge, United Kingdom

CAMBRIDGE UNIVERSITY PRESS
The Edinburgh Building, Cambridge, CB2 2RU, UK
40 West 20th Street, New York, NY 10011–4211, USA
477 Williamstown Road, Port Melbourne, VIC 3207, Australia
Ruiz de Alarcón 13, 28014 Madrid, Spain
Dock House, The Waterfront, Cape Town 8001, South Africa

http://www.cambridge.org

First published 2003

Printed in the United Kingdom at the University Press, Cambridge

Typeface Palatino 10/12.5 pt.   *System* LaTeX 2_ε [TB]

A catalogue record for this book is available from the British Library

Library of Congress cataloguing-in-publication data
Cronin, Bruce, 1957–
Institutions for the common good: international protection regimes in
international society / Bruce Cronin.
   p.   cm. – (Cambridge studies in international relations; 93)
Includes bibliographical references and index.
ISBN 0 521 82480 X (hb.) – ISBN 0 521 53187 X (pb.)
1. Minorities – Civil rights.   2. Ethnic groups – Civils rights.   3. Civil rights.
4. International organization.   5. International relations.   6. National state.
I. Title.   II. Series.
JF1061.C76   2003
341.4'81 – dc21   2003051545

ISBN 0 521 82480 X hardback
ISBN 0 521 53187 X paperback

Contents

Acknowledgments

I gratefully acknowledge those who acted as critical readers for various parts of the manuscript while it was in preparation: Michael Barnett, Barry Buzan, the late Joseph Lepgold, Jon Pevehouse, and Jack Snyder. I also appreciate the help of the staff of the OSCE High Commissioner on National Minorities during my research for chapter 5. I specifically wish to acknowledge the assistance of John Packer, Walter Kemp, Carl Salicath, and the High Commissioner, Max Van der Stoel. Finally, I appreciate the financial support of the Wisconsin Alumni Research Fund, whose grants paid for much of my fieldwork.

1 Introduction: international relations theory and the common good

The protection of foreign populations by collectivities of states is both an anomaly and an enduring practice in international relations.[1] It is an anomaly because in a system of sovereign states, each state is not only the final judge of its own interests, it is also required to provide the means to attain them.[2] Most political leaders recognize that their primary responsibility is toward their own citizens, and they tend to pursue this with extreme prejudice. Protecting groups and individuals within other states traps foreign policy officials into diverting resources from their own security needs without providing a significant domestic political benefit. Thus, the welfare of foreign populations falls well outside traditional definitions of state interest. Moreover, the institution of sovereignty is supposed to limit the jurisdiction of international organizations to regulating the relations *between* states, not *within* them. This has long been maintained through norms of coexistence, diplomatic practice, and international law, all of which are largely designed to shield states from interference in their internal affairs by outside powers.[3]

Yet international protection is also an enduring practice in diplomatic history. Since the evolution of the nation-state system in the sixteenth and seventeenth centuries, collectivities of states have alternately sought to protect religious minorities, dynastic families, national minorities,

---

[1] By foreign, I am simply referring to individuals and groups who are not citizens, subjects, or rulers of the states offering the guarantees.

[2] See Robert Art and Robert Jervis, "The Meaning of Anarchy," in Robert Art and Robert Jervis, eds., *International Politics: Anarchy, Force, Political Economy and Decisionmaking*, 2nd edition (Boston: Little, Brown and Company, 1985), p. 3.

[3] See, for example, Gerhard von Glahn, *Law Among Nations: An Introduction to Public International Law* (Boston: Allyn and Bacon, 1996), p. 133 and Article 3/7 of the UN Charter.

ethnic communities, individual citizens, and refugees. This practice has not been random. Rather, during particular eras certain classes of people have been specifically singled out for protection while others have been consciously ignored. In fact, international commitments to protect groups or individuals within states have been an important component of every major diplomatic settlement since the Peace of Westphalia in 1648. While the institutional mechanisms for implementing these guarantees have varied in both strength and depth, in each case the participating states considered the commitments to be general obligations.

The open-ended nature of these protections suggests a level of commitment that usually is only found in military alliances. Historically the commitments made to target populations have tended to assume the form of general guarantees applied to entire classes of people. While targets have sometimes been selective and enforcement inconsistent, states have established elaborate protection mechanisms through international institutions such as the Holy Alliance, the League of Nations, the Council of Europe, the Organization for Security and Cooperation in Europe, and the United Nations. In each case, they committed themselves to protecting defined classes of people within countries far from their borders.

At the same time, there is no easily apparent conceptual thread that connects the choice of target populations; sometimes the protected group is a ruling class while at others it is a political community. For example, the protection of religious minorities was singled out in the multilateral treaties of Osnabrück and Munster (1648), that ended the Thirty Years War. Catholic and Protestant minorities were guaranteed the right to privately practice their religion without interference from the king, and public discrimination based on religion was prohibited within all realms.[4] No other domestic group was afforded such protection. Following the end of the Napoleonic Wars in 1815, the Holy Alliance extended guarantees toward all recognized European dynastic families but not to the religious minorities within their realms.[5] The existence of national minorities was barely even acknowledged.

The protected group changed again after World War I, when the League of Nations assumed the responsibility for enforcing a wide range of treaties which extended recognition and protection to *national*

[4] For specific provisions see Clive Parry, ed., "Treaty of Osnabrück," in *The Consolidated Treaty Series, vol. 1, 1648–1649* (Dobbs Ferry, NY: Oceana, 1969), Article V, sections 11–44.
[5] See Harold Temperley, *The Foreign Policy of Canning, 1822–1827: England, the Neo-Holy Alliance and the New World* (London: G. Bell and Sons, 1925).

2

(defined as ethnic) minorities.[6] Religious minorities were considered only in so far as their religion formed the basis of a national identity. A generation later, the Council of Europe ignored national minorities in favor of individual citizens as a target class, through the adoption of several broad-based and legally binding human rights conventions and protocols.[7] The signatories agreed not only to establish basic standards, but also to create binding adjudication for enforcement. More recently, with the political and diplomatic integration of Eastern and Western European states the aftermath of the Cold War, the Organization for Security and Cooperation in Europe committed itself to protect the identity and corporate integrity of ethnic communities.[8]

The recurrence of these practices over time suggests that they constitute a definable form of institutional cooperation, which I call International Protection Regimes (IPRs). IPRs are multilateral institutions designed to protect clearly defined classes of people within sovereign states.[9] They are initiated by either international organizations or coalitions of states, whose members make general commitments to defend the target population against violations either by their governments or other segments of their societies.

Any explanation for this phenomenon must confront not only the apparent contradiction between theory and practice, as suggested in the opening paragraphs, but also the concurrent duality of a recurring pattern (international protection) and a secular change (the identity of the protected group). This book does so by examining why collectivities of states make general commitments to protect foreign populations and how they decide which groups to protect. It offers an explanation for this practice by advancing a theory of cooperation that is based on a shared normative and political vision of international order. Its fundamental starting point is not the maximization of individual utility by autonomous actors in a competitive system, although this certainly

[6] See Inis Claude, *National Minorities: An International Problem* (New York: Greenwood Press, 1955), pp. 17–20.
[7] See the Council of Europe, "European Convention on Human Rights and Fundamental Freedoms," Rome, November 4, 1950 and its five protocols: Paris, March 20, 1952; Strasbourg, May 6, 1963 (2 separate protocols); Strasbourg, September 16, 1963; and Strasbourg, January 20, 1966.
[8] See, for example, Conference on Security and Cooperation in Europe, *The Challenges of Change: Helsinki Summit Declaration*, Helsinki, 10 July, 1992, Section II.
[9] An institution is multilateral when it is based on generalized principles of conduct that apply without regard to the particularistic interests of the parties or the strategic exigencies that may exist in a particular occurrence. John Ruggie, "Multilateralism: The Anatomy of an Institution," *International Organization*, vol. 46, no. 2 (1992), p. 571.

explains many forms of statecraft. Rather, the problematique is how a self-selected group of political actors in an international society attempt to maintain a cohesive political order by resolving its internal tensions and adapting to a changing environment. Such an order helps these actors to promote their preferred political values over competing ones and freezes the existing distribution of resources and authority within the region or system.

I begin with the premise that political leaders not only come to the international stage with preferences for particular outcomes, they also bring with them a vision of politics that reflects various forms of knowledge, beliefs, and values about the nature of security, justice, and order. These attributes help to structure their choices and determine what kinds of relationships they wish to create and maintain. From this perspective international politics is as much about defining the structures and rules of interaction as it is about achieving specific material benefits or gaining strategic advantage.

I argue that international protection regimes are part of a class of institutions that are designed to promote the "common good" for a collectivity of states.[10] Unlike functional institutions that seek to provide consumable benefits to their participants, "institutions for the common good" are concerned with the preservation and general welfare of the international order itself. Their development requires a consensus among a group of core states around a basic set of political and normative principles. Since these types of institutions do not allocate resources among individual members, concerns with relative gains are muted; this allows states to make general commitments that apply in unforeseen circumstances. Thus, while these institutions may not provide direct benefits to participating states, they help to advance the broader goals of an international order by helping to maintain a preferred social or political framework through which states can cooperate and compete on the international stage.

Explaining international protection regimes

Traditionally, scholars have explained patterns of institutional cooperation by state interest, necessity, mutual advantage, and domestic

[10] Institutions are relatively stable collections of practices and rules that define appropriate behavior for specific groups of actors in specific situations. James G. March and Johan P. Olsen, "The Institutional Dynamics of Political Orders," *International Organization*, vol. 52, no. 4 (Autumn 1998), p. 948.

politics. That is, institutions have been presented as arenas for advancing parochial strategic or economic interests,[11] as mechanisms for achieving reciprocal gains,[12] and as transmission belts for projecting domestic politics onto the international field.[13] Each of these approaches is "individualist" in the sense that they attempt to explain cooperation by appealing to characteristics of individual actors (such as their internal preferences or capabilities) within their strategic environments.[14]

Typically, individualist-based theories conceptualize institutions as mechanisms for achieving the optimum allocative efficiency of their participants. While there is some debate over the role of power and coercion in creating them, regimes are considered to be the outcome of bargaining among utility-maximizers. Whether the regimes are imposed by hegemonic powers or negotiated by a group of like-minded states, they represent an attempt to reach interdependent decisions by reconciling diverging and converging interests. From this perspective, the "logic of expected consequences" drives state behavior.[15] Such logic is derived from a rational calculation of costs and benefits. While these benefits may sometimes be long term rather than immediate, political actors clearly expect some type of direct payoff.

Consequently, while this literature is highly varied and covers a wide range of cooperative and collaborative practices, its explanatory power is limited to situations in which political actors seek to achieve direct material benefits that cannot be obtained through unilateral action. Yet, the theoretical and empirical puzzles discussed in the introduction arise precisely because the benefits from making broad commitments to foreign populations in unforeseeable circumstances are not directly consumable by the participating states. Consequently, international protection regimes do not fit individualist models of institutions for several reasons.

---

[11] John Mearsheimer, "The False Promise of International Institutions," in Michael Brown *et al.*, eds., *Theories of War and Peace* (Cambridge, MA: The MIT Press, 1998), p. 339.

[12] Robert Keohane, "A Functional Theory of Regimes," in Stephen Krasner, ed., *International Regimes* (Ithaca: Cornell University Press, 1982).

[13] Andrew Moravcsik, "Explaining International Human Rights Regimes: Liberal Theory and Western Europe," *European Journal of International Relations*, vol. 1 (1993).

[14] I borrow the term "individualist" from James Caporaso in "International Relations Theory and Multilateralism: The Search for Foundations," *International Organization*, vol. 46, no. 3 (Summer 1992).

[15] James G. March and Johan P. Olsen, "The Institutional Dynamics of International Political Orders," in Peter Katzenstein *et al.*, eds., *Exploration and Contestation in the Study of World Politics* (Cambridge, MA: The MIT Press, 2000), pp. 309–11.

First, IPRs are not designed to provide a public good, such as open trade routes or reduced hydrocarbon emissions. Nor are they specifically created to solve collaboration problems such as achieving arms control or providing stable currency convertibility.[16] They do not resolve dilemmas of common aversion or common interest.[17] Unlike collective security systems, protection regimes do not affect utility calculations by linking state security with general commitments to protect territorial integrity and promote nonaggression. And, unlike other types of security regimes, they do not attempt to increase each state's relative safety through mutual restraint and adjustment of military policy. Finally, they differ from other forms of collective intervention in that they are not targeted at particular states, but rather at general classes of states, and, more specifically, at general classes of people within these states.

International protection regimes are particularly challenging for neorealist theories of international relations. In a realist world, states are predisposed toward self-help and parochialism and resist becoming entangled in any commitments or institutions that significantly restrict their freedom of action. Great powers therefore hesitate to get involved in potentially violent situations where their vital interests are not threatened, particularly if this means expending their own political and material resources.[18] Participating in multilateral efforts to guarantee the security of foreign populations both constrains a state's ability to act unilaterally while also tying it to open-ended commitments that could apply in circumstances that may not support its strategic objectives in the future.[19] As a result, a realist foreign policy eschews unnecessary foreign entanglements and avoids taking risks that do not further the welfare of either the state or its citizens.[20]

---

[16] Collaboration problems arise when the pursuit of one's preferred strategy results in suboptimal outcome for all sides. Institutions can help resolve this dilemma by facilitating mutual policy adjustment, extending the shadow of the future and sanctioning defectors. See, for example, Lisa Martin, "The Rational State Choice of Multilateralism," in John G. Ruggie, ed., *Multilateralism Matters: The Theory and Practice of an Institutional Form* (New York: Columbia University Press, 1993), pp. 95–100.

[17] See Arthur Stein, "Coordination and Collaboration: Regimes in an Anarchic World," *International Organization*, vol. 36, no. 2 (Spring 1982).

[18] Mearsheimer, "The False Promise of International Institutions," pp. 356 and 357.

[19] This problem in part underlies the realist opposition to collective security regimes. See, for example, Richard K. Betts, "Systems of Peace or Causes of War?," *International Security*, vol. 17 (1992).

[20] See, for example, Michael Mandelbaum, "Foreign Policy as Social Work," *Foreign Affairs* (January/February 1996), pp. 16–32.

From a realist perspective, protecting foreign populations should also have significant relative gains implications that preclude state involvement.[21] To the extent that protection systems strengthen some political actors at the expense of others, this could undermine the government of a potential ally just as it could fortify that of a potential adversary. Without knowing in advance which powers might benefit from a particular protection system, participating states cannot calculate how the regime will ultimately affect the distribution of political influence and strategic advantage in a given region. Indeed, according to realist logic, states should be more likely to try to enhance their own strategic position by exploiting conflicts between domestic actors than attempting to settle them on the basis of an abstract principle.

According to realist approaches, institutions are forums for acting out power relationships and implementing hegemonic preferences.[22] Therefore, in order to account for IPRs, realist theories would have to establish a clear positive relationship between a hegemonic interest in protecting specific populations and the creation of multilateral regimes that do so. Yet the most we can derive from these theories themselves are *ad hoc* explanations that are based on the particularities of each case. Stephen Krasner argues, for example, that intervention to alter the relations between rulers and subjects has been motivated by a variety of factors, all related to the interests of the intervener.[23] Quite simply, protected groups are objects for the pursuit of powerful states' strategic, economic or ideological interests.

From this perspective, a state or group of states may support a foreign population in order to weaken a target government or disrupt a potential alliance with an adversary. In these types of cases, however, theories based on state power and interest can account only for a particular action, not for a *general* guarantee, particularly one of a multilateral nature. Nor can they account for the recurrence of IPRs over time under very different strategic and geopolitical circumstances.

---

[21] On the relative gains problem in international relations, see Joseph Grieco, "Anarchy and the Limits of Cooperation: A Realist Critique of the Newest Liberal Institutionalism," *International Organization*, vol. 42 (1988) and Kenneth Waltz, *Theory of International Politics* (New York: Random House, 1979).

[22] Mearsheimer, "The False Promise of International Institutions," p. 339.

[23] Stephen Krasner, "Sovereignty and Intervention," in Gene M. Lyons and Michael Mastanduno, eds., *Beyond Westphalia? State Sovereignty and International Intervention* (Baltimore: The Johns Hopkins University Press, 1995). For an application of this argument to human and minority rights protection see Stephen Krasner, *Sovereignty: Organized Hypocrisy* (Princeton: Princeton University Press, 1999), chs. 3 and 4.

Neoliberal theories of institutions can more easily accommodate the idea of a multilateral protection regime. Although the study of regimes has tended to focus primarily on economic and social issues, neoliberal theories do not preclude the possibility of establishing multilateral security institutions.[24] Regime theories show how a convergence of self-interest among states can facilitate cooperation in defined issue areas when independent action would result in pareto-inferior outcomes.[25] They argue that the nature and scope of institutional cooperation reflects the strategic incentives and constraints posed by different types of cooperation problems. In doing so, they try to specify the conditions that can lead to the creation of cooperative institutions by showing how regimes can help states to overcome collective action problems, make commitments more credible and reduce uncertainty and mistrust. In short, neoliberals conceive of institutions as solutions to dilemmas of strategic interaction.[26]

By showing how certain types of institutions can overcome relative gains concerns and fears of cheating, institutionalists address some of the neorealist barriers to establishing a multilateral protection regime. While conceding that few states wish to cede their right to self-help, institutionalists nevertheless argue that in an interdependent world, states will accept limits on their operational sovereignty out of necessity when doing so will increase their effectiveness and provide material benefits.[27] Thus, unlike neorealist theories, liberal institutionalist approaches can account for the bargaining processes that could lead to the creation of a protection regime. So long as the participating states find mutual benefit in protecting the populations of other nations, there are few inherent barriers to creating the regime (though there may well be many practical problems).

Like neorealists, however, institutionalists can not account for the motivation to establish one. In a neoliberal world, states participate in

---

[24] For a dissenting view of this statement see Robert Jervis, "Security Regimes," in Stephen Krasner, ed., *International Regimes* (Ithaca: Cornell University Press, 1983). For a supportive study see Harold Müller, "The Internationalization of Principles, Norms, and Rules by Governments: The Case of Security Regimes," in, Volker Rittberger, ed., *Regime Theory and International Relations* (New York: Oxford University Press, 1993).

[25] See for example Robert Keohane, *After Hegemony: Cooperation and Discord in the World Political Economy* (Princeton: Princeton University Press, 1984).

[26] Robert Keohane, "Multilateralism: An Agenda for Research," *International Journal*, vol. 45 (August 1990).

[27] Robert Keohane, "Sovereignty, Interdependence, and International Institutions," in Linda B. Miller and Michael Joseph Smith, eds., *Ideas and Ideals: Essays on Politics in Honor of Stanley Hoffman* (Boulder: Westview Press, 1993), p. 91.

regimes only to achieve *national* objectives in an environment of perceived international interdependence.[28] Governments join the GATT, for example, because they realize that they must trade in order to prosper and their ability to export their own goods depends upon reciprocal reductions in trade barriers. For this reason, institutional theories are primarily concerned with how the benefits of cooperation are distributed and the degree to which all members are in practice made better off by the presence of institutions.[29]

Unlike GATT, however, most of the benefits from a multilateral protection system are not enjoyed directly by the participating states or their domestic constituents, but by the collectivity of states as a whole, and more specifically, by the protected population. It is not clear from neoliberal theory why states should be concerned with the welfare of foreign populations. The institutionalist emphasis on expected utility and reciprocal benefit eliminate the need to consider questions of obligation or justice. This makes it difficult to apply neoliberal theories to explain any common interest that cannot be reduced to the sum of individual interests.

In neoliberal models, norms serve as external constraints and regulatory mechanisms rather than as expressions of preferred values. States follow the rules and procedures of the regime because of the functional benefits they provide. Institutions, however, not only produce benefits to participants; they also reproduce and occasionally alter the structures that define a given system. Returning to the previous example, the GATT has not only been a mechanism for opening markets to participating states, it has also been a major force in promoting and expanding the Western liberal economic order. The idea of a trade regime designed to reduce barriers would be unthinkable without some prior commitment toward a liberal world economy. Therefore, while neoliberal theories can explain a wide range of functional regimes, they cannot explain the development of institutions that emerge primarily to pursue broader social goals.

Liberal theories also approach institutions as mechanisms for realizing national preferences, however their starting point is not state interest but rather that of individuals and groups *within* states. Domestic politics

---

[28] John Donnelly, "International Human Rights: A Regime Analysis," *International Organization*, vol. 40, no. 3 (1984).

[29] Lisa Martin, "An Institutionalist View: International Institutions and State Strategies," in T.V. Paul and John Hall, eds., *International Order and the Future of World Politics* (Cambridge: Cambridge University Press, 1999), p. 93.

is the first cut for explaining state behavior and systemic constraints are less important than internal ones. In the liberal paradigm, the fundamental actors are the autonomous, rational individuals and groups who engage in transactions on the basis of self-interest and risk-averse preferences.[30] Governments represent a subset of their societies whose dominant interests generate and constrain the underlying preferences and identities of states in the international system. The development of international organizations and institutions can therefore best be explained through the sequential analysis of national preference formation and strategic interaction among sovereign states.[31]

From a liberal perspective, then, an international protection regime would represent a convergence of interests among government officials from various countries acting on behalf of the dominant domestic groups within their respective societies. They would emerge through a series of "two-level games" whereby state officials attempt to reconcile the interests of their societies with those of others. Human rights regimes, for example, arise when domestic social movements and interest groups pressure their political leaders to make human rights a priority in the pursuit of foreign policy. Thus, international human rights institutions would emerge among states that already practice human rights domestically themselves.

The advantage of a liberal approach is that it does not place any inherent limits on the kinds of policies that states may choose to pursue. State interest reflects domestic politics rather than some external constraint imposed by the structure of the international system. Therefore, unlike realism, for example, states are not automatically constrained by balance of power considerations nor do international institutions have to necessarily serve some type of state interest. In fact, states could go so far as to cede much of their sovereignty in economic matters if it serves the interests of their domestic constituencies.[32] This creates more space from which one can try to explain international protection regimes.

---

[30] Andrew Moravcsik, "Taking Preferences Seriously: A Liberal Theory of International Politics," *International Organization*, vol. 51 (1997).

[31] See Andrew Moravcsik, "Preferences and Power in the European Community: A Liberal Intergovernmentalist Approach," *Journal of Common Market Studies*, vol. 31, no. 4 (December 1993), p. 481.

[32] See, for example, Andrew Moravcsik, *The Choice for Europe: Social Purpose and State Power from Messina to Maastricht* (Ithaca: Cornell University Press, 1998).

According to the liberal model, the internal political organization of a state is a key variable in explaining the kinds of policies its government would pursue. That is why, for example, democracies are not likely to wage war against other democracies, and liberal states are more likely to conduct their foreign relations on the basis of international law and liberal political norms.[33] One can infer from this that international protection regimes would reflect largely the domestic politics of the states that establish them. For example, liberal states would be more likely to protect individual citizens; monarchies to protect monarchs; and Islamic states to protect Moslems. This would explain how political leaders decide which populations to protect, and would account for the secular change discussed in the introduction (the identity of the target populations).

This still leaves us with the question of *why* domestic individuals and/or groups would wish potentially to risk the lives and treasure of their fellow citizens on behalf of a foreign population. Liberal theory assumes that individuals and groups within society are utility-maximizing and risk-averse and therefore it is difficult to understand how the domestic interest is served in promoting an abstract principle that does not provide any material benefits to the citizenry. While it is conceivable that some domestic interest groups might see an ideological or humanitarian interest in such activities, the influence of these groups on foreign policy tends to be weak, at least in comparison to their influence on domestic policy. In practice, foreign policy elites tend to be more disposed toward making and keeping multilateral commitments than domestic political actors; relationships among diplomats, heads of state, and foreign policy officials are more likely to produce an international consensus than a convergence of domestic interest groups.[34] In fact, studies have shown that the *greater* the autonomy of these elites from domestic pressures, the more likely it is that they will pursue multilateral policies.[35]

---

[33] Anne-Marie Burley, "Toward an Age of Liberal Nations," *Harvard International Law Journal*, vol. 33, no. 2 (Spring 1992), p. 397.

[34] As Theda Skocpol argues, the linkages of states into transnational structures and into international flows of communication may encourage leading state officials to pursue independent policies even in the face of domestic indifference or opposition. See her "Bringing the State Back In: Strategies of Analysis in Current Research," in Peter Evans, Dietrich Rueschemeyer, and Theda Skocpol, eds., *Bringing the State Back In* (Cambridge: Cambridge University Press, 1985), p. 9.

[35] See, for example, Robert Putnam, "Diplomacy and Domestic Politics: The Logic of Two-Level Games," *International Organization*, vol. 42, no. 3 (Summer 1988), p. 449.

Institutions for the common good

If we cannot derive a motivation to extend multilateral protection guarantees to foreign populations from the strategic or economic preferences of individual states, we need a concept of interest that transcends parochial definitions of expected utility. That is, states must recognize some type of benefit or value that cannot be reduced to calculations of individual self-interest, suggesting some type of collective interest. A collective interest differs from overlapping self-interest in that it has an existence independent of the specific actors who comprise the collective at a particular time. For example, lawyers may share a collective interest in safeguarding the integrity of the legal profession, regardless of who happens to be a member of the bar at any particular time. Similarly, political leaders may perceive a collective international interest in maintaining international law or the principle of sovereignty regardless of which states populate the system in a given era. In the following pages, I suggest that a common political interest emerges from within a social structure (or society) when political actors recognize a link between their fundamental goals and the cohesion of the collectivity. Under these circumstances, they will act to preserve the values and institutions of the political order. When they do so, they are acting on behalf of the common good.

The common good is a value that represents the fundamental goals of a collectivity and is in many ways at the core of its *raison d'être*. As such, the common good is concerned with the preservation and general welfare of the collectivity itself.[36] As Aristotle argues, all political associations have some conception of the good; those who cooperate in furthering the progress of the association share of the common good, which is the expressed aim of their association.[37] Similarly, Alasdair MacIntyre defines the common good as the "good" of a type of association that is not reducible to that of the individual members.[38] The stability of any ongoing relationship or association requires individuals to act on behalf of the common good when they believe it to be necessary for the continued progress of the collectivity. Actions that may not be consistent with a parochial definition of interest are sometimes necessary for the

---

[36] Rousseau refers to this as the general will, which he sharply distinguishes from the will of all. The latter is more consistent with the institutionalist concept of mutual self-interest. See Jean-Jacques Rousseau, *Rousseau's Political Writings*, ed. Alan Ritter and Julia Conaway Bondanella (New York: W. W. Norton and Co., 1988), p. 148.

[37] Aristotle, *Politics*, Book III (Oxford: Oxford University Press, 1995), p. 98.

[38] Alasdair MacIntyre, *After Virtue* (Notre Dame, IN: University of Notre Dame Press, 1984).

long-term maintenance of the community or society of which individuals are a part. To the extent that states find value in such a community – such as the "club" of advanced industrial countries or a regional security structure – their leaders often realize the necessity of taking positive action toward its progress. That is why, for example, countries will contribute their own soldiers to serve as United Nations peacekeepers in regions where they have no security or economic interest.

The idea of a common good is not a rejection of individual interest. In fact, it derives from a recognition that parochial interests always exist, often conflict and – all other things being equal – usually dominate. Common interests, Rousseau argues, arise in opposition to the interest of each individual. If there were not any different interests, the common interest would hardly exist and would never meet any obstacle; everything would proceed on its own and politics would cease to be an art.[39] Quite simply, a common good arises precisely because in many cases individual interests can not be reconciled. Thus, for a collectivity – any collectivity – to remain cohesive, the common good must remain apart from individual interest. This idea is fundamental to any political or legal system, including the institution of international law. For this reason, the principle of *pacta sunt servanda* (agreements must be observed) is not a matter of convenience but rather a fundamental value that allows "international relations" to exist at all. While there is always an ongoing tension between parochial interest and the common good, we should expect individuals who are committed to maintaining a particular political order to act on its behalf when they believe that the cohesion of the collectivity or its underlying values are at stake.

Certainly the concept of the "common good" is a controversial one, and not only in the field of international relations. It has often served as a shield under which particularistic interests are promoted under the guise of promoting the general welfare. Most students of international relations are mindful of E. H. Carr's observation that dominant groups often identify themselves with the community as a whole and then use their resources to impose their view of life on the community.[40] Witness, for example, how political leaders often evoke the "international community" to suggest broad support for policies that further their parochial state interests. However, nothing in this discussion implies that a collectivity's definition of the common good is fair, just, or even the best

[39] Rousseau, *Rousseau's Political Writings*, p. 100, fn. 9.
[40] E. H. Carr, *The Twenty Years' Crisis, 1919–1939: An Introduction to the Study of International Relations* (New York: Harper and Row, 1939), p. 79.

one available (in a normative sense). The principles of any international order reflect a specific group of states' collective views of justice, stability, and interest. They are not universal values, only the dominant or prevailing ones. As Inis Claude points out, there is a tendency for a single concept of legitimacy to become dominant in a particular era and political leaders tend to accept obligations that derive from those principles.[41] Those promoting alternative values would likely not agree with the "consensus." Yet all associations have dissidents, and a cohesive political order can usually accommodate them, at least up to a point. It is only when the dissidents' views become mainstream among the members of a society that the consensus unravels.

For this reason, I develop my concept of the common good in international affairs from state practice and the consciousness of state leaders, rather than deriving it from abstract theories of security and anarchy.

The common good and an international society of states

For a common good to arise among a collection of political actors, there must be a shared sense that all members have a positive stake in building and maintaining long-term internal relationships. A system of autonomous units coexisting in an environment of unregulated competition will not provide the sufficient condition for such a situation to develop, even if contacts are frequent. However, when a given group of states choose to formalize their relations and pursue a more cohesive type of political association that promotes a common set of goals and values, they begin to develop a form of structural interdependence. This alters the conditions under which international relations are conducted.

Structural interdependence is a situation in which individual states not only depend on *each other* for their security and prosperity but on the stability and progress of the political system or order itself. It is a deeper, more fundamental condition than one of *functional* interdependence. Functional interdependence is brought about through ongoing interaction and exchange. As the volume, depth, range, and reliability of this interaction increases, political leaders develop rules and institutions to formalize their relations and create a more predictable environment

---

[41] Inis Claude, "Collective Legitimation as a Political Function of the United Nations," *International Organization*, vol. 20 (1966), p. 367.

through which they could compete and cooperate.[42] Over time, this increases states' sensitivity and/or vulnerability to each other's actions. While this offers incentives for continued cooperation, individual states can choose to sever their relationships so long as they are willing to bear the opportunity costs.[43]

On the other hand, under conditions of structural independence, few states can even conceive of severing their relationships since this would dramatically undermine the predictability and stability that allows them to act on the international stage. For example, on the most fundamental level a state's sovereignty is dependent on a stable system of territorial "property rights" through which states recognize each other's borders and agree on the conditions for coexistence.[44] Without the continued operation of a pluralistic system of juridically equal states, the stability of borders and the state's dominance over competing political actors (such as transnational or substate political authorities) would be threatened. The random and unpredictable actions of private transnational "terrorist" organizations suggest how international relations might be conducted in the absence of fundamental rules concerning sovereignty, diplomacy, and the conduct of warfare.

In fact, without a framework of stable institutions and rules, states would find it difficult even to conduct day-to-day transactions. The capacity for states to negotiate, sign agreements, and trust that their commitments will usually be observed is dependent upon the institutions of diplomacy and international law. Although these institutions occasionally break down and the rules are sometimes violated, they have remained durable for several centuries. Thus, even powerful states follow diplomatic procedures in cases where it is not in their immediate interest to do so. While these procedures can be viewed as providing a

---

[42] See Barry Buzan, Charles Jones, and Richard Little, *The Logic of Anarchy: Neorealism to Structural Realism* (New York: Columbia University Press, 1993), p. 78. A similar point is made by Alan Watson, "Hedley Bull, *States Systems and International Societies*," *Review of International Studies*, vol. 13 (1987), p. 151.

[43] See, for example, Richard Cooper, *The Economics of Interdependence: Economic Policy in the Atlantic Community* (New York: McGraw-Hill, 1968) and Robert Keohane and Joseph Nye, *Power and Interdependence: World Politics in Transition* (Boston: Little, Brown and Co., 1977).

[44] On sovereignty as property rights, see Friedrich Kratochwil, "Of Systems, Boundaries, and Territoriality," *World Politics*, vol. 39 (1986) and John Ruggie, "Continuity and Transformation in the World Polity," in Robert O. Keohane, ed., *Neorealism and its Critics* (New York: Columbia University Press, 1986). Ruggie further develops this idea in his later work, "Territoriality and Beyond: Problematizing Modernity in International Relations," *International Organization*, vol. 47, no. 1 (Winter 1993).

utility function (based on the expectation of reciprocity), it is also evident that officials within foreign affairs ministries have been socialized into believing that violating diplomatic norms is not simply a policy choice but a serious breach of binding rules. In this sense, states share a structural interdependence in the maintenance of diplomatic institutions. Thus, even in the face of overwhelming domestic pressures, governments have refused to prosecute foreign diplomats accused of manslaughter.[45]

Even market-driven economic transactions rely on stable institutional structures that go beyond functional cooperation. The ability for states to trade openly with access to each other's markets not only depends upon actions taken by individual states (such as negotiating an agreement to reduce tariffs), but also on the continued progress of a free trade system. Such a system is built upon a relatively stable set of practices and beliefs that enable states to interpret behavior, make judgments, and identify cooperation and defection. This exists apart from the specific rules that states may negotiate in order to facilitate these goals. Political leaders who value free trade will thus develop a commitment toward the institutions and processes that facilitate international commerce, even though at times the rules may not favor their immediate interests. When these break down, as they did during the interwar period, it becomes difficult if not impossible to negotiate new trade rules, even if states believe that it is in their interests to do so.

This suggests a deeper level of interdependence than the liberal concept; it is based not only on a recognition of mutual vulnerability (or sensitivity) to each other's actions, but also on a shared sense that all states have a positive stake in building and maintaining long-term relationships. This condition of structural interdependence is the foundation upon which an international society of states is built. I argue that the existence of such a society provides the best foundation for explaining how and why states develop multilateral commitments to protect foreign populations.

The most extensive conceptualization of international society has been developed by scholars working within a theoretical perspective

---

[45] A classic example of this occurred in 1997, when a Georgian diplomat killed a seventeen-year-old girl in a drunk driving incident in Washington, DC. Although the Georgian government eventually waived the diplomat's immunity, the US government would neither arrest nor prosecute the driver until the American waiver request was officially granted. See Ruben Castaneda and Karl Vicks, "Diplomat Unlikely to Be Prosecuted in Crash, Officials Say," *Washington Post*, January 7, 1997, page B1.

informally dubbed the "English School" of international relations. The English School evolved from the British Committee on the Theory of International Politics in 1958, and was particularly indebted to the work of Martin Wight, Herbert Butterfield, and Adam Watson.[46] It became an important part of international relations theory in the United States with the publication of Hedley Bull's *Anarchical Society* in 1977.

Theories of international society seek to account for the prevalence of order in international affairs despite the absence of a central authority or common world culture. They do so by stressing the social context of international relations. As such, English School theories focus on how political leaders create rules and institutions in pursuit of common goals for a diverse and pluralistic collectivity of states. At a minimum, these institutions provide a standard through which states can make collective judgments about the types of actors who may join the society of nations and how sovereignty may be created and transferred when states break up or amalgamate.[47]

Within international society, formal and informal rules structure interaction by providing a foundation for making judgments of legitimate and illegitimate conduct; for advancing claims concerning mutually accepted rights and duties; and for seeking vindication and redress when rules are violated, rights infringed, and duties ignored.[48] States may sometimes violate the rules – and when they do there may be few coercive mechanisms to sanction them – however, all members are expected to observe them and in most cases they consider them to be binding.[49] Thus, for example, in 2003 the US government hired dozens of lawyers to advise military leaders which targets they might legally attack in a war with Iraq.[50] In practice, even powerful states accept constraints on their autonomy as a condition for participation in international institutions, and, more basically, as the cost of membership in an international

[46] For an excellent overview of the evolution of this school, see Timothy Dunne, *Inventing International Society: A History of the English School* (London: Macmillan, 1998).
[47] See Martin Wight, *Systems of States* (Leicester: Leicester University Press, 1977), p. 153.
[48] See Terry Nardin, *Law, Morality, and the Relations of States* (Princeton: Princeton University Press, 1983), pp. 34–35.
[49] In a study on state compliance with international law, for example, Louis Henkin concludes that "almost all nations observe almost all principles of international law and almost all of their obligations almost all of the time." See *How Nations Behave: Law and Foreign Policy* (New York: Columbia University Press, 1979), p. 47. See also, Thomas Franck, *The Power of Legitimacy Among Nations* (New York: Oxford University Press, 1990).
[50] Steven Komarow, "US Attorneys Dispatched to Advise Military," *USA Today*, March 11, 2003, p. 9A.

society of states. A state that regularly violates widely accepted norms is seen by other states not only as acting in a hostile manner, but as breaching the most fundamental rules that they all value.

In distinguishing between an international society and an international system, contemporary English School scholars develop theories of state obligation that are not based on natural law, moral imperative, or traditional bonds of common sentiment. Rather, since international societies are contractual and constructed rather than sentimental and traditional, they reflect the collective wills of their members.[51] Thus, although some of the early English School theorists saw international society as emerging from a common (European) culture, the "constructivist" concept of society suggests that cultural unity is not a necessary condition.[52] This enables us to derive principles of obligation from state practice without becoming entangled in the classic debate between realists and idealists over moral judgment and the harmony of interests.[53] Rather, research focuses on trying to determine which beliefs or principles represent a consensus of the members of an international society at a given time, what the substance of that consensus is and what its limits are. At the same time, it also enables us to determine which actors reside within this consensus, which remain outside, and why. In this sense, international society is not only an analytical concept, but also an empirical reality.[54]

For Hedley Bull, the field's best-known international society theorist, there is a fundamental set of goals that provide the foundation for any international society. These include the preservation of

---

[51] This distinction between a *gemeinschaft* and a *gesellschaft* understanding of international society was suggested by Barry Buzan. See his, "From International System to International Society: Structural Realism and Regime Theory Meet the English School," *International Organization*, vol. 47, no. 3 (Summer 1993), p. 333.

[52] Martin Wight, in particular, held that a degree of cultural unity was necessary for the development of an international society. See his *Systems of States*, p. 33.

[53] See Carr, *The Twenty Years Crisis*, especially chs. 4 and 5 and Hans Morgenthau, *Politics Among Nations: The Struggle for Power and Peace* (New York: McGraw-Hill, 1993 [1948]), pp. 14–16.

[54] Alan James argues that the existence of any society can be demonstrated empirically through the presence of the following: a plurality of members, regular communication among them, and a set of binding rules that provide a foundation for interaction. See his "International Society," *British Journal of International Studies*, vol. 4, no. 2 (1978), fn. 15. Robert Jackson holds that an international society can be identified through the existence of customary and positive international law and the community of diplomacy that has been sustained over the centuries. See his "International Community Beyond the Cold War," in Gene Lyons and Michael Mastanduno, eds., *Beyond Westphalia: State Sovereignty and International Intervention* (Baltimore: The Johns Hopkins University Press, 1995), p. 62.

the nation-state system, the stability of territorial possession, mutual recognition of sovereignty, limitations on violence, and the sanctity of agreements.[55] Beyond this, collectivities of states have at various times developed secondary goals such as maintaining dynastic sovereignty in Europe, promoting a liberal economic order, providing for national self-determination, facilitating the peaceful settlement of disputes, and expanding the European state system into new areas of the world. This study is concerned with these "thicker" types of international society.

Under these conditions, states assume external responsibilities and/or obligations that derive, not from domestic politics, natural law, or universal moral principle, but rather from their membership in international society. These obligations are neither universal nor unchanging, but rather reflect the collectivity's "constitutional structures."[56] While political leaders may generally consider domestically generated preferences to be their primary guide in defining their interests, sometimes they must act also to preserve the fundamental principles of international society. To do otherwise would threaten the political foundations of international life that they value.

Like any political or social structure, the depth of an international society can vary from minimal to highly cohesive.[57] The greater the consensus over a larger range of values and goals, the more cohesive the association. As the level of consensus deepens, we should expect those states that are part of the regional or global society of states to develop stronger commitments toward the preservation and progress of

[55] See Hedley Bull, *Anarchical Society: A Study of Order in World Politics* (New York: Columbia University Press, 1977), pp. 16–19.

[56] Christian Reus defines constitutional structures as coherent ensembles of intersubjective beliefs and principles that define what constitutes a legitimate state, the nature of state rights and obligations, the conditions under which these rights can be legitimately exercised, and the situations in which international society is licenced to intervene to compromise these rights. See his, "The Constitutional Structure of International Society and the Nature of Fundamental Institutions," *International Organization*, vol. 51, no. 4 (1997), p. 566.

[57] Andrew Hurrell posits three levels: minimalist, pluralist, and solidarist. The goal of a pluralist society of states is to maintain an "ethic of difference" while providing rudimentary rules of coexistence. While this requires some type of shared consciousness of international society among state officials, it is not as deep as a "solidarist" level in which far more extensive social goals and common values (such as the preservation of human rights) exist. See his "Society and Anarchy in International Relations," in B. A. Roberson, *International Society and the Development of International Relations Theory* (London: Continuum, 2002), p. 32. This distinction between pluralist and solidarist forms of international society was first suggested by Hedley Bull in his earlier work, "The Grotian Conception of International Society," in Herbert Butterfield and Martin Wight, eds., *Diplomatic Investigations* (London: Allen and Unwin, 1966).

international society. This is because under conditions of high structural interdependence states link their futures, at least in part, with those of the collectivity. Within this environment, states will construct institutions that further the primary and secondary goals of the collectivity. I consider any regime that is created primarily to promote, preserve and/or extend the principles of a regional or global political order or collectivity (as opposed to providing direct benefits to its members) to be an institution for the common good. Modern examples of these include the International Criminal Court, United Nations specialized agencies (such as the office of the UN High Commissioner on Refugees) and UN peacekeeping missions. In each case, the institution reflects a particular principle that is fundamental to the collectivity (human rights, humanitarian assistance and peaceful resolution of disputes, respectively).

International society and International Relations theory

In the previous section I suggested that international protection regimes are part of a class of institutions that are designed primarily to promote the common good for an international society of states. The existence of such a society provides the permissive condition from which institutions for the common good can develop. In an international society, political leaders create political institutions that promote the goals of the collectivity and designate the range of appropriate or legitimate ways to pursue them. The goals can be minimal – for example, as Bull suggests, simply maintaining the essential principles of the nation-state system – while the means may be broad – including, for example, the right to use force. They can change over time. Their depth and scope can vary across time and space. They may be confined to a single region of the world (for example, Western Europe) or they could include a wide variety of countries from many regions. In short, we should expect considerable variation in behavior within the environment of an international society.

This raises a problem in attempting to use an international society approach in order to explain a particular pattern of behavior. Like Waltz's international system, the concept of international society allows for a limited set of generalizations about state behavior. While English School theories suggest that states are guided by a fundamental set of norms in their relations with each other, they do not claim that all or even most behavior is determined by either the internalization of norms or adherence to institutional practices. Martin Wight and Hedley Bull, for example, argue that in addition to the existence of some type of international society of states, the global environment also contains aspects of a Hobbesian (realist) state of nature and a Kantian (cosmopolitan) world community. While at any given time or place one of these elements may dominate, at no time do any of them cease to exert at least some influence on state behavior.[58] Thus, within the international environment the sources of state interest and responsibility are threefold: within one's own domestic society or state institutions, the international society of states, and the world community of humanity in general, usually in that order. To some degree, world politics is largely about balancing these three levels of responsibility.

Yet there is little in the body of English School theory that specifies the conditions under which states are most likely to act according to the demands presented by one of these levels as opposed to the others, at any given time. All we can say at this point is that sometimes states will pursue parochial policies (some of which may conflict with the interests of international society), while at other times they will meet their responsibilities toward a broader collectivity.

This variation in state behavior has limited the ability of English School theories to explain some of the broader issues within the field of international relations. I argue that the protection of foreign populations reflects the desire by political leaders to promote and protect their collective goals and values. Yet in order to derive an interest in protecting foreign populations from states' participation in international society, it is necessary to specify the conditions under which a defined group of states will act in defense of the norms and institutions of international society as opposed to domestic or global concerns. I address this task by building upon the following premises: first, during any given period, some political actors will have a greater stake in the progress of international society than others;[59] second, these actors are more likely to act in support of its fundamental institutions than those with a peripheral commitment; and third, they are most likely to do so when the cohesion and stability of the collectivity is at stake.

---

[58] Martin Wight, *International Theory: Three Traditions*, ed. Gabrielle Wight and Brian Porter (Leicester: Leicester University Press, 1991), and Bull, *Anarchical Society*, p. 24.

[59] I am using the term "political actors" to designate those individuals who maintain formal, ongoing relationships with each other in international affairs. Such individuals include high government officials, diplomats, and representatives from international and transnational organizations.

As Barry Buzan points out, international societies create outsiders as well as insiders, and, even among the insiders, one can usually find a wide variance in levels of commitment.[60] While the "core" members will most likely exhibit the greatest cohesion, others can share in some but not all of the values of an international society and participate in some but not all of the regimes and institutions generated by the core. At the same time, since international societies do not necessarily develop evenly across the globe, their depth and scope can vary from region to region and from era to era. Therefore, we can expect a greater level of commitment from core states in regions where international society is firmly entrenched and its institutions are highly durable.

The idea of core and peripheral memberships is not unique to the concept of international society. Most collectivities are stratified, with some classes or groups having a greater stake in the progress of the collectivity than others. And, like most collectivities, the institutions of international society will most likely reflect the vision and interests of the core states, particularly those that were instrumental in their development and that stand to benefit from their stability. Over time these states often develop "habits of cooperation," that can lead to a greater commitment toward the collectivity.[61] The logic of sunk costs suggests that as a state's level of commitment deepens, its willingness to act in support of the institutions increases as well.

For example, Germany and France have demonstrated a far stronger commitment to the progress of the European Union and the advancement of Europeanism than Great Britain. While this is partly the result of ideological and domestic factors, it also reflects their respective relationships to the other states of Western Europe. Since Britain has long held an ambiguous relationship toward Europe, it has far less invested in the success of the European project. For this reason, Germany and France have been in the forefront of each new level of institutionalization within the Union, while Britain has lagged far behind.[62]

---

[60] Buzan divides states into four classes, characterized by their relationship to the institutions of international society: core (belonging to most regimes), peripheral (belonging to some), minimal (accepts mutual recognition and diplomatic practices), and outsiders. See Barry Buzan, "International Society and International Security," in Rick Fawn and Jeremy Larkins, eds., *International Society After the Cold War: Anarchy and Order Reconsidered* (New York: St. Martin's Press, 1996), pp. 270–71.

[61] The phrase "habits of cooperation" is from Oran Young, "International Regimes: Toward a New Theory of Institutions," *World Politics*, vol. 39 (October 1986), pp. 104–22.

[62] Desmond Dinan, *Ever Closer Union? An Introduction to the European Community* (Boulder: Lynne Rienner Publishers, 1994), part I.

The relative importance that political leaders attach to their external relationships is a key factor in determining their degree of willingness to tie their fortunes to those of the collective, in this case international society. While power considerations may be paramount in an environment where individuals do not have a long-term stake in maintaining relationships with each other, in a pluralistic society there are at least two other factors that influence the way political actors react to differences in preferences: the importance they attach to creating or sustaining legitimate relationships, and their beliefs about legitimate procedures and outcomes.[63] The more that individuals value a particular set of relationships or institutions, the more willing they will be to accept procedures and outcomes that benefit the collective rather than individual members.

As a result, core states within international society are more likely to act on behalf of the collectivity in cases where the cohesion and progress of the society is at stake. As I will argue in chapter 2, international protection regimes help promote the progress and cohesion of a regional or international political order by creating stability within the participating states. This is the primary factor motivating their creation.

Argument and alternative explanations

In the following pages, I will argue that international protection regimes emerge from within international society when the leaders of the major powers believe it to be necessary for the cohesion and stability of a regional or international political order that they value. The goal is thus regional stability and the preservation of the status quo, both of which contribute to the common good of the political order. At the same time, however, neither "stability" nor "the status quo" are abstract entities; the creators of IPRs attempt to protect a particular kind of status quo, usually in the face of a perceived challenge. The conditions of stability (for example, whether target governments will be pressured to grant specific rights to their populations or be protected from members of the populations demanding said rights) reflects the type of political order the core states are promoting. Thus, their primary concern in establishing IPRs is therefore not their own power and security, but rather the stability of the political order. From this argument I hypothesize that the

[63] Alan Lamborn, "Theory and the Politics in World Politics," *International Studies Quarterly*, vol. 41 (1997), p. 193.

motivation for states to construct IPRs will vary directly with their level of commitment to the cohesion and progress of the political order. The type of IPR (who gets protected and how) reflects the values promoted by the core states.

As with other institutions for the common good, the primary purpose of these IPRs is to advance the welfare and principles of the collectivity. In chapter 2 I develop a theory of international orders that explains how the protection of foreign populations furthers this goal. I argue that IPRs are formed in the aftermath of a major systemic change as core states attempt to build a consensus around a set of fundamental principles for a new political order. During these periods there is a strong tendency for large numbers of states to break up, become reorganized, or be created anew. When new states are created or old ones reorganized, individuals and groups are forced to adopt new identities; this alters their relationships with each other and with their governments.

Under these conditions, international institutions will usually require that all new or reorganized states accept principles of governance that are consistent with those of the new political order. This helps to ensure both the stability of the states and the cohesion of the system. In this way, the collectivity not only influences the institutional development of the state, but also regulates internal political relationships. It does so by making specific commitments to monitor and sometimes enforce the standards it establishes. Depending on the type of states that are built, this could mean protecting the population from the government, the government from the population, or one segment of the population from another.

This argument is not a "rejection" of realism or liberalism. As stated above, I accept the proposition that realist and cosmopolitan factors are present in most aspects of state behavior. The force of rules and institutions derives both from considerations of legitimacy (and how law helps to define membership criteria for a society of states) and from considerations of mutual advantage and reciprocal benefit.[64] The protection of foreign populations therefore occurs within an environment in which political leaders are faced with a variety of conflicting pressures, domestic as well as international. At the same time, a desire to promote the cohesion of the international order is the *primary* factor that motivates states to construct IPRs. Stability and order, rather than power and security, are the principle values. And as Patrick Riordan suggests, both

---

[64] See Hurrell, "Society and Anarchy in International Relations," p. 32.

24

the institutions that are created from the concern for public order (in the midst of threatening disorder) and the body of ideas that support these institutions constitute the common good for those who cooperate in designing and operating them.[65]

In advancing this argument in the empirical chapters, I will also consider two alternative explanations for the development of international protection regimes. The first suggests that IPRs are established by hegemonic powers to advance their state interests and/or those of their alliance partners. This is consistent with a realist or neorealist explanation. From this perspective, the purpose of an international protection system is to enhance the economic or strategic position of the protecting states relative to potential or actual competitors. The "common good" is actually the parochial interest of this dominant state or alliance. This explanation constitutes the null hypothesis in that it suggests that there is neither a pattern nor a single explanatory variable that accounts for the protection of foreign populations. IPRs arise whenever hegemonic powers determine that it is in their interest to construct them and this varies with the interests of the dominant states. There is therefore no relationship between the principles of the international order and the creation of an IPR.

Contrary to the thesis argued in this book, for example, Stephen Krasner holds that foreign intervention into the relationship between governments and their populations demonstrates the *lack* of an international society, since even its most fundamental constitutive principle (sovereignty) is routinely violated.[66] IPRs therefore do not promote the goals of an international society, but rather reflect the existence of power asymmetries, competing domestic demands, and the absence of authoritative institutions to restrain state behavior. Since there are few formal mechanisms for choosing among mutually inconsistent norms, political leaders follow whichever principles or rules are convenient for promoting their parochial interests.[67]

Robert Gilpin's work can offer a more complex realist explanation for the creation of IPRs by arguing that the stability of a multilateral security order is often in the national interest of a hegemonic state. Hegemonic

---

[65] Patrick Riordan, *The Politics of the Common Good* (Dublin, Ireland: Institute of Public Administration, 1996), p. 70.

[66] Krasner, *Sovereignty: Organized Hypocrisy*.

[67] See Stephen Krasner, "Globalization and Sovereignty," in David Smith, Dorothy Solinger, and Steven Topik, eds., *States and Sovereignty in the Global Economy* (New York: Routledge, 1999).

states therefore tend to take a sophisticated view of international order, and accept responsibilities that go beyond immediate self-interest. Since such orders reflect the long-term interests of the hegemon, they can be expected to act on its behalf and enforce the rules when they deem it to be necessary.[68] IPRs, then, are created by hegemonic states to support their long-term interest in maintaining a favorable political order that supports their preferences.

A second competing explanation is that IPRs are motivated by humanitarian or ideological concerns generated by transnational social movements or strong domestic constituencies. This model would posit the protection of populations as an end in itself, based on a strong normative appeal generated by "norm entrepreneurs" and nongovernmental organizations.[69] In considering this alternative, I refer to the literature on transnationalism. From this perspective, the common good would emerge not from states or their leadership but from international civil society and nongovernmental organizations within key states.

International civil society can be understood as networks of knowledge and interaction created by decentralized nonstate actors across juridical borders.[70] These networks are built upon independent social, economic, and cultural links among individuals and organizations from different societies in the pursuit of specific social goals. The literature on transnationalism emphasizes the role of nongovernmental organizations, social movements and policy networks in transforming state interest and influencing state policy.[71] Actions by these organizations can change the principles upon which government policy is based through direct political pressure and the dissemination of ideas.

[68] Robert Gilpin, *War and Change in World Politics* (Princeton: Princeton University Press, 1981).

[69] See, for example, Martha Finnemore and Kathryn Sikkink, "International Norm Dynamics and Political Change," *International Organization*, vol. 52, no. 4 (August 1998).

[70] Ronnie Lipschutz, "Reconstructing World Politics: The Emergence of Global Civil Society," in Rick Fawn and Jeremy Larkins, eds., *International Society After the Cold War: Anarchy and Order Reconsidered* (New York: St. Martin's Press, 1996), p. 102. For other work on international civil society, see *inter alia*, M. J. Peterson, "Transnational Activity, International Society and World Polity," *Millennium*, vol. 21 (1992), pp. 37–88; Paul Ghils, "International Civil Society: International Non-Governmental Organizations in the International System," *International Social Science Journal*, vol. 44, no. 3 (1992); and, from a different theoretical vantage point, John Meyer, "The World Polity and the Authority of the Nation-State," in George Thomas *et al.*, eds., *Institutional Structure: Constituting the State, Society and the Individual* (Newbury Park: Sage Publications, 1987).

[71] See Thomas Risse-Kappen, *Bringing Transnational Relations Back In: Non-State Actors, Domestic Structures and International Institutions* (Cambridge: Cambridge University Press, 1995), p. 4 and Margaret E. Keck and Kathryn Sikkink, *Activists Beyond Borders: Advocacy Networks in International Politics* (Ithaca: Cornell University Press, 1998).

This approach is reflected in much of the literature on human rights. Jack Donnelly, for example, posits that human rights regimes are triggered by transnational social movements, which spark a conceptual transformation in moral beliefs. This in turn creates a crossnational demand for state action.[72] Similarly, Risse and Sikkink argue that the diffusion of human rights norms is brought about by the establishment of networks among domestic and transnational actors who manage to link up with international regimes. This alerts both public opinion and governments.[73] In these models, the benefits of a protection regime are enjoyed not by states but by domestic constituencies and transnational organizations, whose members pressure their own governments to provide guarantees to specific populations. Since the principal forces are non-state actors who define their interests in cosmopolitan rather than national terms, the distribution of benefits among states is not a major factor.

Case selection, method, and evidence

In order to examine my theories and those of the two alternative explanations, the second section of the book will investigate four cases where collectivities of states sought to protect foreign populations. These cases span a century and cover different types of protected populations and different types of protecting states. The protected groups include national minorities, individual citizens, ethnic communities, and displaced peoples, while the protecting states include monarchies, liberal democracies, and national states. The institutional mechanisms to implement the regimes include formal, informal, regional, and universal organizations. This range allows for greater generalizability.

In deciding which cases to choose for examination, I surveyed the historical literature for all instances where coalitions of states or international institutions made sustained commitments to protect clearly defined classes of people within states other than their own. I rejected any cases that involved populations with whom the protectors either shared a pre-existing affinity or had an historic attachment. Thus, for example, I do not examine the protection of Christians within the (Islamic)

---

[72] See Jack Donnelly, "International Human Rights," p. 636.
[73] Thomas Risse and Kathryn Sikkink, "The Socialization of International Human Rights Norms into Domestic Practices: Introduction," in Thomas Risse, Stephen Ropp, and Kathryn Sikkink, eds., *The Power of Human Rights: International Norms and Domestic Change* (Cambridge: Cambridge University Press, 1999), p. 5.

Ottoman Empire by European powers. I also did not include the protection of dynastic families by the Holy Alliance during the early nineteenth century – even though this is an important case – because I examined this case in some detail (albeit in another context) in a previous work.[74] Finally, I limited my case selection to those that met the criteria to be considered as IPRs, as discussed at the beginning of this chapter.

Since I am examining only instances where IPRs were actually constructed rather than those where they were not, the universe of potential cases is relatively small. While an investigation of "negative cases" (where populations were not protected) could yield some interesting data, they do not require an explanation, since the structures of sovereignty and anarchy should make this the predictable behavior of states. At the same time, I tried to account for the possibility of selection bias by choosing cases where the principal actors had mixed motives, where their actions were not always consistent, and where the regimes were not always successful in reaching their goals. In this way, the cases are not inherently confirming. This allows for the possibility that state participation in the regimes could be based on a more narrowly defined self-interest disguised as international responsibility.

Since my investigation concerns how and why political leaders establish IPRs, my method is centered on discovering the "original intent" of the creators and tracing the process through which the principal parties created these institutions. I am more interested in explaining a stream of behavior through time than I am in correlating independent with dependent variables in discrete cases. Consequently, the focus of this study is on motivations, political goals, beliefs, and perceptions rather than on outcomes (which in each case is the same). At the same time, I examine the context surrounding this process by examining the distribution of capabilities, the strategic situation, and the political environment in the regional or global system. Therefore, my case studies focus almost exclusively on the origin of the regimes rather than on their operation.

In presenting the cases, I consider two types of evidence that would support or refute the three alternative explanations.

The first concerns the *process* through which the IPRs were created. A realist explanation would predict that the IPRs would have been imposed on the system by the most powerful states (principally a hegemonic power) through coercion or inducement. The IPRs should

---

[74] Bruce Cronin, *Community Under Anarchy: Transnational Identity and the Evolution of Cooperation* (New York: Columbia University Press, 1999), ch. 3.

therefore reflect the self-defined interest of the most powerful states. A transnational or domestic explanation should reveal considerable influence by powerful domestic interest groups and/or transnational advocacy networks in the construction of the IPRs. The regime should reflect these self-same interests. An IS approach would suggest that IPRs are created through the development of a consensus among those states having the greatest stake in the cohesion of the new political order. To support this explanation, the evidence would have to show that the creators build this consensus by advancing a clear set of values and common goals for the collectivity that goes beyond reducing trade barriers and maintaining national security (goals that are typically found in the institutionalist and realist literature). This requires a demonstrable direct link between the principles of the international order, the form of state promoted by the protectors, and the choice of which populations to protect.

A second type of evidence concerns the motives of the creators. Since realists argue that political leaders place the greatest value on state security and the distribution of power, a realist account should find that the IPRs were designed to advance the strategic interests of the dominant states and that they attempted to influence the relative military capabilities of states in the region. Moreover, we should find a direct link between specific state interests and the choice of a protection regime as the means to promote these interests. Transnationalist theories would predict that ideological or humanitarian goals were predominant, and that concern for the welfare of the protected populations was the primary motivating force in their creation. We should therefore be able to find a link between the preferences of domestic or transnational groups promoting their welfare and a high level of influence on political leaders in obtaining the outcome. Finally, an English School explanation should reveal an interest in stabilizing specific types of states and a concern for stability and the values of the international order.

In order to trace the process and determine the motives of political leaders, I examined published historical accounts and official minutes and records of deliberations of those organizations involved in constructing the regimes. Such documents were available for the Council of Europe, the Organization for Security and Cooperation in Europe (OSCE), and the United Nations (chapters 4, 5 and 6, respectively). For the chapter on the protection of ethnic communities (chapter 5), I also conducted extensive on-site interviews with staff and officials in the office of the OSCE High Commissioner on National Minorities at The

Hague. Unfortunately this was not possible in the other cases, since few of those with first-hand knowledge of the original deliberations were still alive. For the chapter on minority protection (chapter 3), I relied primarily on memoirs, historical research, and the published notes from those who participated in the Paris Peace Conference. Finally, in addition to tracing the deliberations, I examined the justifications (both public and private) offered by the key political leaders for protecting specifically defined foreign populations. To control for self-serving statements aimed at particular constituencies, I specifically looked for patterns of discourse that remained constant regardless of the audience and circumstances.

Organization of the book

The second part (chapters 3 through 6) will focus on the four cases that constitute the heart of the study. In each of the cases, a group of political actors is confronted with a series of dilemmas and tensions that arise within a specific region in the aftermath of a major systemic crisis. In establishing the political/strategic environment through which these actors operated, I begin each case study by examining which political actors are directly involved in the process of reconstruction, their strategic choices, the domestic and international pressures they faced, and their beliefs concerning the nature of security, order, and justice. After this, I trace the process through which these actors weighed competing alternatives and negotiated the creation of the regimes.

Chapter 3 examines the minority-rights protection regime established in the early twentieth century. It shows how this system emerged from the reorganization of central, southern, and eastern Europe following World War I. The allied and associated powers tried to build a new European order based on the principles of nationality, self-determination, and collective security. The leaders attending the conference at Versailles believed that there could be neither justice nor peace so long as national (that is, ethnic) communities were denied the right to choose their own political affiliation. At the same time, the allies also recognized the inherent contradiction between the unified national state and the presence of significant ethnic minorities. They thus attempted to maintain the cohesion of new and reorganized national states by requiring the newly established governments to sign minority-rights treaties. This was supposed to make the minorities into loyal citizens of the state. In trying to solidify the national state as the foundation for the new order, the League of Nations established an elaborate monitoring and protection system.

Chapter 4 focuses on the efforts by West European leaders to create a regional liberal order after World War II, based on the principles of democratic governance, the rule of law, and economic cooperation. It shows that these leaders believed that this could only be maintained by the proliferation of liberal states in the region. In order to facilitate this form of political organization, European institutions developed a concept of European citizenship and sought to empower individuals through a complex and extensive system of human rights protections. In particular, they created the Council of Europe to facilitate cooperation among European democracies, and the European Court of Human Rights to enforce their human rights treaties. This highly intrusive protection system allowed European institutions to pass judgment on the legal and political systems of West European states and provided a set of rights for individuals that emanated from the European (rather than the domestic) level. Under this system, individual citizens could challenge their own governments in European courts, thereby ensuring that each state would remain democratic and liberal.

Chapter 5 examines the dilemmas faced by West European and North American powers after the collapse of the Soviet Union and revolutions in Eastern Europe. With few exceptions the successor states legitimized themselves on the principle of ethnic nationalism and sought to build explicitly national states. However, learning the lessons from the failure of the national state after World War I, the OSCE rejected the assimilationist approach that would be necessary to create such states. They concluded that the existence of large numbers of national minorities within the new national states endangered the stability of the new European order because the solutions to the minority dilemma (assimilation, domination, or elimination) were incompatible with the principles of New Europe. The chapter suggests that European officials recognize this and that the solution they developed was to transform the political organization of the target states from ethnic nationalism to civic multiculturalism.

Chapter 6 focuses on the protection of refugees in the twentieth century. It argues that the notion of international responsibility for their protection is directly tied to changes in the international order and the domination of the nation-state. More specifically, I show that an international protection regime for refugees emerged after World Wars I and II as part of broader efforts to stabilize the nation-state system and build coherent international orders centered around the League of Nations and United Nations, respectively. During both periods, political leaders recognized refugees to be the by-products of a transformation from an old political order into a new one.

The chapter also shows that the regimes created after both world wars reflected the priorities and values of those building the postwar order, and that in both cases the refugee system helped to reinforce the type of order favored by the participating states. In the interwar period, the League of Nations only recognized as refugees those displaced persons who were members of specific ethnic groups. The choice of which groups would qualify was not random but rather represented those who could not integrate into the newly created and reorganized national states of the postwar era. On the other hand, during the post-World War II period, ethnic criteria were not even considered. Rather, those creating the regime did so on the basis of human rights and individual choice. Refugees were reconceptualized as those denied the protection of their state and who in fact faced persecution by the very entity that was created to ensure their basic rights and fundamental freedoms.

Chapter 7 reviews and evaluates the evidence from the empirical chapters and discusses how it supports or refutes the various theories offered in the first two chapters. Building on these findings in the previous chapters, it seeks to contribute to the debate in three areas of International Relations theory: first, it offers suggestions for resolving the tension between the "solidarist" and "pluralist" conceptions of international society. Second, it attempts to advance the broader debates within the discipline by expanding the conception of "institutions for the common good" to other issue areas. Finally, it offers suggestions for better understanding contemporary politics by adopting a conceptualization of the international environment as a complex interaction between realist, pluralist, cosmopolitan, and solidarist elements.

2 International protection regimes in an international order

Martin Wight argues that the fundamental political task of an international society is to provide order and security, from which law, justice, and prosperity can then follow.[1] On one level, we can equate order with stability and define security in terms of freedom from threat. In this sense, both can be viewed as environmental conditions. Thus, we consider international life to be ordered if it is based on predictable, recurrent relations, and secure so long as the units remain independent and free from physical danger.[2] On another level, however, order can be viewed as a pattern of activity that sustains particular social goals, and security can be defined as the protection of particular social institutions. From this perspective, order is a social structure that represents the institutionalization of a particular set of values. "International ordering" is the construction of political and social relations among independent actors.

While both conceptions reflect elements of international life, for the purposes of this study I consider order to be a social structure rather than an environmental condition. Therefore the key question is not how order can be maintained in international relations but rather what kind of order political actors seek to maintain. In this chapter I examine how political leaders define order and the means they employ to sustain it. In particular, I focus on the efforts of core states to develop a consensus around a set of fundamental principles of order and how the protection of foreign populations helps to promote these principles. Since international protection regimes are built within the context of an international

[1] Martin Wight, *Systems of States* (Leicester: Leicester University Press, 1977), p. 192.
[2] This concept of order can be traced to the theories of Thomas Hobbes and more recently to political realism. See Thomas Hobbes, *Leviathan* (Baltimore: Penguin Books, 1968) and Gilpin, *War and Change in World Politics*, ch. 1.

order, the first part of this chapter will examine in some detail the concept of political orders in world politics.

International orders in international society

Within the basic framework of an international society of states, there are many possible ways of organizing political, security, and economic relations among the units. Each of these various arrangements constitutes a definable international order. For example, although a form of international society existed in both eighteenth and twentieth-century Europe, the European dynastic system operated on a very different set of political principles than the Western liberal order of the Cold War era. Trade rules, diplomatic practices, mechanisms for facilitating state succession, requirements for recognizing new states, conditions for legitimate collective intervention, and even the identities of the main actors varied.

One way to distinguish among different types of orders is to focus on forms of governance. Ikenberry, for example, holds that there are three primary varieties of political order within an international system: balance of power, hegemony, and constitutional. Each represents a different way in which power and authority are distributed and exercised.[3] This aspect of order is defined by the organizing principle (anarchy, hierarchy, rule of law), the concentration of power (multipolar, bipolar, hegemonic), the restraints placed on this power, and the source of systemic stability. However, while this approach captures the structural features of a political order, it does not address questions of substance, for example, the particular values and social goals that the "governors" pursue.

Another approach is to distinguish between orders according to the political principles upon which an order is built. Hedley Bull, for example, argues that order in social life is not based on *any* pattern in the relations among the units but rather a *particular* pattern that leads to a specific result, that is, an arrangement that promotes specific goals or values.[4] Similarly, Richard Falk conceives of order as an arrangement of power and authority designed to promote a set of goals that are deemed

---

[3] G. John Ikenberry, *After Victory: Institutions, Strategic Restraint, and the Rebuilding of Order After Major Wars* (Princeton: Princeton University Press, 2001), pp. 21–24.

[4] Bull, *Anarchical Society*, p. 4.

to be beneficial to the members of a society.[5] In both conceptions, the focus is on the substance rather than the structure.

International orders comprised both elements. For the purpose of this study, international orders can be understood as cohesive systems of political practices, institutions, and structural arrangements that reflect the political consensus of a collectivity of states regarding the conditions for security, prosperity, justice, and stability.[6] As such, they are social structures that states construct in the pursuit of their common goals and values. The construction of a political order involves defining *which* elements in international life will be ordered, *how* these elements will be ordered, and *who* will be involved in the ordering. Political leaders therefore construct a political order by identifying the principles and actors, establishing relationships to facilitate desired transactions, and determining the geographic or cognitive boundaries that the order will encompass.[7]

James Rosenau and Robert Cox both argue that international political orders operate at three levels: ideational, behavioral (or material), and institutional. The first involves values and belief systems, the second consists of recurring, patterned activities that express these beliefs, and the third is the formal mechanisms that the actors develop in order to pursue their ideational goals.[8] Political actors derive conceptions of the common good from the values that underlie the order, and the institutions are designed in part to promote and protect this good. Therefore, the common good is not an abstract, unchanging, or universal concept that is promoted for the "betterment of humankind." Rather, it is reflective of a dominant set of political values at a given time and within a given geographic or cognitive region.

[5] Richard Falk, "Contending Approaches to World Order," *Journal of International Affairs,* vol. 31 (Fall/Winter, 1977).

[6] This definition is a hybrid of concepts drawn primarily from James N. Rosenau, "Governance, Order, and Change in World Politics," in James N. Rosenau and Ernst-Otto Czempiel, eds., *Governance Without Government: Order and Change in World Politics* (Cambridge: Cambridge University Press, 1992) and Andreas Osiander, *The States System of Europe 1640–1990: Peacemaking and the Conditions of International Stability* (Oxford: Clarendon Press, 1994).

[7] See Steve Smith, "Is the Truth Out There?," in Rick Fawn and Jeremy Larkins, eds., *International Society after the Cold War: Anarchy and Order Reconsidered* (New York: St. Martin's Press, 1966), pp. 99, 101.

[8] James N. Rosenau, "Governance, Order, and Change in World Politics," in T. V. Paul and John Hall, eds., *International Order and the Future of World Politics,* (Cambridge: Cambridge University Press, 1999), pp. 14–15 and Robert Cox (with Timothy Sinclair), *Approaches to World Order* (Cambridge: Cambridge University Press, 1996).

A variety of scholars from divergent perspectives have argued that states attempt to construct these international orders to promote particular principles and values in world affairs.[9] Gordon Craig and Alexander George, for example, suggest that a viable international system requires an agreement among the principal actors concerning their aims and objectives that reflect the dominant values that they are seeking to preserve and enhance. Lacking this basic agreement, the system will be unstable and conflict among the principal actors would be likely. When a community of states reaches this broad level of consensus, they can develop a set of procedural norms, rules, and institutions to achieve their common objectives.[10] Ikenberry refers to this as a "constitutional" order.[11] This framework of political, social, and economic institutions provides the material foundation for the international order. In this sense I agree with Steve Smith that international orders are something that actors construct, not something we "discover."[12]

For example, after World War II political leaders in North America and Western Europe sought to build a transatlantic liberal political order based on the principles of free trade, economic cooperation, democratic governance, and multilateralism.[13] These principles reflected a robust and sophisticated set of beliefs about security, prosperity, and the causes of war and depression.[14] At least some American political analysts believed that they could best provide for security within the West by promoting international law, building international organizations, and supporting the spread of liberal democracy.[15] Toward this end they established a set of institutions (such as the European Economic Community, NATO and GATT) that often required states to act on behalf of the

[9] See, *inter alia*, G. John Ikenberry, *After Victory*; Osiander, *The States System of Europe*, especially, pp. 8–9; Gilpin, *War and Change in World Politics*, ch. 2; and Henry Kissinger, *A World Restored: Metternich, Castlereagh and the Problems of Peace, 1812–1822* (Boston: Houghton Mifflin, 1959) , especially the introduction.

[10] Gordon Craig and Alexander George, *Force and Statecraft: Diplomatic Problems of Our Time* (New York: Oxford University Press, 1995), p. x.

[11] Ikenberry, *After Victory*, pp. 29–37.

[12] Smith, "Is the Truth Out There?," p. 103.

[13] See, for example, the eight principles contained in the Atlantic Charter, August 14, 1941 and the principles cited in the preamble of the North Atlantic Treaty, April 4, 1949.

[14] G. John Ikenberry, "Liberal Hegemony," in T. V. Paul and John Hall, eds., *International Order and the Future of World Politics* (Cambridge: Cambridge University Press, 1999), p. 126.

[15] This obviously reflects the idealist side of American political thinking. See David Callahan, *Between Two Worlds: Realism, Idealism, and American Foreign Policy After the Cold War* (New York: HarperCollins Publishers, 1994), p. 57.

collectivity, even when they did not directly benefit.[16] Thus, for example, political leaders have often defied powerful domestic constituencies when they believed that the cohesion of the EEC or NATO was at stake.

History suggests that political leaders tend to create political orders in the aftermath of major wars and/or widespread revolution. Systemic crises often undermine existing authority and weaken the political foundation of international relations. Rapid change tends to produce uncertainty and insecurity both within states and among political actors who interact at the international level. Political life loses its spontaneity and the norms and principles that legitimized domestic authority and power relations can no longer be taken for granted. On another level, widespread unrest and war also provide an opportunity for a winning coalition to restructure the system and redefine commitments and obligations. This provides permissive conditions for a dramatic reorganization of international relations.

At the same time, there are also positive factors that encourage states to develop more cohesive relationships and institutions than are typically found in international society, creating what may be termed a "solidarist moment." A solidarist approach to international order is one where the interests of the collective form an important foundation of international relations, and thus a greater degree of consensus around common values and goals are present. Such a moment is made possible by the two factors: a sense of solidarity that develops among the creators from a shared experience of high intensity and long duration and a convergence of domestic political structures. For example, political leaders developed close bonds by working together as allies during World War I, as a transnational Resistance movement during World War II, and as a liberal democratic community during the Cold War. These experiences reduce the conceptual barriers that divide states and increase their perception of interdependence.[17] It also enables them to consider the foundation for maintaining these relations on a longer-term basis. This inevitably involves developing common goals and values. This is enhanced by a

---

[16] I am aware that many security studies specialists consider NATO to be a strictly military alliance, however many scholars also conceptualize the organization as a type of transatlantic security community. See, for example, John Ruggie, "Consolidating the European Pillar: The Key to NATO's Future," *Washington Quarterly*, vol. 20 (1997).

[17] For the sociological foundation of this phenomenon in international relations, see Cronin, *Community Under Anarchy*, ch. 2.

convergence in the dominant political values among groups of states sharing a common form of domestic political structure.[18]

In considering the composition of a postwar order, then, states often look beyond simply creating a regional security order (for which sophisticated realism can account) toward one that builds upon shared values such as national self-determination, human freedom, or cultural pluralism.

The construction of an international order is a therefore a process by which a group of political elites establishes new principles, institutions, and practices that shape the political environment through which they interact. States construct them by synthesizing their national preferences into a consensus agenda.[19] Once they agree on a broad set of political values and goals, they try to reconcile their often-conflicting parochial interests through negotiation in the pursuit of a common program. This is usually a difficult process that is not always successful. The creation of a Western liberal economic order after World War II, for example, reflected the resolution of several tensions that existed among the creators, such as Anglo-American versus continental political philosophies, security versus economic priorities, American globalism versus European regionalism, and liberal capitalism versus social democracy.[20]

On one level, the synthesis of preferences requires individual states to adopt a collective approach toward defining and addressing the major issues within international society.[21] For example, the creation of the Concert of Europe after the Napoleonic Wars involved more than simple

---

[18] For an examination of solidarism through a convergence of domestic political structures, see R.J. Vincent, "Western Conceptions of a Universal Moral Order," *British Journal of International Studies*, vol. 4, no. 1 (1978), pp. 20–46 and Fred Halliday, "International Society as Homogeneity: Burke, Marx, Fukuyamam," *Millennium*, vol. 21, no. 3 (1992), pp. 435–61.

[19] I am using the term "synthesis" in a dialectical sense. More than simply the sum of individual interests, a synthesis of preferences is a process through which the tension between conflicting interests is resolved. The result is a new, independent outcome that reflects, but cannot be reduced to, the individual inputs. See Georg Wilhelm Friedrich Hegel, *The Science of Logic*, vol. I (London: George Allen and Unwin, 1929), pp. 63–67.

[20] John Ruggie refers to the resolution of the latter as the "compromise of embedded liberalism." See his "International Regimes, Transactions, and Change: Embedded Liberalism in the Postwar Economic Order," in Stephen Krasner, ed., *International Regimes* (Ithaca: Cornell University Press, 1983).

[21] Historian Paul Schroeder refers to this as "systemic thinking," while Osiander calls it "systemic-consciousness." See Paul Schroeder, "The Transformation of Political Thinking, 1787–1848," in Jack Snyder and Robert Jervis, eds., *Coping With Complexity in the International System* (Boulder: Westview Press, 1993) and Osiander, *The States System of Europe*.

cooperation among independent actors; it also demanded that the participating states approach the issue of security from a European rather than a strictly national perspective.

On another level, the construction of an international order also requires that states incorporate the needs of the collective into their own definitions of interest. Thus, for example, Egypt's attempt to build a pan-Arab political order in North Africa during the 1950s required that its leadership at least publicly broaden its definition of state interest to include the advancement of Arab nationalism.[22] This dialectical process of harmonizing the individual with the collective produces a concept of a common good in which the group consensus reflects both individual preferences and collective interests. While states continue to retain their own parochial interests, this process creates a new set of preferences and incentives that political leaders must then take into account.

Developing a consensus around what constitutes the common good is a difficult and complex process. At any particular moment in history there are a variety of alternative principles and values competing for supremacy and legitimation within international society. In cases where political leaders cannot reconcile them there will be either multiple international orders (for example, on the Eurasian continent during the Cold War) or none at all (for example, in Europe during the interwar period). As a necessary condition for a consensus agenda, there must exist among a group of states some compatibility of world views and a willingness to compromise in order to achieve a common vision. At the same time, there are a variety of other factors that influence whether or how competing values are ultimately reconciled: the number and relative strength of revisionist powers, the influence of transnational social movements, the impact of domestic politics on the national leadership, and the influence of external events (such as a recent war or revolution).

For many International Relations theorists, the cohesion of an international order is determined by the distribution of power. Robert Gilpin and Stephen Krasner, for example, both argue that a stable international order requires the presence of a dominant state with the willingness and ability to impose a set of rules on the system. The features and dynamics of the political order reflect the parochial interest of the hegemonic state,

---

[22] For one study on the tension between state sovereignty and Arab nationalism, see Michael Barnett, "Sovereignty, Nationalism and Regional Order in the Arab States System," *International Organization*, vol. 49 (1995).

not a systemic or regional consensus.[23] The so-called collective interest is actually the interest of the hegemon imposed on the system.

Yet while a regional or global empire could theoretically form through imposition and domination, balance of power theory clearly predicts that the other great powers would act to prevent a single power from dominating the system for any significant period of time. In the absence of a general agreement on the conditions of international stability and justice, any attempt by one state to impose a regional or global political order on the system will likely be countered by a balancing alliance.[24] As a result, a pluralistic political order (such as that which would exist in an international society of states) requires some level of consensus. Under these conditions, politics involves negotiation to achieve *interdependent* outcomes through an aggregation of individual preferences into collective actions.[25]

The greater the desire to reach some form of consensus, the less power considerations matter. In circumstances where political leaders value their relationships with each other, strategic interaction is not so much about winning or dominating, but rather about developing a set of procedures and principles that will help to maintain the common goals of the group. Political leaders participate in these processes because they see an inherent value in both the process and the institution. In doing so, they identify some of their interests with those of the collective. For example, while members of the Group of Seven bring their own national preferences to each forum, they tend to treat each other as partners rather than competitors. In fact, the United States and others will sometimes act *against* their parochial or domestic interest in order to strengthen and further the goals of the group. This is most likely to occur when its leadership determines that the cohesion of the community of advanced capitalist democracies is at stake. Thus, *the more the actors value their common goals as an objective, the more likely that they will be willing to aggregate*

[23] Gilpin, *War and Change in World Politics*, ch. 1. Stephen Krasner, "State Power and the Structure of International Trade," *World Politics*, vol. 28, no. 3 (1976).

[24] See, *inter alia*, Arnold Wolfers, "The Balance of Power in Theory and Practice," in his *Discord and Collaboration: Essays on International Politics* (Baltimore: The Johns Hopkins University Press, 1962), ch. 8; Hans Morganthau, *Politics Among Nations: The Struggle for Power and Peace* (New York: Knopf, 1973), part IV; Waltz, *Theory of International Politics*, pp. 123–28; Barry R. Posen, *The Sources of Military Doctrine: France, Britain, and Germany Between the World Wars* (Ithaca: Cornell University Press, 1984). For critiques of balance of power theory, see Inis Claude, *Power and International Relations* (New York: Random House, 1962), chs. 2 and 3, and Ernst Haas, "The Balance of Power: Prescription, Concept, or Propaganda," *World Politics*, vol. 5 (July 1953), pp. 442–77.

[25] Lamborn, "Theory and the Politics in World Politics," pp. 191, 202.

their individual preferences in ways that produce a consensus around a common good. This establishes a foundation for a self-sustaining, cohesive international order.

Over time, international orders can become durable and self-sustaining through both domestic and international processes. As political leaders become more deeply involved with the institutions of an international order, its fundamental principles can become embedded within the political and social structures of their societies and state institutions. The deeper the links that states develop with various networks of international and transnational social relations, the more that these interactions will help to shape their perceptions of the world and their role within it.[26] This can have important effects domestically. For example, the links between the democratizing states of Eastern Europe and West European institutions such as the European Union, the OSCE, and NATO, have helped to institutionalize many of the democratic principles of New Europe within these states.[27]

At the same time, the principles and procedures that help to define the relationships among political leaders can become adopted as customary and habitual, particularly if there are no compelling reasons to change them. John Ikenberry argues that over time many institutions develop a "lock-in" effect that solidifies valued relationships and commitments and that raises the costs of change.[28] This is accomplished in part through "institutional binding," a process by which states agree to accept mutual constraints by adopting multilateral treaties, interlocking organizations, and joint management responsibilities. This web of commitments makes it difficult and costly to defect in the future.[29] Thus the institutions of an international order can help to socialize political leaders by providing a standard for evaluation and a medium for interaction. In fact, for some, the most important feature of a stable international order is its spontaneity and "taken-for-grantedness."[30]

As a consequence, as an international order becomes more established, the entrance requirements for new participants become less

---

[26] See Martha Finnemore, *National Interests in International Society* (Ithaca: Cornell University Press, 1996), p. 2.

[27] See Jon Pevehouse, "Democracy from the Outside-In? International Organizations and Democratization," *International Organization*, vol. 56, no. 3 (Summer 2002).

[28] Ikenberry, "Liberal Hegemony," p. 136.

[29] See Daniel Deudney, "Binding Sovereigns: Authorities, Structures, and Geopolitics in Philadelphian Systems," in Thomas Biersteker and Cynthia Weber, eds., *State Sovereignty as Social Construct* (Cambridge: Cambridge University Press, 1996).

[30] See, for example, Kissinger, *A World Restored*, introduction.

flexible. This is particularly true for newly formed or reconstituted states and "outsiders" wishing to join the institutions of the order.[31] Thus, for example, the European Union has placed very strict conditions on Turkey's attempt to join the institutions of Western Europe, particularly in the areas of human rights and economic liberalism.

State identity and the principles of international order

Andreas Osiander argues that as states construct a new international order, they attempt to develop a consensus around a fundamental set of assumptions concerning three structural aspects: the identity of the units that will dominate the new order, their relative status *vis-à-vis* one another, and the distribution of territories between them.[32] He labels the sum of these shared assumptions and principles as a consensus agenda. I contend that the identity of the units is the primary aspect, and that the other principles are derivative of this. This provides the foundation upon which international protection regimes are built.

On the most fundamental level, the identity of the units refers to the primary actors in international affairs. For the past several centuries, this has meant territorial states. For neorealists such as Waltz, one does not need to differentiate among types of states in order to understand behavior at the systemic level. In an environment of unregulated competition, the logic of anarchy forces all states to act similarly in their relations with each other. Thus, states are far less concerned with the internal organization or identity of each other than with their capabilities.[33]

At the same time, the stability of the nation-state system requires a legitimizing principle for sovereign statehood. Without some standard for determining how territory, populations, and authority would be distributed, it would be impossible to sustain a state system. As an institutional entity, the state has no natural boundaries; absent some commonly accepted principle of organization, a system composed of such units is likely to experience ongoing and enduring conflict.[34] The distribution

---

[31] Although as David Armstrong has demonstrated, new entrants such as revolutionary states can also influence the direction of world politics by introducing new principles of order. This could be considered a form of "reverse socialization." See his *Revolution and World Order* (Oxford: Oxford University Press, 1996).

[32] Osiander, *The States System of Europe*, p. 5.

[33] Waltz, *Theory of International Politics*, pp. 97–98.

[34] See Buzan, "International Society and International Security," p. 176.

of territory among competing authorities would be arbitrary and unstable. States would routinely expand and contract according to their
capabilities and opportunities. Populations would have no clear identity, and their allegiances would be constantly changing. However, once
the idea of the state was broadened to include territorial and social criteria (for example, dynastic or ethnic lineage), it becomes a more fixed
and defined object. Given an agreement on these definitions, conflicts
over territory have been minimized.

Moreover, while states may behave similarly under conditions of high
threat and insecurity, the determination of whether they become status
quo or revisionist powers is usually related to their compatibility with
the principles of the international order.[35] Thus, to the degree that domestic politics affects foreign policy, the internal political organization
of states greatly influences their external behavior. For these reasons,
states have always been concerned with the *types* of states that populate
a regional or global political system.[36] The organizing principle upon
which a state is based has long provided the primary criteria for membership in international society. That is, the institutionalization of the
nation-state rests with the notion that there are external social requirements for statehood; a state is supposed to look a certain way and do
certain things.[37]

Over the past several hundred years, the nation-state system has
been highly successful in accommodating various forms of authority
within the institution of sovereign statehood. Thus, we have had dynastic states, legitimized through family lineage and legal titles to territory;
national states, legitimized through the principle of ethnic and cultural
autonomy; theocratic states, legitimized through divine law; civic liberal states, legitimized through social contract; and civic multicultural
states, legitimized through the principle of cultural pluralism. In each
case, legitimate sovereignty has resided within different political actors
in society. From this perspective, one can define a "form of state" by the
location of sovereign authority within it. This in turn helps to determine

---

[35] For an in-depth discussion of revisionist states and their relationship to systemic stability, see Randall Schweller, "Bandwagoning for Profit: Bringing the Revisionist State
Back In," *International Security*, vol. 19, no. 1 (Summer 1994), p. 105.

[36] For an interesting study of how states attempt to influence the type of governmental
system in other states, see John M. Owen IV, "If Regime Type Doesn't Matter Why Do
States Act Like it Does?," Paper presented at the annual meeting of the International
Studies Association, Washington, DC, February 19, 1999.

[37] See, for example, Connie McNeely, *Constructing the Nation-State: International Organization and Prescriptive Action* (Westport, CT: Greenwood Press, 1995), p. 37 and Wight,
Systems of States, p. 153.

who has the legitimate "title" to the territory, where the borders would be drawn, and who can speak for the population.

In a monarchic or dynastic state, sovereignty resides within a recognized royal family, and thus the population has no independent political existence. Such families usually retain their territories through legal titles and historical possession, both of which have long been recognized under international law. This principle was well articulated by King Louis XVI, who argued that, "the sovereign power of the kingdom (state) belongs to the king alone . . . he is accountable only to God for the exercise of his supreme power."[38] When this form of authority dominated in Europe, populations were regularly "bartered about" and "reassigned" to other states, either as compensation to sovereigns or to facilitate the balance of power. Accordingly, sovereignty could only be transferred legally by royal will or marriage compact. As the Austrian Emperor Francis II put it: "A Prince can, if he wishes, cede a part of his country and all of its people" to create a new state or enlarge an existing one. "If he abdicates, then his rights are passed on to his legitimate heirs."[39] While dynastic sovereignty is becoming increasingly less common, it still exists in many parts of the world.

In a theocratic state, sovereignty resides within the body of the faithful (represented by a recognized religious leader) and is legitimized through divine law. The identity of the population is fixed; however, borders that divide those of the faith are not recognized. For example, the Islamic principle of *umma* holds the community of Moslems to be the basic political unit. All members of that community are bound together by ties of religion, rather than nationality or lineage.[40] This was the foundation of Iran's call for a "revolution without borders," and underlies the claim by some Moslem countries that they have a right to support and arm Moslem communities *within* other states.[41]

In a national state, sovereignty rests with a defined ethnic or cultural community. Political association is based on "objective" characteristics of the population such as a common language, culture, ethnicity and/or shared history (which may be real or imagined). Citizenship is derived

[38] Quoted in Albert Sorel, *Europe and the French Revolution: The Political Traditions of the Old Régime*, trans. and ed. A. Cobban and J. W. Hunt (London: Collins, 1969), p. 221. Parenthetical mine.

[39] Quoted in Guglielmo Ferrero, *The Reconstruction of Europe: Tallyrand and the Congress of Vienna, 1814–1815* (New York: G. P. Putnam and Sons, 1941), p. 261.

[40] See Reinhard Bendix, *Kings or Peoples: Power and the Mandate to Rule* (Berkeley: University of California Press, 1978), p. 39.

[41] See David Armstrong, *Revolution and World Order*, chapter 4.

from membership in that community. This community exists apart from the individuals that comprise it, and its members *inherit* their identities.[42] While citizenship within a liberal state (below) is inclusionary within defined boundaries, a state legitimized through the principle of nationality is potentially exclusionary and is not necessarily limited by political borders. The state exists as the institutional expression of nationhood. Thus territory is significant only inasmuch as co-nationals populate it or at least did at some crucial time in the historical past.

In a liberal state, sovereignty resides with the body of legally recognized citizens, each of whom enjoys juridical equality. The four principles that underlie such a state include: (1) the rule of law (government operates according to a specified set of rules that apply equally to all individuals including government officials); (2) some form of popular participation in government (usually through representative institutions); (3) the autonomy of civil society; and (4) a body of individual rights guaranteed by the state. Unlike a national state, citizenship in a liberal state is derived from political association – and legitimized through a "social contract" – rather than through membership in a particular community.[43] "Nationality" in this context does not have a legal existence; rather it is a political rather than a cultural or ethnic concept that encompasses the entire body politic. This idea is rooted in the thought of Rousseau and the practice can be traced to the French and American revolutions.[44] Thus, in theory, the liberal state is stripped of all identifiable characteristics such as ethnicity or religion in favor of abstract civic concepts that unite the citizenry.[45]

A civic multicultural state is also based in part on the citizen as the primary unit of society. However, unlike the liberal state, cultural groups are legally recognized and there is no concerted effort to homogenize the population into a single nationality. The multicultural state is therefore one that moves beyond tolerance and equal rights toward institutionalized cultural plurality. More specifically, a multicultural state actively promotes the public expression of national or ethnic identities and provides to such groups at least a moderate degree of cultural

---

[42] See, for example, Walker Connor, *Ethnonationalism: The Quest for Understanding* (Princeton: Princeton University Press, 1994) and Ernest Gellner, *Nations and Nationalism* (Ithaca, NY: Cornell University Press, 1983).

[43] See, for example, Julian Franklin, *John Locke and the Theory of Sovereignty: Mixed Monarchy and the Right of Resistance in the Political Thought of the English Revolution* (Cambridge: Cambridge University Press, 1991).

[44] See, for example, Rousseau, *Rousseau's Political Writings*, p. 103.

[45] John Rawls, A *Theory of Justice* (Cambridge, MA: Harvard University Press, 1999).

(although not necessarily territorial) autonomy. This institutional form allows for multiple cultural identities to exist within a single political community or polity. Sovereignty is therefore shared between the citizen and the cultural group, with no single language or ethnic group legally dominant. The promotion of national culture is conducted in both the public and private spheres.[46]

Finally, the twentieth century saw the emergence of a new form of state that could be called "bureaucratic authoritarian."[47] Such a state is one in which sovereignty is held by the institutions of the state and power is concentrated in the hands of a small group of elites – either military or civilian. The government itself is administered through a bureaucratic apparatus that relies on coercive force to regulate and/or control the institutions of civil society. Bureaucratic authoritarian states are usually created to pursue some type of social goal, such as rapid economic development or national unity, and their base of power is concentrated within a coalition of social groups, such as business or religious groups. European fascist states of the 1930s, for example, fused militant nationalism with bureaucratic authoritarianism as a way of reordering their societies. Stalinist states in the former Soviet Union and Eastern Europe would also fall within this category.

A regional or global order based on each of these state forms would lead to a different allocation of territory and population. For example, the ecclesiastical borders of the sixteenth century differed significantly from the dynastic boundaries of the eighteenth, which in turn differed dramatically from the national borders of the twentieth.[48] That is why political leaders find that some type of legitimizing principle is necessary

---

[46] The institutional mechanisms for governing such a state can vary. In some cases, such as the Swiss canton system, the organizational principle is territorial federalism. In other cases, for example in Belgium, each national group is guaranteed administrative and cultural autonomy. Thus while Belgium remains a unified nation-state with a distinct national identity, Belgian society equally reflects the cultures of the Walloons and Flemish.

[47] Guillermo O'Donnell coined the term "bureaucratic authoritarian regime" to describe a form of government that developed within Latin America during the 1970s and 1980s. He focused specifically on the role of authoritarian leaders in trying to "modernize" their societies through the coercive power of the state in coalition with various social groups. I am using the concept in a broader sense to describe a form of state that encompasses a wider cagagory of regimes than those discussed by O'Donnell. See his *Modernization and Bureaucratic-Authoritarianism: Studies in South American Politics* (Berkeley: Institute of International Studies, University of California, 1979).

[48] See Robert Jackson, "Boundaries and International Society," in B.A. Roberson, ed., *International Society and the Development of International Relations Theory* (London: Continuum, 2002), p. 157.

as a baseline for weighing competing territorial and authority claims. At its most basic level, a legitimizing principle informs the global collectivity who could become a state, where to draw the borders, and the essential prerogatives and obligations that sovereignty would entail. This would in turn directly influence the nature of interstate relations, since by empowering specific authorities it alters the structure of domestic politics.

Under normal circumstances, the legitimation of authority and the identity of the state are not key factors in the conduct of diplomatic relations. In practice, there have always been a variety of state forms coexisting within the international system, and international law and diplomatic tradition do not generally discriminate among them. Thus, monarchies have carried on diplomatic relations with liberal republics, ethnic nations with civic multiethnic states and so on. Moreover, the right to "continued existence" (the preservation of a state's corporate integrity) creates a presumption that states will not be reorganized or abolished.[49] This strongly favors the status quo.

At the same time, state succession is a persistent feature of diplomatic history. The creation, break-up, amalgamation, and reorganization of new and existing states in the aftermath of major wars or revolutions have been common since the beginnings of the state system. During these periods of systemic change, political leaders are forced to consider the legitimation of authority and the internal organization of states. State identity becomes a particularly important systemic issue, and political leaders are compelled to examine the compatibility of state forms with the principles of international order. When collectivities of states and international institutions recognize a new state or regime, they endow the new entity with a range of entitlements and responsibilities, which are the concomitants of sovereignty.[50] As Hedley Bull argues:

> Whatever rights are due to states or nations or other actors in international relations, they are subject to and limited by the rights of the international community ... The rights of sovereign states (thus) derive from the rules of the international community or society ...[51]

These rights and obligations are usually imposed by the collectivity of states.

---

[49] See von Glahn, *Law Among Nations*, pp. 102–03.
[50] Thomas Franck, "Legitimacy in the International System," *The American Journal of International Law*, vol. 82 (1988), p. 726.
[51] Hedley Bull, *Justice in International Relations: The 1983–84 Hagey Lectures* (Waterloo, Ont.: University of Waterloo), p. 11.

This view is captured in the following statement by French Prime Minister Clemenceau following World War I:

> It has for long been the established procedure of the public law of Europe that when a State is created . . . the joint and formal recognition of the Great Powers should be accompanied by the requirement that such States should, in the form of a binding international Convention, undertake to comply with certain principles of Government.[52]

For Clemenceau, however, it was not only the new or reorganized state that must accept certain obligations; the collectivity is also responsible for ensuring that the relations between the rulers and their populations reflect these principles of governance: "There rests, therefore, upon these Powers an obligation, which they cannot evade, to secure in the most permanent and solemn form guarantees for certain essential rights which will afford to the inhabitants the necessary protection."[53]

While states may be concerned about the balance of power implications inherent in the break-up or reorganization of existing states, they must also deal with competing claims from political actors within the newly emerging units. Postwar congresses and international institutions usually help to settle these claims by favoring one set of legitimizing principles over others.

During these periods, political leaders find that they must address the issue of legitimate statehood for very practical reasons: borders need to be drawn, redrawn, and/or reconfirmed, new governments need to be recognized or installed within territories where authority has collapsed or is contested, and a new set of workable diplomatic arrangements need to be created among states. While some decisions are inevitably made on the basis of convenience and opportunity, international institutions still need a set of principles to determine how to resolve conflicting claims from competing authorities. These principles reflect the type of political order the participating states wish to construct.

Under these conditions, states are concerned with each other's internal development not only because it influences the distribution of power in the system, but also because it affects the type of international order that will evolve. In this sense, states socialize each other and adopt a common set of practices and standards for judgment. Thus, the types of states that populate the system, the rules governing their relationships,

---

[52] Quoted in C. A. Macartney, *National States and National Minorities* (New York: Russell & Russell, 1968 [1934]), p. 238.
[53] Quoted in ibid., p. 238.

and the common assumptions that are shared by its members directly influence the kind of world in which they coexist. The maintenance of a system of preferred states becomes a common good.

In constructing a postwar or post-revolutionary order, diplomats and political leaders are particularly concerned with creating a stable environment that would promote and protect the values that Craig and George argue underlie any viable system.[54] Thus, every major settlement since the Peace of Westphalia in 1648 has focused on building a stable international order that would last at least a generation.[55] While much of the literature is concerned with efforts to create balances of power and/or collective security systems to protect the territorial integrity of states, political leaders have also been very concerned about the *types* of states that exist within the new political order. This is because the new order cannot remain cohesive and stable if it is populated by states whose organizing principles are inconsistent with those of the order.

For example, a system in which territory is allocated according to ethnicity/nationality would be unstable if a significant portion of the states were multinational empires. National self-determination requires congruence between the ethnic or cultural composition of the population and the political boundaries that define the state. It cannot remain a political principle of a regional order if the territorial organization of the region violates it. Similarly, a dynastic system cannot endure in a region populated by liberal or national states.

For this reason, after major wars winning coalitions have routinely reorganized the internal structure of the losing states. In most cases, they do so because they believe certain types of states to be inherently more aggressive and less stable. For example, after the Napoleonic Wars, the Quadruple Alliance not only stripped France of its military capabilities, they also reinstated the Bourbon monarchy. This was done in part because leaders such as Metternich believed that liberalism and nationalism were a threat to European monarchy and were therefore inherently disruptive.[56] Similarly, the allied powers after World War II reorganized Germany, Japan, and Italy into liberal states by purging the

---

[54] Henry Kissinger, for example, argues that legitimacy (and following from this, stability) implies that all of the major powers accept the framework of the international order (*A World Restored*, p. 102).

[55] See the cases in Osiander, *The States System of Europe*.

[56] Kalevi Holsti, *Peace and War: Armed Conflicts and International Order, 1648–1989* (Cambridge: Cambridge University Press, 1991), p. 117.

governments of all fascist institutions and imposing Western-style constitutions on them. While balance of power theory can explain why such a coalition might place limits on a losing states' armed forces or ability to wage war, it does not tell us why they should be concerned about their internal structure. In a balance of power system, states are only concerned about capabilities, not intentions or state identity.[57] Rather, it is a concern for stability and a compatibility with the principles of the new order that motivates this behavior.

International orders and international protection regimes

The above discussion suggests that the cohesion and stability of an international order is linked to the types of states that comprise it. Once a collectivity of states has agreed on the principles upon which new states could be created or transitioning states reorganized, they need to address the consequences of its decisions. These consequences are felt most strongly within the domestic arena of the new or reorganized states. The character of any state is defined largely by the political and social relationships that exist among various segments of the population and the relationships that develop between these groups and the state elite. The creation or reorganization of a state often requires individuals and groups to adopt new identities and redefine their relationships with each other and with their governments. This increases the potential for social conflict.

For example, as T. A. Elliot demonstrates, tribal identities in Africa had to become reclassified as national when they became attached to a particular territory after decolonization.[58] In this sense, the population had to be made into "citizens" within a centralized polity, a process that has met with limited success. As the world witnessed in Rwanda, Somalia, and Congo during the 1990s, a nation-state cannot endure in a society where the population's primary loyalties are directed toward tight-knit localized communities. Similarly, when national states are created, the population needs to adopt the nationality of the dominant group, even though many may be large ethnic minorities within the new polity. For this to occur, the population must accept their membership in their home

---

[57] Waltz, *Theory of International Politics*, ch. 6.
[58] T. A. Elliot, *Us and Them: A Study in Group Consciousness* (Aberdeen, Australia: Aberdeen University Press, 1986).

state rather than their kin state. And as we are currently witnessing in many parts of the world, governments in newly democratizing states find that they must balance their desire to maintain social order with the need to accommodate the upsurge in public participation that is encouraged by the creation of a liberal state.[59]

Under these conditions, states constructing an international order have an interest in seeing that particular actors are protected because a dissatisfied population or ruling elite may be prone to revolt, secede, or annex themselves to a neighboring state. The effects of this on the stability of an international order are obvious. Moreover, an international order cannot remain cohesive if there is a disjuncture between the principles of the political order and those of the states that comprise it. For example, an international order based on national self-determination can only endure if it is populated by cohesive national states. As a result, the stabilization of specific forms of state is necessary for the progress and cohesion of the international order and therefore becomes a common good for the collectivity.

When such situations develop, international institutions will usually require as a condition of recognition that all new, reorganized or reconfirmed states accept principles of governance that are consistent with those of the new order. This helps to ensure both the stability of the states and the cohesion of the system. At the same time, stability and cohesion also require that vulnerable segments of the population be secure from threat by the newly emerging dominant segments. Depending on the type of states that are built, this could mean protecting the population from the government, the government from the population, or one segment of the population from another. The leading states will thus establish mechanisms to protect populations within states that could potentially disrupt the political order. These mechanisms are the heart of the international protection regime.

In general, a protection regime contains the following three elements: (1) a legitimizing principle that provides a political or normative foundation for singling out a specific population; (2) one or more multilateral treaties or agreements that codify the commitment to protect them; and (3) some type of institutional mechanism to articulate and implement the guarantees. These mechanisms may be weak (standard-setting or monitoring) or strong (coercive enforcement), but they must be viewed

---

[59] See, for example, Jack Snyder, "Averting Anarchy in the New Europe," *International Security*, vol. 14, no. 4 (Spring 1990).

as obligations by the participating states.[60] Thus, *ad hoc* actions under-taken on behalf of a population by one or more states do not constitute a regime, nor does a series of interventions by an alliance promoting a strategic goal.

An IPR also involves three categories of participants: the protectors, the target states, and the protected groups. The protectors are the ini-tiators and guarantors of the regime; the target states are the objects and the protected groups are the beneficiaries. In some cases the protec-tors and targets could overlap, particularly when the protectors subject themselves to the same rules that they impose on others. Whichever way the institution is organized, however, to be considered a regime, the participants in all three categories must be well defined and each group must be aware of its role. At the same time, not all states in a given system need participate in the regime for it to be a coherent institution (although for it to remain cohesive it must have at least tacit support from a broad range of states). Only those states that could potentially defend or disrupt the political order are vital participants.

At its center, an IPR requires a core of states with the capabilities, willingness, and legitimacy to provide security guarantees to the tar-get populations. The protectors can be either a concert of powers or a multilateral organization with the authority to implement international norms. Formal treaties, protocols, or binding resolutions (in an inter-national organization) are necessary to codify these guarantees into political and/or legal obligations. They are important also for estab-lishing procedures and limits that would prevent protecting states from acting arbitrarily or unilaterally. In order to maintain legitimacy and check each other against unilateral acts, collectivities of states tend to coordinate IPRs through multilateral institutions such as the Concert of Europe, the League of Nations, the United Nations, the Organization for Security and Cooperation in Europe, or the Council of Europe. Such institutions have historically addressed the collective action problem by relying on deliberative bodies to authorize a particular action rather than responding to automatic "triggers."[61] They have also generally used consensus decisionmaking rather than majority voting to ensure broad support.

---

[60] Jack Donnelly distinguishes between four different types of regimes based on their degree of coercion: declaratory, promotional, implementational, and enforcement. See Donnelly, "International Human Rights," p. 633.

[61] See, for example, ch. 7 (Articles 39–51) of the United Nations Charter.

Target states are those whose internal political relationships could pose a threat or challenge to the principles and cohesion of the political order. Since this is most likely to occur within new or reorganized states, such states tend to be the primary targets. Their participation in the regime is usually secured through binding agreements that commit them to observe certain principles of governance as the cost of membership in international society. In making these commitments, the targets implicitly or explicitly agree to accept a form of multilateral intervention that could range from simple monitoring to coercive enforcement.

At the same time, there is no single model of enforcement that can apply to all IPRs. Generally, the range of enforcement measures will vary according to the will and capabilities of the protectors as well as the level of commitment the institution coordinating the regime is willing and able to make. There will inevitably also be political considerations that are factored in, for example the quality of the violator's relationship to the protectors or the costs the protectors would have to bear in a particular adventure. At the minimum, violators can expect to be excluded from the institutions of the political order. Beyond that, enforcement mechanisms can range from diplomatic sanctions to collective military intervention.

This does not mean, however, that all non-conformist states will be targets. As suggested in chapter 1, international societies create outsiders as well as insiders and international orders tend to have geographic and/or political boundaries. Theories of international society do not suggest that insiders will necessarily attempt to either socialize or forcibly incorporate outsiders. In fact the histories of colonialism and slavery suggest that insiders are more likely to exploit outsiders and exclude them from their institutions.[62] States that remain outside of the political order (so-called pariah states) are not subject to the norms of the regime. Thus, for example, the transatlantic community after World War I did not extend minority rights protection to other regions of the world, nor did the West European powers include non-Europeans in their human rights regime after World War II.

Like the identity of the target states, the identity of the target populations depends upon the type of international order the dominant states

---

[62] For two discussions of how "insiders" have historically viewed "outsiders" in selected cases, see Gerrit Gong, *The Standard of Civilization in International Society* (Oxford: Oxford University Press, 1984) and Donald Puchala and Raymond Hopkins, "International Regimes: Lessons from Inductive Analysis," in Stephen D. Krasner, ed., *International Regimes* (Ithaca: Cornell University Press, 1983), especially p. 80.

seek to construct. Since the purpose of IPRs is not primarily humanitarian, target populations are not chosen on the basis of their suffering. While many segments of the population may be potentially threatened, the protectors are most interested in the security of those whose abuse could endanger the cohesion of the state and by extension the international order. This is determined by the type of target state. For example, the cohesion of a monarchy requires that the line of succession not be threatened, and that the subjects remain loyal to the king or royal family. For this reason, a protection regime in a dynastic order will guarantee the security of the monarchy from the population. Since the ethnic composition of the population is politically irrelevant in such a state, national minorities as such do not exist, and are therefore neither recognized nor protected.

On the other hand, in a national state, the treatment of ethnic minorities poses a potential threat, since their nationality does confer a political status *vis-à-vis* the dominant ethnic group. Such a state would not be stable if members of these groups failed to consider themselves as citizens of their home country, but rather favored affiliation with their kin state. As a result, the nineteenth-century Holy Alliance sought to protect dynastic families in order to maintain the stability of the European dynastic order, while the League of Nations tried to protect ethnic minorities in support of the national state.

Since IPRs are created to support specific types of political orders among a given collectivity of states, they do not represent the institutionalization of universal values. We should therefore not expect the protecting states to apply the norms of the regime consistently or evenly. As suggested above, the regime is targeted specifically at those states that have the potential for disrupting the institutions and principles of the order. Thus the regime is potentially but not necessarily an association of equals. Unlike conventions, in which states agree to observe certain codes of conduct regardless of how others behave, IPRs do not necessarily require the protecting states to make any adjustments to their own internal policies, although they may in fact decide to do so.

Still, the protecting states and/or the organization coordinating the regime assume a political and legal obligation to enforce the norms of the regime even when it is not in their immediate interest to do so. While the extent to which individual protectors actually meet their obligations is not a main focus of this study, one can posit a variety of international and domestic factors that influence this. Internationally, protecting states are more likely to act when the stability and cohesiveness of the international order is at stake, particularly if they value the progress of the order. Moreover, the smaller and more cohesive the group of protectors, the more likely they will be able to overcome the potential collective action problems that are inherent in these types of enterprises.[63] For this reason, a concert of great powers is more likely to be effective than a broader, more representative body.

At the same time, while political elites from various states may be able to achieve a consensus among themselves, they may not be able to sell it domestically. This could mitigate some of the factors cited above. Although theories of state agency generally assume that the composition of the political leadership reflects the outcome of domestic political struggle, this outcome may be tentative and thus unstable. This can help to explain why international institutions often act inconsistently and hesitantly in enforcing their commitments, even in cases where there are no substantial disagreements among the leaders. Thus, the ability of a collectivity to promote a cohesive international order is conditioned upon a substantial degree of internal political unity within the member states.

The next four chapters will examine how these principles have been applied in practice.

---

[63] On the link between size and cohesion see Mancur Olson, *The Logic of Collective Action: Public Goods and the Theory of Groups* (Cambridge, MA: Harvard University Press, 1965), ch. 1.

3   The national state and the protection of ethnic minorities

Hannah Arendt argues that the creation of the "national minority" as a permanent institution – a *modus vivendi* between different ethnic groups living in the same territory – was one of the most unique initiatives introduced in the aftermath of World War I.[1] While the fate of religious minorities had long been an international issue with countries that had a state religion, the political existence of national or ethnic minorities had never before been officially recognized by international institutions.[2]

So long as the states of Europe were conceived as either political/ economic institutions or as the territorial realm of a monarch or emperor, they remained separate from considerations of nationality. This did not change significantly even after the "age of nationalism" swept the continent. Ever since the end of the "great migrations" of the early Middle Ages, there had been relative stability in the composition of the populations within Western Europe.[3] As a result, when these territories became states and later developed a concept of "nationality," there was a fair degree of ethnic homogeneity within them, at least as "ethnicity" came to be defined in the West.[4]

At the same time, the vast prewar empires of central, eastern and southern Europe had been truly multinational, with no single ethnic group holding a majority. At its height, the Russians comprised only

---

[1] Hannah Arendt, "Concerning Minorities," *Contemporary Jewish Record*, vol. 8, no. 3 (1945), p. 359.

[2] The exception to this was the status of the Polish populations within Russia and the Hapsburg Empire at the Congress of Vienna in 1815. The Polish question was unique inasmuch as Poland had been eliminated as a nation-state and partitioned among the Hapsburgs, the Russians, and the Prussians at the end of the eighteenth century.

[3] T. H. Bagley, *International Protection of National Minorities* (Geneva: Georg, 1950), p. 10.

[4] This, of course, was not true in all cases. Switzerland and Belgium, for example, never had a dominant nationality.

44 percent of the Romanov empire, the Germans less than 37 percent of Austria-Hungary and the Magyars only 48 percent of the Hapsburg's Hungarian territories.[5] Political loyalties were directed toward the emperors and kings who ruled the territories, not toward one's ethnic community. Minorities and majorities had mathematical significance only. In fact, with a few exceptions (such as the Poles, Magyars, and Croats), the ethno-linguistic groups within the great empires were not even "nationalities" in an historical sense, since they had never before constituted independent political communities.[6] Consequently, the concept of "national minority" only gained political significance when nationality (defined in ethnic terms) became the central factor in the definition of the state. This was one of the most important legacies of the postwar era.

How and why the principal political actors of the postwar period decided to single out national minorities for special recognition and protection in the new European order is the focus of this chapter. Little has been written in the political science literature about the protection of national minorities after the war, however a standard realist argument might view the regime as a reflection of the power preferences of the dominant states.[7] From this perspective, one could hypothesize that the allied powers sought to protect national minorities in eastern and central Europe in order to facilitate a favorable balance of power and/or to ensure that their security interests be preserved. France, for example, was particularly concerned with containing Germany and reducing its power. All of the allies wanted to prevent Russian expansion into eastern and southern Europe, particular after the Bolshevik revolution. Toward this end, one can hypothesize that minority protection would help to maintain stability within a ring of "buffer states" that would surround Germany and Russia.

Another explanation for the creation of the regime is the spread of transnational norms facilitated by nongovernmental organizations and

[5] Raymond Pearson, *National Minorities in Eastern Europe, 1848–1945* (New York: St. Martin's Press, 1983), pp. 148–49.
[6] Jean Bérenger, *A History of the Habsburg Empire, 1700–1918,* C. A. Simpson, trans. (London: Longman, 1997), p. 213.
[7] Jennifer Jackson Preece and Stephen Krasner are two of the few political scientists who examine this issue, each from a very different perspective. Krasner's project does not seek to explain why the great powers tried to protect minorities, but rather to demonstrate that they did so with little regard for the norms of sovereignty and nonintervention. See his *Sovereignty: Organized Hypocrisy,* pp. 90–96. Preece's comprehensive study explores the question of national minorities from an historical perspective. See her *National Minorities and the European Nation-States System* (Oxford: Oxford University Press, 1998).

entrepreneurial leaders. The principle of national self-determination had been gaining widespread support among the populations and intellectual circles of Europe and the United States for at least a decade prior to the war. As Jennifer Jackson Preece argues, national minority rights were an attempt to offset the widespread violations to the prevailing rule of legitimacy, that is national self-determination as the criterion for statehood.[8] To the extent that national minorities were being denied their right of self-determination, idealist "norm entrepreneurs" such as Woodrow Wilson had humanitarian and ideological motives for seeing that they were protected from repression. In this quest he received considerable support from nongovernmental organizations. During and after the war, peace societies, transnational organizations, and domestic Jewish groups in the United States and Britain put political pressure on their governments to monitor the behavior of states toward their kin.

In the following pages, I argue that neither of these factors was significant in the decision to build an international protection regime for national minorities. Rather, the decision by the allied powers to create a European order based on the national state led them down a path that ultimately required their direct intervention in the relationship between the governments of the newly created and reorganized states and the national minorities living within the borders of these states. I hold that the primary purpose of this intervention was to promote the values of the new European order by facilitating the cohesion and stability of the new national states. By counterfactual inference, I also suggest that this would not have occurred had a different type of order – for example liberal or socialist – emerged from the ruins of the war.

In considering this argument – and the competing explanations for the construction of the national-minority protection regime – I trace the process through which the victorious powers attempted to settle the outstanding issues raised at the end of the war. In particular, I examine how they attempted to resolve the internal tensions that developed in the process of reconstruction, and the way they chose to adapt to the changing environment following the end of World War I. I also examine the strategic interests of the victorious powers, the competing visions of international order, the roles played by transnational organizations,

---

[8] Preece, *National Minorities and the European Nation-States System*, p. 123.

and the prevailing ideas and beliefs of the primary actors concerning security, justice, and order.

The political and strategic environment

World War I occurred in an environment where radically different types of states coexisted. Britain and France were liberal states, Italy and Serbia national states, Germany a national empire, Austria-Hungary and Russia dynastic empires and Ottoman Turkey a theocratic empire. The political order that governed the relationships among these disparate units had been established almost four decades earlier at the 1878 Congress of Berlin. In many ways, the Congress had confirmed an uneasy – and ultimately unstable – coexistence that had evolved in Europe in the years following the European revolutions of 1848 and the wars of German and Italian unification.

The 1848 revolutions occurred simultaneously in fifteen countries, undermining the legitimacy of dynastic rule on the continent. Kings and princes were forced to abdicate, royal families fled, governments resigned, and revolutionary leaders established parliaments and other forms of popular government. Yet in virtually all cases the popular movements were divided between those advocating a sovereignty based alternatively on the nation (the nationalists), class (socialists), and citizens (liberal republicans).[9] Their inability to agree on a common program prevented the creation of a consensus agenda either domestically or within Europe. Consequently, while the traditional authorities were not able to re-establish the *ancien régime*, the revolutions ended in a political stalemate, without any particular form of state or international legitimizing principle dominating.

Compounding these dramatic changes, the integration of Italy and Germany changed the political and geographic map of central and southern Europe. For the first time in European history, the national state became a political force on the continent, empowering the disparate nationalist movements that had been evolving since the middle of the

---

[9] Priscilla Roberts argues that the overriding question of 1848 was whether one's loyalty should be to one's monarch, class, or nation. See her *Revolutions of 1848: A Social History* (Princeton: Princeton University Press, 1971), ch. 1. Other works examining the revolutions and their causes include: Frank Eyck, *The Revolutions of 1848–49* (New York: Barnes and Noble Books, 1972); J. A. S. Grenville, *Europe Reshaped: 1848–1878* (Sussex: Harvester Press, 1976); and David Ward, *1848: The Fall of Metternich and the Year of Revolution* (New York: Weybright and Talley, 1970).

century. This lead to semi-autonomy for the Magyars (Hungarians) in 1867 and the creation of new national states in Serbia, Montenegro, and Romania following the Russian–Turkish war of 1877–78.[10] Yet the nationalists were not the only political force on the continent. In France, Britain, and Belgium republicans and liberals gained power and the parliamentary monarchies of these countries began to transform into liberal states. Countering this trend, socialist movements grew throughout both eastern and western Europe, offering yet a different vision for the future of Europe.[11] In short, by the end of the nineteenth century, European politics was simultaneously moving in contradictory directions.

The Congress of Berlin did not attempt to resolve these tensions. Rather, it simply confirmed a new balance of power in Europe and within the colonial territories, without creating a consensus agenda. Among the many permissive causes of World War I stands this lack of political cohesion among the states of Europe. Thus, one way to look at the peace negotiations after World War I is as an attempt to address the "unfinished business" of the late nineteenth century.

The national-minority protection regime that was established by the great powers emerged from the reorganization of central, southern and eastern Europe following World War I. This reorganization was necessitated by the collapse of four empires, the desire of the allies to prevent future conflicts, and widespread domestic unrest aimed at undermining traditional authority in the region. Yet the question of *how* Europe would be reorganized was an open one for most of the war; indeed even in the immediate postwar period it was not clear which of several competing visions would ultimately win out: Bolshevism, liberal democracy, national self-determination, or geopolitical realism. Each of these visions would have required a different distribution of territory and different types of states inhabiting it. Following from this, the relationships between the new governments and their populations would have differed as well.

On the eve of the war, more than half of Europe's territory (and well over half of its population) was controlled by four empires: Ottoman, Austro-Hungarian (Hapsburg), Russian (Romanov), and German.[12]

---

[10] South Slav nationalism was particularly strong toward the end of the nineteenth century; as a political force it contributed toward the decline of the Ottoman empire and to the independence of Serbia and Montenegro. See A. J. P. Taylor, *The Struggle for Mastery in Europe, 1848–1918* (Oxford: Oxford University Press, 1986 [1954]), ch. 11.

[11] Ibid.

[12] Bagley, *International Protection of National Minorities*, p. 11.

Despite challenges from nationalists within the Bohemian and Slavic territories, on the eve of the war the Austro-Hungarian empire was a prosperous and cohesive great power.[13] However, its rocky history over the previous half century also suggested uncertainty both internally and within the European state system. More significantly, the tsarist regime in Russia was under siege by social democrats, nationalists, and Bolsheviks, and the Russian revolution – which was at least partly facilitated by the war – threatened the cohesion of the Romanov territories. The Ottoman empire had been slowly decaying since the early nineteenth century and its European territories were being whittled away through war and social unrest.[14] And while no one thought that Germany would break up even if it were defeated, there was much reason to assume that the Hohenzollern territories, which formed the core of the German empire, would be reorganized after the war.

This uncertainty over the future of central, southern and eastern Europe, as well as the growing competition among various ideologies, raised fundamental questions about the kind of political and social system that would govern the continent after the war. The allied powers realized that much of Europe would likely become engulfed in civil conflict among competing authorities unless they could develop a coherent principle for determining which (if any) territories would remain empires, which would become new states, which authorities would be recognized as the legitimate rulers within these polities, and where the borders would be drawn. It was not clear, however, which of the principles would ultimately provide this foundation. The outcome was influenced by a combination of external events and prevailing beliefs about stability, justice, and security held by the allied powers. In this sense, the determination that the new order would be one based on national self-determination and national states emerged from a combination of realist, idealist, and solidarist motives.

External events – the development of "facts on the ground" – created conflicting expectations concerning the future of postwar Europe. Declarations of independence by the Czechs, Croats, Poles, and other nationalities during the latter part of the war suggested that the prewar empires would break apart and be replaced by national states.[15] Nationalist

[13] Bérenger, *A History of the Habsburg Empire*, p. 253.
[14] See Marian Kent, ed., *The Great Powers and the End of the Ottoman Empire* (London: Frank Cass, 1996).
[15] Thomas Musgrave, *Self Determination and National Minorities* (Oxford: Clarendon Press, 1997), p. 25.

agitation within the Hapsburg territories had grown dramatically as the war dragged on, creating a serious source of internal weakness for the empire. The Ottoman empire also was unstable after a rapid string of defeats dramatically accelerated the disintegration of its rule, particularly within its southern European lands. Russia lost its territories in Poland, Ukraine, Finland and the Baltic provinces after signing the treaty of Brest-Litovsk with Germany. The allied leaders knew that conflicts among "nationalities" was one of the many causes of the war, and that the brutality of the fighting had only fed these passions.[16] From this perspective, nationalism appeared to be the dominant force on the continent.

This factor, however, was challenged by other events that suggested alternative scenarios. In some areas, for example Hungary, Berlin, and Baden, the spread of civil unrest and revolution at the end of the war raised the possibility that some form of Bolshevism or socialism would expand throughout eastern and central Europe.[17] In other areas, such as Britain, France, Poland, Austria, and Finland, the Russian revolution had emboldened socialist, social democratic, and other leftist political movements, raising the possibility that a leftist, if not a Bolshevist, political program would triumph within the industrialized West.[18] The Bolsheviks fueled the popular discontent with the war in late 1917 by publishing the secret treaties between the tsar and the other allies. They did so in an effort to discredit the reigning governments in favor of a radical alternative. Had the leftist alternative triumphed, international solidarity might have trumped nationalism as the legitimizing principle for the new Europe. While the reigning governments obviously did not relish such an outcome, its possibility forced them to consider making concessions that would accommodate the aspirations of their societies' more radical forces.

Countering this trend, however, was the prospect that an allied victory would spark a liberal democratic revolution throughout the continent. President Woodrow Wilson's emphasis on liberal democracy as the

---

[16] Gordon Craig and Alexander George argue that World War I began as a political crisis and ended almost as a religious one, in which each side viewed the other not as an opponent but as a kind of anti-Christ who must be extirpated. See their *Force and Statecraft*, p. 44.

[17] William Keylor, *The Twentieth Century World: An International History* (Oxford: Oxford University Press, 2001), p. 87.

[18] E. J. Hobsbawm, *Nations and Nationalism Since 1780: Programme, Myth, Reality* (Cambridge: Cambridge University Press, 1992), pp. 123–30. See also Sara Moore, *Peace Without Victory for the Allies, 1918–1932* (Oxford: Berg Publishers, 1994), pp. 21–25.

cornerstone of security and stability suggested that the allies would seek to democratize the newly liberated regions and establish liberal states after the defeat of the central powers.[19] In fact Wilson's original concept of self-determination had little to do with nationality, but rather with self-government and popular sovereignty.[20] Toward this end, Wilson appealed directly to the populations of Europe and gave strong moral and ideological support to grassroots democratic organizations throughout the continent.[21] While the conservative leaders of Europe were less enthusiastic in pursuing such agitation, Wilson's program was very popular among the liberal political parties and reformers in both eastern and western Europe.

Any of these three scenarios would have made ideology a key factor in determining the distribution of territory and the legitimation of authority within the vast regions of Europe where authority had either collapsed or was contested. Yet until 1918 the most likely possibility was not the construction of new states in central and eastern Europe based on either principle or ideology, but rather the maintenance of large centralized units capable of securing a lasting balance of power on the continent. This was the geopolitical realist alternative. While the allied leaders had some sympathy for the nationalist aspirations within the Hapsburg, Ottoman, and Russian empires, the great powers also feared that a widespread "Balkanization" of the pre-war territories could lead to a proliferation of small, ineffective, and weak states, creating a power vacuum in central Europe.[22] This fear, shared by leaders on both sides of the Atlantic, suggested that the allies would place a greater priority on stability and balance and therefore would seek to maintain the cohesion of the central European empires. Thus, during the early years of the war, nearly all political leaders considered the most likely postwar settlement to be one based on a new balance of power on the continent, albeit one that favored the victorious states.[23]

The British and the French were especially concerned about establishing a new balance in central Europe, in particular containing the

---

[19] See, for example, Harold Temperley, *A History of the Peace Conference*, vol. I (London and New York: Oxford University Press, 1969 [1920]), p. 142. Arthur Link, *Woodrow Wilson: Revolution, War and Peace* (Arlington Heights: Harlan Davidson, 1979), p. 13.

[20] Musgrave, *Self Determination and National Minorities*, p. 23.

[21] Link, *Woodrow Wilson*, p. 13.

[22] See Alan Sharp, *The Versailles Settlement: Peacemaking in Paris, 1919* (New York: St. Martin's Press, 1991).

[23] Victor Tapié, *The Rise and Fall of the Hapsburg Monarchy* (New York: Praeger, 1971), p. 385.

Germans and Russians.[24] The British believed that their own security interests required either the unity of Austria-Hungary or the formation of a federation of Hapsburg states.[25] As late as December 1917, the British Prime Minister Lloyd George stated as one of Britain's aims that Austria-Hungary should remain intact, although provisions could be made for autonomy among some of the constituent nationalities.[26] France concurred with this policy, believing that the Hapsburgs would act as a check against German and Russian expansion.[27] In fact, in November of 1917, the French still sought a separate peace with the Hapsburgs that would have maintained the cohesion of the empire after the war.[28] Even the United States assumed that the empire would remain after the war. Both Woodrow Wilson and his chief aide, Colonel Edward House, thought that the cohesion of the empire was an absolute necessity for the stability of Europe.[29]

In addition, for most of the war the large majority of Czechs, South Slavs, and Ruthenes favored a settlement to the nationality question that kept them within the empire but with a fair amount of autonomy.[30] It was not until early 1918 – after the Russian revolution and the publication of the allied war aims – that the Czech, Polish, and South Slav politicians within the empire began agitating for complete independence.[31] Had the allies persisted with the policy they held for most of the war, any concessions to nationalist demands within central and eastern Europe would have been accommodated through various forms of autonomy within large, economically viable and militarily effective states.

In short, despite the popular view of nationalism as an unstoppable force sweeping eastern and central Europe during the war, there was no "natural outcome" for the postwar settlement. Depending upon which

---

[24] See Walter McDougal, *France's Rhineland Diplomacy, 1914–1924: The Last Bid for a Balance of Power in Europe* (Princeton: Princeton University Press, 1978), chs. 1 and 2.

[25] Michael Dockrill and J. Douglas Gould, *Peace Without Promise: Britain and the Peace Conferences, 1919–1923* (Hamden, CT: Archon Books, 1980), p. 90.

[26] David Lloyd George, *British War Aims Statement on January 5, 1918* (authorized version as issued by the British government) (London: R. Clay and Sons, 1918).

[27] Harold Temperley, *A History of the Peace Conference*, vol. IV, p. 176; Taylor, *The Struggle for Mastery in Europe*, p. 560.

[28] Bérenger, *A History of the Habsburg Empire*, p. 279.

[29] Edward Mandell House, *The Intimate Papers of Colonel House*, vol. III, Charles Seymour, ed. (New York: Houghton Mifflin Company, 1928), p. 346.

[30] Z. A. B. Zeman, *The Break-Up of the Habsburg Empire, 1914–1918* (Oxford: Oxford University Press, 1961).

[31] John Mason, *The Dissolution of the Austro-Hungarian Empire, 1867–1918* (London: Longman, 1985), pp. 79–80.

of the various competing alternatives triumphed, the new European order would have looked very different. This in turn would have influenced the types of states that emerged from the war, the relationships between these states and their populations, and the degree to which (if at all) the victorious powers would have intervened to protect one group or another. At the same time, the powers were not driven simply by the historical forces of nationalism; they were active participants in helping to bring about a Europe of nations.

The national state as an unintended consequence

Several factors eventually forced the allies to abandon their initial geopolitical approach to postwar order: nationalist agitation within the Hapsburg and Ottoman empires; the disintegration of the Romanov empire following the Russian revolution; the allies' public commitment to specific "war aims"; and the influence of transnational organizations. These factors would ultimately convince the allied leaders that a European order based on self-determination and the national state would be both the most stable and the most just. Yet this also produced contradictory political factors that created tensions within the postwar European community. These tensions would ultimately force the allies to become directly involved in regulating the relations between the newly installed governments of central and eastern Europe and their populations.

Whatever visions for the future the allied leaders may have had early in the war, they were eventually forced to re-evaluate them; as the war progressed, events began to spin out of their control. The biggest challenge came from within the Austro-Hungarian empire. The Entente had fostered nationalist agitation within the Hapsburg territories during the war as a strategic move to weaken the morale and legitimacy of the central powers.[32] However, this had the unintended effect of strengthening the movements for independent statehood, even though none of the allies had committed themselves to such a policy. In October and November of 1918, the empire began to break apart in a series of coups, revolutions, and rapid transfers of power. On November 11, the Hapsburg Emperor Charles I renounced his authority in Hungary and Serbia. Romanian and Czech militias responded by seizing power in

[32] Macartney, *National States and National Minorities*, p. 185.

their own regions. Croats and Poles within the empire also declared their intention to secede.[33]

The allies, however, were not mere spectators in this process. According to some historians, the ultimate demise of the empire was the result of concerted action by at least some of the allies, particularly the French. François Fejtö, for example, argues that the new self-proclaimed states within the Hapsburg territories would never have survived had the allies concluded a separate peace with Austria-Hungary and refused to support these secessionist movements.[34] He holds that the "radical republicans" within France in effect formed an informal alliance with the nationalists in order to rid Europe of the last vestiges of monarchy and clericalism, that is, the Hapsburg empire.

Once the allies abandoned the emperor, however, they no longer had the luxury of debating the future of the empire; they had to determine what type(s) of unit(s) would replace it. At the same time, the creation of national states was not the only option. Possibilities for other types of units to replace the empire were discussed. Otto Bauer and Karl Renner, for example, offered an alternative to the Wilsonian national state. They suggested creating larger economically efficient states based on national cohesion tempered with cultural self-administration.[35] This would have retained some form of multiculturalism but allowed for local autonomy.

In addition to these external events, the allies placed constraints on their own postwar options by making a series of public commitments during the latter days of the war. For most of the conflict the Entente states avoided any discussion of a postwar program, fearing that this could lead to political conflicts within the alliance.[36] This is because neither the coalition of central powers nor that of the Entente were based on any particular ideology, nor did either group share a common vision for the future. Russia was primarily interested in restoring

---

[33] Musgrave, *Self-Determination and National Minorities*, p. 25; Sharp, *The Versailles Settlement*, p. 147.

[34] François Fejtö, *Requiem pour un empire défunt: histoire de la destruction de l'Autriche-Hongrie* (Paris: Lieu commun, 1992).

[35] For a discussion of these ideas see Otto Bauer, *The Question of Nationalities and Social Democracy*, Joseph O'Donnell, trans. (Minneapolis: University of Minnesota Press, 2000).

[36] The only substantive discussion of common goals was held during the period leading up to the Treaty of London, a pact that was signed by Britain, France, Russia, and Italy in April 1915. This secret agreement, however, focused exclusively on how the allies would divide up the European and colonial territories that would be considered the spoils of war. Nothing was said about the type of political order that would emerge after the conflict.

its international position through territorial gains in the Balkans. The French wanted to regain territories lost in previous wars and reduce the power of Germany.[37] Britain wished to re-establish a balance of power in Central Europe and secure its naval supremacy.[38] Italy's goals were strictly limited to expanding its own territory. In addition, the allied leaders initially believed that they could underline the unity of their adversaries by concluding a separate peace with one of the central powers; specifying a set of goals could prevent this possibility.[39]

As the war dragged on, however, the populations grew weary of the conflict, and the Entente realized that it needed to develop a set of "war aims" that would give their efforts a *raison d'être*. This belief was strengthened in late 1916 when President Wilson issued a public declaration asking all countries involved in the war to state their goals concerning the terms of peace and the arrangements that would prevent future conflicts. Both sides were eager to garner the favor of the United States; the Entente hoped that the United States would enter the war on its side while the central powers wanted America to remain neutral.[40] The British and French were particularly anxious to avoid an inconclusive peace that would leave Germany undefeated, and feared that the United States could facilitate such an outcome.[41]

This need to develop war aims became even more urgent after leaders of the Bolshevik revolution proposed their own detailed agenda for the reorganization of postwar Europe. Their six-point program became the foundation from which the Soviets would later conclude a bilateral peace agreement with the central powers.[42] The core of this program was the realization of national self-determination for peoples throughout Europe, a proposal that drew particular favor with the nationalist movements challenging the Hapsburg monarchy. The allies knew that they needed to develop a program of their own if they hoped to compete for the hearts and minds of the public and forestall the spread of Bolshevism among the disaffected populations of eastern and central Europe.[43]

---

[37] James Joll, *The Origins of the First World War* (New York: Longman, 1984), p. 47; McDougal, *France's Rhineland Diplomacy*, ch. 1.

[38] Dockrill and Gould, *Peace Without Promise*, pp. 17–18. [39] Ibid., p. 18.

[40] See Temperley, *A History of the Peace Conference*, vol. I, p. 180.

[41] Lawrence Martin, *Peace Without Victory: Woodrow Wilson and the British Liberals* (New Haven: Yale University Press, 1958), pp. 20–22.

[42] The text of this program can be found in Arno Mayer, *Political Origins of the New Diplomacy, 1917–1918* (New York: Random House, 1970), pp. 296–97.

[43] Hobsbawm, *Nations and Nationalism Since 1780*, p. 131.

As a result, government agencies within Britain and France began to develop proposals for the organization of postwar Europe. The principles upon which these programs were based provided a goal for their war efforts and served to distinguish the allies from both the central powers and the Bolsheviks. The substance of these publicly stated war aims would ultimately constrain the allies' future considerations for a postwar order.

While the policymakers of the allied governments did not consult with one another over the substance of their programs, they each developed a similar approach toward reconstruction. Reacting to the turn of events in eastern and central Europe, the allied powers adopted the position that the national state would most likely provide the most stable foundation for a cohesive postwar order. In making these proposals, the allies assumed that this policy would appeal to the various nationalities within the Hapsburg and Ottoman empires and undercut the appeal of Bolshevism. As a result, each of the allies began to express publicly support for a new Europe based on the principle of nationality. This made it difficult to consider the maintenance of the Habsburg empire after the war, since its multinational character was inconsistent with the allies' publicly announced principles.

The first formal statement of war aims issued by the Entente in 1917 clearly committed the alliance to pursue such a political order. For example, their declaration called for: 'the reorganization of Europe guaranteed by a stable regime and based at once on respect for nationalities . . . (and) the liberation of the Slavs, Roumainians and Czecho-Slovaks from foreign domination . . .'[44]

The British Foreign Office had already committed itself to this policy in a key state paper issued in late 1916. This document boldly stated that nationality must be the primary standard for postwar territorial adjustments and argued that frontiers "based as closely as possible on ethnic lines would help to assure a just and stable future for all."[45] A stable peace, the paper argued, must give "full scope to national aspirations as far as practicable."[46] Toward that end, the Foreign Office proposed that eastern and central Europe should be reorganized in accordance with the principle of nationality. Other agencies within the government

[44] See Temperley, *A History of the Peace Conference*, vol. I, pp. 172–73.
[45] Erik Goldstein, *Winning the Peace: British Diplomatic Strategy, Peace Planning, and the Paris Peace Conference, 1916–1920* (Oxford: Clarendon Press 1991), p. 230 and Dockrill and Gould, *Peace Without Promise*, p. 20.
[46] See David Lloyd George, *War Memoirs*, vol. II (London: Adhams, 1938), p. 32.

were coming to the same conclusion. James Headlam-Mosley of Britain's Political Intelligence Department (the primary agency charged with developing Britain's postwar policy) argued that it should be Britain's postwar objective to establish national states in central and eastern Europe. He reaffirmed this position in an influential memorandum issued in November of 1918. Headlam-Mosley argued that: "States based on the conscious existence of a common nationality will be more durable and afford a firmer support against aggression than the older form of State, which was often a merely accidental conferees of territories . . ."[47]

This view had already been official government policy after Prime Minister David Lloyd George's key address to the British Trades Union League in January of 1918. In stating British goals for the postwar organization of Europe, Lloyd George referred several times to the "general principle of national self-determination" and a "territorial settlement based on (this) right" as the foundation for a just peace.[48] This address is particularly noteworthy because it occurred several days before President Wilson's highly influential Fourteen Points speech.

The French had already adopted this principle in January of 1917, officially stating that their war aims would include the "liberation" of various national communities throughout the continent.[49] Prime Minister Georges Clemenceau would later declare "the right of nations to govern themselves" to be "the basis of all civilization."[50]

Still, Woodrow Wilson's comprehensive program was particularly important for solidifying the Entente's commitment to the national state. As a relatively detached party and latecomer to the conflict, Woodrow Wilson was able to provide the coherent political vision that the allied coalition had been lacking. While collective security and democratization were his primary plans for preventing future aggression, national self-determination was the core principle for reforming the European state system. As I suggested earlier, Wilson initially had equated self-determination with self-government and popular sovereignty, both of which are liberal concepts of governance. As the United States became more involved in European affairs, however, he began to shift his position toward a definition that was based on a congruence between the

[47] British Foreign Office, "The Settlement," memorandum by the Political Intelligence Department, 18 November 1918, FO 608/435.
[48] David Lloyd George, *British War Aims Statement on January 5, 1918*.
[49] This was articulated in an official note from French Prime Minister Aristide Briand to the US ambassador. See Derek Heater, *National Self-Determination: Woodrow Wilson and his Legacy* (New York: St. Martin's Press, 1994), p. 29.
[50] Quoted in Osiander, *The States System of Europe*, p. 268.

national and political units.[51] Democracy, he argued, would follow from national self-determination; the former could not emerge without the latter. Thus, for Wilson, the promotion of national self-determination would provide stability, order, and justice for the European/North Atlantic community. As such it would be a common good from which all countries would benefit.

Wilson's belief in the desirability of national states dated back to his experience with the Mexican revolution and the Philippine movement for independence.[52] These beliefs were strengthened during the course of World War I, inasmuch as he believed that the denial of self-determination to national communities was a primary cause of the conflict. In his "Four Principles" speech to Congress, for example, he argued that: "This war had its roots in the disregard of the rights of small nations and of nationalities which lacked the union and force to make good their claim to determine their own allegiance . . ."[53]

More generally, Wilson viewed "arbitrary and opportunistic" juridical borders as the underlying cause of territorial conflict. There could be neither justice nor order, Wilson argued, so long as national (that is, ethnic) communities were denied the right to choose their own political affiliation.[54] His solution would be a readjustment of borders and a redistribution of territory based on the ethnic composition of the population. "All well-defined national elements," he asserted, "should be accorded the utmost satisfaction that can be accorded them . . ."[55] It was this world view that provided the political vision for the new European order, and the key idea that linked his principal wartime speeches: the Fourteen Points address, the Four Principles, the Four Ends and the Five Particulars.[56]

Taken as a whole, these highly publicized declarations of the allies created a moral basis for a just postwar settlement. This in turn raised public expectations that the principle of nationality would be universally recognized as the new legitimacy in the European order.[57] In this

---

[51] Heater, *National Self-Determination*, ch. 1.

[52] See Thomas Knock, *To End All Wars: Woodrow Wilson and the Quest for a New World Order* (New York: Oxford University Press, 1992).

[53] Woodrow Wilson's address to Congress, 2/11/18 in Temperley, *A History of the Peace Conference*, vol. I, p. 437.

[54] Musgrave, *Self-Determination and National Minorities*, p. 23.

[55] Temperley, *A History of the Peace Conference*, vol. I, p. 195.

[56] The text of these speeches can be found in Albert Fried, ed., *A Day of Dedication: The Essential Writings and Speeches of Woodrow Wilson* (New York: Macmillan Press, 1965).

[57] See Pearson, *National Minorities in Eastern Europe*, p. 135.

way, vague "war aims" over time became transformed into public commitments, a transformation that would greatly constrain future considerations for the victorious powers.

In addition to external events and government commitments, transnational organizations and social movements also played an important role in developing a consensus around the national state as the foundation for a just and lasting peace. The war sparked the rise of peace societies throughout the United States and Europe, most of which promoted plans for a "just reorganization of the continent." In particular, the international Organisation Centrale pour une Paix Durable (based in the Netherlands) and the British League of Nations Society helped to mobilize public opinion behind the cause of national self-determination. This activity culminated in the organization of the Congress of Oppressed Nationalities in Rome in April 1918. The Congress brought together nationalists from throughout eastern and central Europe, particularly Romanians, Poles, Czechs, and south Slavs. This meeting had a strong impact on political leaders on both sides, not the least Woodrow Wilson, whose attitude toward the future of the Austro-Hungarian empire changed dramatically after the Congress.[58] Following the conference, he shifted his position in favor of independence for the national communities within the empire.

This suggests that a general consensus had begun to develop among the allied powers even before the war had ended. They not only agreed on the broad conditions for ending the war and preventing future aggression, they also laid the foundation for a consensus agenda for a new European order based on the principle of national self-determination. The foundation of this order would be the creation of new national states and a reorganization of existing ones along national lines. Multiethnic empires, theocracies, monarchies, and even multicultural liberal states would be inconsistent with this principle. Under these conditions, the allies could not remain indifferent to the types of states that would form in central and eastern Europe. This led them down a path that ultimately required their direct involvement in the internal relations between the new governments and their populations.

The Paris Peace Conference and the new Europe

The war effectively ended in November 1918 when the German kaiser abdicated and his regime was replaced by a social democratic

[58] Temperley, *A History of the Peace Conference*, vol. I, p. 199.

government willing to sign an armistice based on Wilson's Fourteen
Points. The Ottoman empire had already signed such an agreement the
previous month. Continuing a tradition that dated back to 1648, the
victorious states called an international conference in Paris to formally
end the war and determine the conditions for a peace settlement. The
Paris Peace Conference had two main objectives: to draft peace treaties
between themselves and the central powers and to plan for a postwar reconstruction. In general these are the primary objectives all postwar conferences. Yet, like most congresses, the goals of the allies were broader:
they also sought to determine the kind of political and social order that
would replace the one that had collapsed during the war. As a British
delegate to the conference commented, "We were journeying to Paris,
not merely to liquidate the war, but to found a new order in Europe."[59]

In addition to developing a set of principles and institutions that
would govern such an order, the allies also knew that they would have
to recognize, reorganize, and in some cases create new states out of the
ruins of the Hapsburg, Russian, German, and Ottoman empires. From
this perspective, the fundamental task of this conference was to produce a coherent and stable international order founded on the principle
of self-determination.[60]

One thousand and thirty-seven delegates and seventy plenipotentiaries came to Paris to attend the conference.[61] They represented not
only European states and nationalities, but also countries in Latin
America, Asia, and the Middle East. However, as with most of the previous postwar peace congresses, the real decisionmaking authority did
not rest with the formal delegates but with the leaders of the victorious powers. Those states that were not formally considered to be an
"allied or associated power" were referred to as "powers with special
interests."[62] They were given seats on committees that dealt with issues that directly affected them, but were not included in discussions
dealing with the peace settlements with Germany and Austria or with

---

[59] Harold Nicolson, *Peacemaking 1919* (London: Methuen, 1964), p. 31.
[60] This is the claim offered by historian Alfred Cobban in his *The Nation State and National
Self-Determination* (New York: Crowell, 1970), p. 15.
[61] Temperley, *A History of the Peace Conference*, vol. I, p. 243, fn. 1.
[62] Documents from this period refer to the Western coalition as the "allied and associated
powers." The United States did not want to formally join the alliance and therefore was
considered to be an "associated" power. The alliance itself was originally called the
"Triple Entente," and was composed of Britain, France, and Russia. Italy was initially
a member of the central alliance, however when the war broke out it declared its neu-
trality. Upon signing the Treaty of London in 1915, Italy joined the Entente and Russia
withdrew after the Bolshevik revolution.

the organization of Europe after the war. These discussions were re-served for those "powers with general interests," that is, the victorious coalition of great powers.[63] Consequently, when the Conference opened on January 12, 1919, it began with an informal meeting of the heads of state and foreign ministers of the four principal allies: the United States, Britain, France, and Italy. This group was essentially an extension of the Supreme War Council that had directed the war effort.

The early days of the conference were chaotic and unfocused, and it was unclear exactly who would be involved in setting the agenda and drafting the peace settlements. In fact there were no plans even for how the conference would be organized. The allies eventually agreed to establish a Council of Ten, a group comprising the prime ministers/ presidents and foreign ministers of the four principal allies, plus Japan. However, this soon proved to be unwieldy. Continuous delays and the inability to reach quick decisions led the allies to replace the Council of Ten with one comprising solely heads of state from the Supreme War Council. This became known as the Council of Four (Japan was excluded), and was in fact the main decisionmaking body of the con-ference. Complaints from the Japanese delegation and the need to deal with details beyond the competence of the prime ministers led the Coun-cil to create yet another consultative body, the Council of Five, which included the foreign ministers of the four allies plus Japan.

The initial meetings of the Council of Four (also known as the Supreme Council) dealt primarily with immediate problems such as the with-drawal of military forces, territorial claims by Italy and France, the degree to which Germany should pay reparations, and other practi-cal matters. France's concern with containing Germany was addressed in the German peace treaty, which was drafted by the Council and presented to the Germans for their signature. At the same time, the Council also wished to create a territorial and political settlement that was permanent, and consequently began to discuss how to provide for long-term security and order in Europe. The consideration of these broader matters inevitably raised questions of legitimate statehood, the distribution of contested territory and the social and political foundation for relations within Europe. In these areas the principles of nationality and self-determination became prominent.

---

[63] This distinction between principal or great powers and secondary powers dated back to the 1815 Congress of Vienna. See Harold Nicholson, *The Congress of Vienna: A Study in Allied Unity, 1812–1822* (New York: Harcourt, Brace, 1946), p. 137 and Charles Webster, *The Congress of Vienna, 1814–1815* (London: Thames and Hudson, 1934), p. 80.

Aside from specific political payoffs and security concerns, the Council generally applied the principle of nationality in creating and recognizing new states. Upon officially acknowledging the dissolution of the Ottoman and Austro-Hungarian empires, the allies established a firm principle that the creation of new states would be based on the principle of national self-determination. As Wilson explained, "we (the Council) are trying to make an equitable distribution of territories according to the race, the ethnographical character of the people inhabiting those territories."[64] While the Council did not attempt to abolish or reorganize existing states on the continent, national self-determination became the standard from which they judged competing claims for statehood in central and eastern Europe.

Unlike a century earlier when the Congress of Vienna created and reorganized states according to the "legitimist principle" of dynastic sovereignty, the Versailles treaties only recognized new states that could claim to represent a specific ethnic or cultural community. This was reflected in the general terms of the peace settlement. The first three principles specified self-determination, nationality, and the equality of nations as the foundation upon which the settlement would be based.[65] This principle was further acknowledged in the allied rejoinder to the German peace note, which stated that peace would only be possible with the "recognition of the principle of nationalities and of the free existence of small states."[66] The allied powers reaffirmed this policy in a memo sent to the German government following the conference: "Every territorial settlement of the Treaty of Peace has been determined upon the most careful and labored consideration of all the religious, racial and linguistic factors in each particular country."[67]

Some ethnic states (such as Hungary, Estonia, Latvia, Poland, and Lithuania) and pan-nationalist states (such as Czechoslovakia and Yugoslavia) were created anew.[68] Others, such as the core territories of the Austro-Hungarian and Ottoman empires (Austria and Turkey),

[64] Macartney, *National States and National Minorities*, p. 232.
[65] Temperley, *A History of the Peace Conference*, vol. I, p. 408.
[66] Oscar Janowsky, *Nationalities and National Minorities* (New York: Macmillan Press, 1945), p. 10.
[67] Macartney, *National States and National Minorities*, p. 429.
[68] The creation of Czechoslovakia as a compound state was based on the principle that the Czechs and Slovaks were sufficiently ethnically related to form a coherent core for a new state; any other assignment of these populations was viewed as being a greater injustice to the principle of nationality. The pan-Slavic idea that justified the creation of Yugoslavia (originally the Kingdom of Serbs Croats and Slovenes) was based on a common language and the fact that at the end of the war all of the Slavic units

were reorganized into national states. Still others, such as Bulgaria and Albania, were officially recognized, although their borders were readjusted to better reflect the ethnic distribution of the populations.[69] Although Greece had achieved independence during the nineteenth century, its borders were greatly expanded and readjusted to include many new territories and populations.

In addition to establishing a basis for recognizing new states and drawing juridical borders, the Council developed elaborate provisions for identifying populations by nationality within these states. For example, Article 85 of the German peace treaty included the following:

> Within a period of two years from the coming into force of the present Treaty, German nationals over eighteen years of age habitually resident in any of the territories recognized as forming part of the Czecho-Slovak State will be entitled to opt for German nationality. Czecho-Slovaks who are German nationals and are habitually resident in Germany will have a similar right to opt for Czecho-Slovak nationality.[70]

Although Wilson had hoped that the new national states would also become democratic, the allies did not require any state created or reorganized after World War I to establish democratic political institutions or adhere to liberal principles of government. These were not liberal states, and thus nations, not citizens, were recognized as sovereign. Consistent with this policy, the allies organized plebiscites in Schleswig-Holstein, Upper Silesia, and Saarland, not for the purpose of choosing a form of government or a constitution, but to determine which nationality the inhabitants of these territories considered themselves to be.

The application of the nationality principle was clearly limited to Europe, a fact that became apparent when the Council discussed the future of the Ottoman empire's Middle East territories. While the norm of self-determination (and Wilson's insistence on this point) made it impossible for the victorious powers to colonize these regions, only Turkey became a new state. Syria, Lebanon, Palestine, and Iraq became "mandates": territories that would be held in trust by the League of Nations

proclaimed their desire to form a union with Serbia. See Maccartney, *National States and National Minorities*, p. 305.

[69] Arthur Walworth, *Wilson and His Peacemakers: American Diplomacy at the Paris Peace Conference, 1919* (New York: Norton, 1986), chs. 3, 14, and 18. A list of new states created and/or recognized during this period can be found in Temperley, *A History of the Peace Conference*, vol. V, pp. 161–2.

[70] Fred Israel, ed., *Major Peace Treaties of Modern History, 1648–1967*, vol. II (New York: Chelsea House Publishers, 1967), p. 1325.

through the great powers until they were deemed capable of governing themselves. The political boundaries of international society after the war did not extend to the Middle East.

Still, this was the first time that the international community attempted a systemic effort to draw the political map along national lines.[71] Their efforts were moderately successful: the Versailles settlement reduced by half the number of people living in states governed by members of a different ethnic or national group.[72] Yet this created new tensions requiring direct intervention by international institutions.

Stabilizing the national state through minority protection

It was not the purpose of the settlement to redraw the entire map of Europe, but rather to establish a stable peace and integrate the eastern and western regions of the continent after the collapse of the great empires. The Council tried to make the new and reorganized states consistent with the principles of the new Europe by establishing nationality as the foundation for legitimate authority within them. In pursuing these goals, however, the principle of nationality had to compete with other considerations such as economic viability, wartime promises, security concerns, and the ethnic distribution of the populations. This created internal tensions both within the new states and within the new European order.

In some cases the allies were constrained by agreements they had made during the course of the war. In particular, the 1915 Treaty of London, which was the foundation for the alliance, provided for political and territorial benefits that were based on expediency rather than principle. Italy, for example, had demanded extensive territorial concessions as its price for joining the alliance. In turn, Britain and France wanted control over Germany's African colonies and France wanted territories it had lost to Germany in the Franco-Prussian war almost fifty years earlier. The allies could not and would not renege on these promises even if they had to violate a strict adaptation of self-determination.

In other cases, balance of power concerns prevailed. In considering the fate of Germany, for example, the principle of self-determination

[71] Hobsbawm, *Nations and Nationalism Since 1780*, p. 133.
[72] Pearson, *National Minorities in Eastern Europe*, pp. 148–49.

had to be balanced against the security interests of other nations, many of which wished to limit Germany's size and power. A merger between Germany and Austria – a demand made by both countries on the grounds of nationality – was politically impossible in the aftermath of the most destructive war in human history to date. Nor was Germany permitted to annex those regions of Czechoslovakia and Poland that contained large German populations. After much debate, the new borders ultimately reflected a balance between the principle of nationality and the principle of stability. Germany remained a national state but its borders did not fully coincide with the distribution of German populations in central Europe.

The allies also realized that no territorial settlement based on the principle of nationality – no matter how sophisticated or complex – could completely satisfy the requirements of an ideal-type national state. Even with the best of intentions, it was simply not feasible for the Council to create a state for every ethnic/cultural group that made a claim to independent statehood. Nor was it possible to make the new states culturally homogenous, short of a policy of ethnic cleansing. The allies recognized that the mere impulse of an ethnic group to constitute an independent state is not always a sound foundation upon which to build a secure, prosperous society. The creation of new national states required sensitivity not only to the ethnic distribution of the population but also to the economic and strategic viability of the state.[73] Thus, for example, although the Sudetenland comprised largely German-speaking people, the Council decided that its mineral resources and mountain defenses were vital to the viability and security of the new Czech state.[74]

Further complicating the situation was the ethnographic distribution of the population in central and eastern Europe. Unlike the western regions of the continent, eastern and central Europe had experienced large-scale migrations and invasions resulting in territories and populations frequently changing hands. Since the idea of national states was relatively new in Europe, ethnic populations had long ago become intimately intertwined throughout most of the region. Traditionally, "nationality" was determined by the identity of the royal family and later on by the identity of the state that ruled in the name of the people. Therefore, until the late nineteenth century, one's ethnicity did not have political significance and migration patterns did not reflect national

[73] Eric Hobsbawm refers to this as the "threshold principle." See his *Nations and Nationalism Since 1780*, p. 31.
[74] Sharp, *The Versailles Settlement*, p. 149.

preferences. Consequently, most of the newly created and newly reorganized national states had significant national minorities within their borders.[75]

This raised a problem for the Council. The application of national self-determination provided for national communities to form their own state, that is, to create a homeland. This did not mean, however, that all individuals could decide for themselves with which state they wished to affiliate. The right of national self-determination is held by communities not individuals, and the nation-state system is, at its root, based on territory not population. The creation of a homeland satisfies the requirement of self-determination even if some ethnic kin do not live within its borders.

The allies considered the idea of population transfers as a method for creating more unified and homogenous national states. In some cases they even experimented with this possibility. The Treaties of Neuilly and Lausanne, for example, provided for "reciprocal and voluntary" transfers between ethnic populations in Greece and Bulgaria and Greece and Turkey, respectively. Through this process, more than 2 million people were transferred under the supervision of the League of Nations.[76] Yet these population transfers produced the same effects as refugees: economic and social dislocation, border tensions, discrimination, and violence. It soon became clear that even a benevolent and "voluntary" form of ethnic cleansing would not create homogenous national states.

The members of the Council realized that disgruntled nationalities could pose the greatest threat to the national state, and, by extension, to the new European order. Yet they had no plan for how to address this problem. The issue of minorities had barely been considered during the planning for reconstruction. Most of the focus had been on how the reorganized territories could be made compatible with the principle of self-determination. The question had not been addressed in any of the wartime or postwar documents or speeches by the allied leaders nor was it mentioned in any of the proclamations of war aims.

The Council was in a bind. Having recognized nationality/ethnicity to be the foundation of political authority and legitimacy in the new Europe, something had to be done with the "unlucky remnants of nationalities (that were) left over after the rights of national self-determination

---

[75] By the end of the conference, there were still 30 million people living in states in which they were not part of the dominant nationality. See Sharp, *The Versailles Settlement*, p. 155.

[76] Pearson, *National Minorities in Eastern Europe*, pp. 139–41.

had been carried out."[77] The allies expected that the minority populations within the new and reorganized states would eventually become
identified with the political culture of the majority.[78] However, unless
they could be made into loyal citizens, the stability and legitimation of
the national state would be in doubt. Drawing from their own experiences living in liberal, relatively homogenous societies, the British and
French assumed that minorities would be willing to integrate into the
majority culture so long as the state granted them legal equality and
protected their civil and political rights as citizens. As the French Prime
Minister Clemenceau remarked:

> We believe that these (minority) populations will be more easily recon-
> ciled to their new position if they know that from the very beginning
> they have assured protection and adequate guarantees against any
> danger of unjust treatment or oppression.[79]

Recognizing that the actions of the Peace Conference largely created
this problem, Clemenceau argued that the Conference had an obligation
to protect those peoples whose future minority status was determined
by the decisions made in Paris. Similarly, Manley Ottmer Hudson, legal advisor to the American Peace Commission at the Conference, remarked that the Peace Conference had assumed a great responsibility in dealing with the political fortunes of large numbers of Czechs,
Poles, Serbs, Romanians, Greeks, Germans, Austrians, Magyars, and
Bulgarians living in transferred territories.[80] Placing the idea of mutual
obligation in terms of the common good, Wilson stated the principle
most succinctly: "All new states should enter into solemn obligations
under responsibility to the whole body of nations, to accord to all racial
and national minorities within their jurisdictions exactly the same status
and treatment, alike in law and in fact, that are accorded to the majority
of people."[81]

It was during the process of trying to reconcile the national state with
national minorities that an international protection regime developed.

---

[77] Quote is from Arendt, "Concerning Minorities," pp. 356–57.
[78] Royal Institute of International Affairs, *Nationalism: A Report* (New York: Oxford
University Press, 1939), p. 293.
[79] Quoted in a letter from Clemenceau to Paderewski in Janowsky, *Nationalities and
National Minorities*, p. 182.
[80] Manley Ottmer Hudson, "The Protection of Minorities and Natives in Transferred Territories," in Edward Mandell House and Charles Seymour, eds., *What Really Happened
at Paris: The Story of the Peace Conference, 1918–1919 by American Delegates* (New York:
Charles Scribner's Sons, 1921), p. 208.
[81] Walworth, *Wilson and His Peacemakers*, pp. 472–73.

The regime grew out of a proposal that was brought to the Council by the US and British delegations concerning the obligations the newly formed states would have toward the international community. The initial concern was the plight of the German and Jewish populations in Poland. The former had become a minority in a land in which they had lived for generations and the latter lacked a national state of their own. The allies addressed this concern by inserting in the German peace treaty a clause that obligated both Poland and the allies to "protect the interests of inhabitants of Poland who differ from the majority of the population in race, language and religion."[82] This became the foundation for minority rights protection guarantees in the Polish peace treaty and eventually in all subsequent treaties.

In developing a regime to protect the rights of national minorities, the Council drew from practices and precedents that had been established in the late nineteenth century, in particular the provisions for religious protection that were attached to state recognition for Serbia and Romania.[83] At the same time, they also responded to proposals and political pressure from transnational organizations and domestic interest groups. In particular, the central and east-European-based Comité des Délégations Juives auprès de la Conférence de la Paix (Committee of Jewish Delegates at the Paris Peace Conference), the Congress of Minorities and the Association for a Durable Peace were very active in developing plans for a national minority protection regime.[84] In fact, the Comité des Délégations presented the Council with a detailed proposal for including minority rights protection in the peace treaties.[85] In addition, Jewish societies in Britain and the United States had lobbied their governments heavily for guarantees of protection for their kin. US delegate Hunter Miller acknowledged that this influenced his thinking about the relationship between minorities and majorities in the new states.[86]

At the same time, the members of the Council realized that protecting minorities within a national state posed special problems inasmuch as

[82] See Article 93 of the Treaty of Peace Between the Allied and Associated Powers and Germany in Temperley, *A History of the Peace Conference*, vol. V, p. 164.

[83] See Article XXVII of the Treaty of Berlin, July 13, 1878, in Israel, ed., *Major Peace Treaties of Modern History*, pp. 985–86.

[84] The Association had issued a Draft International Treaty on the Rights of National Minorities as far back as 1916.

[85] Macartney, *National States and National Minorities*, pp. 220–21.

[86] David Hunter Miller, *My Diary of the Peace Conference* (New York: Appeal Printing Company, 1924), p. 261.

they did not wish to undermine the ethnic foundation or institutional cohesion of these states. As a result, the Council constructed an elaborate regime that sought to balance minority protection with the maintenance of national unity. In doing so, they created obligations for the protecting states, the target states, and the protecting groups.

From the beginning, the Council sought to establish a single set of principles, obligations, and rights regarding the protection of minorities that would apply equally to all new and reorganized states.[87] Toward this end, the Council set up a Committee on New States and the Protection of Minorities to address issues related to the rights and obligations of newly created and reorganized states. In this sense, the Committee was to determine the conditions that would be attached to state recognition. All of the allied powers (including Japan) were represented on the Committee, and after the creation of the League of Nations a representative from that organization was added. The protection of national minorities soon became the primary condition for the recognition of new states by the great powers and for admission of enlarged states into the League of Nations.

The Committee used the minority rights provisions of the Polish Treaty as the model from which all subsequent agreements were drafted. This treaty guaranteed full nationality and citizenship to all inhabitants (Articles 3–6), provided for nondiscrimination in civil and political rights, and the right for all citizens to use their own language and maintain their own charitable and social institutions (Articles 7–8).[88] The treatment of national minorities by the governments, the treaty stated, would "constitute obligations of international concern." Any member of the League of Nations Council would have the right to raise an issue concerning its implementation.[89] Few disagreed with the need for such a regime. Debates among the members of the Council revolved around detail and process, not principles or obligation.

In all, five states were required to sign minority rights treaties (Czechoslovakia, Yugoslavia, Greece, Romania, and Poland), four had to accept minority rights obligations as part of the peace treaties (Austria, Hungary, Bulgaria, and Turkey), and five issued public declarations on the protection of minorities to the Council of the League of Nations as the condition of admission to the organization (Albania, Estonia, Iraq,

---

[87] Macartney, *National States and National Minorities*, p. 231; Temperley, *A History of the Peace Conference*, vol. V, p. 126.
[88] See Claude, *National Minorities*, pp. 17–20.
[89] Macartney, *National States and National Minorities*, p. 230.

Lithuania, and Latvia).[90] By 1922, twelve states had agreed to accept oversight by the League.[91]

Having created a political foundation for an international protection regime for national minorities, the Council had to consider how they would implement these obligations. The procedures for implementation had to be developed *ad hoc*, since there was no precedent for overseeing such a wide-ranging and complex protection system. The allies knew that this would require an institutional structure to provide legitimacy for such a high level of intrusion into the sovereignty of the new and reorganized states. Toward this end, they inserted a provision into the Polish treaty, transferring the adjudication and enforcement of all minority rights agreements from the Allied and Associated Powers to the League of Nations. Article IV stated in part that:

> The stipulations in the foregoing Articles so far as they affect persons belonging to racial, religious or linguistic minorities, constitute obligations of international concern and shall be placed under the guarantee of the League of Nations. They shall not be modified without the assent of a majority of the Council of the League of Nations.[92]

This article transformed a series of bilateral treaties and declarations into a generalized multilateral protection system in which obligations were owed not to the victorious powers, but to the international community. It also removed disputes from the political sphere to a judicial one by placing them under the authority of the Permanent Court of International Justice.[93]

The foundation for the League system of implementation was the Tittori Report, which defined the nature of the general guarantees as comprising the following principles: that the provisions for the protection of minorities were inviolable; that the League Council was responsible for ensuring that these provisions were observed; that the Council was required to take action in the event of an infraction; and that only members of the Council could bring a complaint to the body.[94] Based on this report and on subsequent discussions within the Council,

---

[90] See Janowsky, *Nationalities and National Minorities*, appendix I, pp. 171–72.
[91] Heater, *National Self-Determination*, p. 86.
[92] See the "Treaty of Peace Between the United States of America, the British Empire, France, Italy, and Japan and Poland," Signed at Versailles, June 28, 1919, in Temperley, *A History of the Peace Conference*, vol. V, appendix IV, pp. 434–44.
[93] See Temperley, *A History of the Peace Conference*, p. 442.
[94] League of Nations, *Protection of Linguistic, Racial, or Religious Minorities by the League of Nations* (Geneva: League of Nations, 1921).

the League of Nations committed itself to protect national minorities through extensive monitoring and enforcement. The League Council itself was empowered to enforce all minorities rights provisions in cases of "any infraction or danger of infraction."[95]

To maintain this system, the signatories to the League Covenant established a Minorities Section of the Secretariat and created a provision to establish three-member *ad hoc* Minorities Committees to address any complaints that were lodged. The Council president was named as an ex-officio member of each committee. Under these procedures, any minority or state could file a Minority Petition with the League; the Committee would then initiate a process of follow-up and possible sanction against the country being charged. The process for dealing with the petitions was cumbersome and long, moving through the Minorities Section, the secretary-general, and the Council and the *ad hoc* committee. Between 1921 and 1929 as many as 150 committees were established.

Why an international protection regime?

The decision by the allied powers to create the most elaborate and complex protection regime to date was motivated primarily by a desire to maintain the stability and cohesion of the national state in central and eastern Europe. This is confirmed by the documents and statements released by the allied leaders. Although the treaties were ostensibly aimed at protecting national minorities, the minorities themselves were the objects, not the subjects, of the regime.[96] The targets of the regime were states, and, more specifically, governments. The documents released by the Supreme Council and the League of Nations Council do not refer to "national minorities" as a group or political community. This would have granted them political recognition. Rather, the League system extended protection to "persons belonging to" national minorities, a recognition of the rights of minorities but not of national communities within sovereign states.[97] In fact, the Council specifically rejected a proposal to include a provision for "national cultural autonomy for

---

[95] See Hudson, "The Protection of Minorities and Natives in Transferred Territories," p. 221.

[96] C. A. Maccartney observes that the primary object of the treaties was the internal stability of the treaty states (that is, the newly created and reorganized national states). See his *National States and National Minorities*, p. xx.

[97] See, for example, Article 12 of the "Treaty of Peace Between the United States of America, the British Empire, France, Italy, and Japan and Poland," Signed at Versailles, June 28, 1919, in Temperley, *A History of the Peace Conference*, vol. V, appendix IV.

all minorities" on the grounds that it would seriously undermine the authority and unity of the state.[98] Moreover, the treaties explicitly authorized the establishment of an official language; the new states were clearly national, not multicultural or liberal.

The motivation for the regime, then, was to promote the assimilation of ethnic minorities into the broader national community. The civil and political rights of the minorities would be protected but only as a means toward making them into loyal citizens of the state in which they lived. The members of the Council may have feared the consequences of a jingoistic national state, but they did not challenge the fundamental assumption that a single national culture should prevail and that all individuals should be subject to the will of the majority. As the French Foreign Minister Aristide Briand stated, the goal of minority protection was: "a kind of assimilation which will increase the greatness of the nation as a whole without in any way diminishing the importance of the smaller family."[99] The British Foreign Secretary Austen Chamberlain echoed this sentiment, arguing that: "the object of the minorities treaties was to secure for the minorities that measure of protection and justice which would gradually prepare them to be merged into the national community to which they belong."[100]

As historian Alfred Cobban observed, "a hostile critic might suggest that minority rights treaties were directed more to protecting the (national) state against its minorities than the minorities against the oppression."[101]

Consistent with a general practice that had been common for at least a century, the focus of the regime was on new and reorganized states. Neither Germany nor Italy was required to accept minority rights obligations, nor did the allied powers impose these requirements on the already existing states of western Europe. Representatives from Czechoslovakia, Romania, and Poland objected to the treaties as one-sided and an invasion of their sovereignty. Other smaller states argued that they were willing to accept general regulations that were adopted by all League states but not those that were confined to only certain ones.[102] Yet the leaders of these states did not understand that

---

[98] Maccartney, *National States and National Minorities*, p. 226.
[99] *League of Nations Official Journal* (Geneva: League of Nations, 1929), p. 529.
[100] *League of Nations Resolutions and Extracts*, Minutes of the 37th Council, February, 1926, p. 142.
[101] Cobban, *The Nation State and National Self-Determination*, p. 37. Parenthetical, mine.
[102] Temperley, *A History of the Peace Conference of Paris*, vol. V, p. 129.

the object of minority protection was to stabilize the European order, not to implement abstract principles. As historian Harold Temperley observed: "The Supreme Council never claimed to be laying down general principles to be applied to all states; they had to deal purely with certain difficulties caused by decisions made at the Conference."[103] Since the purpose of the regime was to promote the stability of a European order based on national states, the targets of the system were limited to those states whose internal political relationships could pose a threat or challenge to that order.

The allied leaders were quite clear on these points. In defending the one-sided nature of the treaties, Wilson stated that:

> If this Conference is going to recognize these various powers as new sovereignties within definite territories, the chief guarantors are entitled to be satisfied that their territorial settlements are of a character to be permanent and that the guarantees given are to insure the peace of the world.[104]

The failure of the regime

Ultimately the regime broke down, primarily due to the weak foundation upon which the European order was built. While the consensus in favor of the national state enabled the allied and associated powers to establish an elaborate protection regime, American isolationism and the withdrawal of Germany and the Soviet Union from the League made it impossible for either the League or the European order to remain cohesive. The national minority protection system rose and fell with the League itself. This allowed several factors to emerge that were destructive of the regime.

First, with the withdrawal of the United States from European affairs, the other great powers were not willing to enforce the rules of the regime. Like the United Nations, the League depended on the participation and leadership of its members and the refusal of the United States to join the organization it had created left a vacuum of leadership. The absence of the United States, and secondarily Germany and Russia, led to significant collective action problems among the body of great powers. Since the League could not adequately perform its most basic security functions, it should not be surprising that it could not enforce its secondary ones.

---

[103] Ibid.
[104] Musgrave, *Self Determination and National Minorities*, p. 41.

Second, many of the minorities used the protection system as a vehicle to promote autonomy and undermine their host governments. Often they received assistance from their kin states in these efforts. This, of course, was the opposite of what the allies had intended when they established the system.

Third, as a result of these two factors, many of the target states eventually refused to comply with their obligations. As argued in chapter 2, an international protection regime requires that the protectors, the target states, and the protected population be well defined and aware of their role and obligations. This creates an interdependent relationship among them. When one of the actors fails to act, it has a direct effect on the willingness and ability of the others to do so. After years of this situation, Polish Foreign Minister Josef Beck publicly repudiated the Polish peace treaty on September 13, 1934; characteristically, the League failed to take action and the regime was dead.[105]

Ironically, however, the broad consensus around the principle of nationality helped to undermine both the political order and the regime. The rise of fascism, an ideology that glorified the national state, challenged the European system. Taking the logic of nationalism to its extreme, fascism defied the idea that national minorities should be protected. Quite the contrary, German and Italian nationalism was based on superiority and domination, not liberation and autonomy. Ethnic minorities were considered to be political aliens, a threat to the unified national community upon which the state was built. Nazi Germany exploited the nationality principle to justify its program, claiming (with some justification) that the borders drawn at Versailles failed to reflect the distribution of national populations in central Europe, particularly in Germany.[106] In effect, they used the Versailles *principles* to challenge the Versailles *settlement*.

Conclusion

The evidence presented in this chapter strongly suggests that the primary purpose of national-minority protection was to promote the internal cohesion of the newly recognized and newly created national states by making ethnic minorities into loyal citizens. The regime was the result

[105] Janowsky, *Nationalities and National Minorities*, p. 127.
[106] See the 1937 Nazi Party platform in Frederick L. Schuman, *The Nazi Dictatorship: A Study in Social Pathology and the Politics of Fascism* (New York. Knopf, 1937), pp. 112–16.

of decisions made in Paris concerning which authorities should be recognized as legitimate and where the juridical borders should be drawn. Had one of the other competing legitimizing principles been adopted, for example liberalism or Bolshevism, it is unlikely that national minorities would have been granted political recognition or protection by the international community.

The allies did not undertake the recognition and creation of these states in a random manner. Their actions were based on a general consensus that the principle of national self-determination would provide the most stable, peaceful, and just foundation for the new European order. This consensus arose from a variety of material and ideational factors: external events, unintended consequences, dominant belief systems, and the need to adjust to the changing conditions brought about by the war and its aftermath. Thus, the protection of minorities was undertaken on behalf of the common good, that is, for the preservation and general welfare of the collectivity (Europe).

There was little evidence that strategic calculation, power balancing, or economic or military advantage were significant motivations in creating the regime. The allies were clearly concerned about the potential power of Germany (and to a lesser degree, the Soviet Union) after the war, but the creation of the protection regime did little to address this. Rather, the winning states addressed their security concerns in more traditional ways: limiting the size of Germany's armed forces, depriving it of strategic resources, and creating an international organization aimed at restraining aggressive behavior. In fact, the replacement of the Hapsburg empire with militarily weak and economically tenuous states in eastern Europe benefited the most powerful central and east European powers – Germany and the Soviet Union – more than it did the victorious allies. The protection of national minorities helped to maintain these weak states.

While one may argue that the ring of new states separating the Soviet Union from the west was designed to create a *cordon sanitaire* (sanitary zone) to prevent the spread of Bolshevism, the empirical evidence does not indicate that this was a significant factor in the decision to create an international protection regime.

Despite popular assumptions, then, the decision to build a new European order based on the principle of nationality was not the result of an idealist vision promoted by a strong personality (Woodrow Wilson) representing a dominant state. The historical record clearly demonstrates that political leaders in France and Britain had simultaneously developed versions of this approach, with little evidence of coercion or external political pressure. American power therefore cannot account for this outcome. In fact the historical evidence suggests that the "idealism" that is often considered to be the underlying motivation for Wilson and his allies was in reality a concern for stability, security, order, and justice.

The allies did not make the fine distinctions between stability and justice that is often made by political scientists. For Wilson, Lloyd George, Clemenceau, and others, the issues of order and justice were linked. They not only considered the national state to be the most just foundation for the new European order, they also saw it as the best approach toward maintaining stability and security after the break-up of the Hapsburg, Ottoman, Russian, and German empires. They also considered it to be the approach most likely to promote the political values favored by the winning coalition.

For all of the problems of enforcement and fairness, most political leaders and international law scholars at the time interpreted minority protection to be a general guarantee.[107] The protection of minorities had become a common good, a necessity for maintaining the coherence of the collectivity. While the welfare of minorities under the League system was secondary to the maintenance of peace, it became the foundation upon which the entire system was built.[108]

At the same time, the protection of national minorities does not appear to be primarily the result of humanitarian concerns. While domestic and transnational nongovernmental organizations (NGOs) interested in the minorities' welfare did influence the postwar settlement, ultimately the leaders of the allied powers acted with little accountability to their constituents. Most of the deliberations in Paris were conducted in secret, and the meetings were limited to the heads of state, foreign ministers, and close personal advisors.[109] Domestic and international pressure from NGOs may have had an effect on the thinking of these leaders, but the historical evidence strongly suggests that the allies were motivated primarily by considerations of stability and order.

---

[107] Macartney, *National States and National Minorities*, chapter 9.

[108] Ibid., p. 275.

[109] There are no official minutes of any meetings conducted by the Council of Four, although some of the participants kept notes of their own which they subsequently published. See, for example, Edward Mandell House, *The Intimate Papers of Colonel House*; Edward Mandell House and Charles Seymour, eds., *What Really Happened at Paris: The Story of the Peace Conference, 1918–1919 by American Delegates* (New York: Charles Scribner's Sons, 1921); and Temperley, *A History of the Peace Conference*.

This conclusion partially supports Jennifer Jackson Preece's thesis that national minority rights have been subservient to international peace and that international bodies will only take action when circumstances compel them to do so in the interests of systemic stability.[110] I say partially, because there are a variety of ways to approach the question of systemic stability and order. Minority rights do not always become an international issue whenever borders are changed and territory is transferred, as Preece's argument implies. The question of minorities only arises in a serious way when the political order is based on national states. As argued in chapter 2, the term "nation-state" notwithstanding, the legitimation of the state does not necessarily rest with the principle of national self-determination defined in ethnic terms. Had one of the other alternatives triumphed after World War I – liberalism, Bolshevism, or geopolitical realism – the protection of national minorities would likely not have arisen as an international issue.

---

[110] Preece, *National Minorities and the European Nation-States System.*

4   The liberal state and the protection of European citizens

The experience of the inter-war period and World War II shifted international opinion away from the principle of nationality as the foundation for a cohesive, secure, and just international order. As the war drew to a close, political leaders and resistance fighters began to consider the type of political order that would arise from the ruins of post-Versailles Europe. Gone from the discourse was the emphasis on national self-determination and minority rights. Despite the attempted extermination of ethnic and national minorities that had occurred on the eve of the war, few spoke of renewing the institutional commitment to protect minorities, nor was there talk of granting statehood to dispossessed nations. Sovereignty would be restored to states under German occupation, however there was little interest in redrawing borders to accommodate national claims of self-determination. Nationality would be restricted to the cultural sphere, devoid of any political significance.[1] Instead, the focus shifted toward the citizen as the foundation of sovereign authority. Human rights, not national rights, would be the guiding principle.

Most scholars agree that the development of human rights as an international *issue* was largely the result of the Holocaust and the partial triumph of liberalism as an ideology after the defeat of the Axis powers.[2] However the institution of human rights *protection* did not sweep the

[1] See, for example, William Neumann, *Making the Peace, 1941–1945: The Diplomacy of the Wartime Conferences* (Washington, DC: Foundation for Foreign Affairs, 1950).

[2] See, for example, Jack Donnelly, *International Human Rights* (New York: Westview Press, 1998), ch. 1; Henry Steiner and Phillip Alston, *International Human Rights in Context: Law, Politics, Morals* (Oxford: Clarendon Press, 1996), pp. 56–125; Kathryn Sikkink, "The Power of Principled Ideas: Human Rights Policies in the United States and Western Europe," in Judith Goldstein and Robert Keohane, eds., *Ideas and Foreign Policy: Beliefs, Institutions, and Political Change* (Ithaca: Cornell University Press, 1993); Burns Weston, "Human Rights," in R. P. Claude and B. J. Weston, eds., *Human Rights in the World Community* (Philadelphia: University of Pennsylvania Press, 1999).

globe after the war, even in those regions under strong Western influence. Despite the normative commitment toward individual liberty enshrined in the United Nations' Universal Declaration of Human Rights, an international protection regime only developed in Western Europe. If, as Stephen Krasner argues, the spread of human rights was largely the result of American hegemony,[3] why was there no human rights protection regime in Latin America, the region most directly under US influence and control?[4] Similarly, if transnational nongovernmental organizations and political entrepreneurs were responsible for the spread of human rights norms, why was this influence limited to Western Europe when there were other areas of the world that were also ripe for liberal concepts of governance?

This chapter examines how and why West European leaders created an international protection regime for human rights through the Council of Europe after the end of World War II. In addressing this issue, I consider several possible explanations. One approach is to focus on the power of principled ideas fueled by the rapid growth of epistemic communities and nongovernmental organizations after World War II (particularly in Western Europe).[5] In the waning days of the war, many domestic and transnational human rights organizations became increasingly active throughout Europe and the United States. In addition to these networks, prominent norm entrepreneurs such as Eleanor Roosevelt and Winston Churchill (who became a private citizen when he lost power immediately following the end of the war) initiated public campaigns for human rights, focused on influencing government policies in the West. This had a definite impact on the beliefs and policies of the reigning governments. From this perspective, the protection of human rights was an end in itself.

Another approach is to examine how the protection of human rights contributed to West European security in the face of Soviet domination in the East. Although there is little in the realist literature that discusses the development of human rights in Europe during this period, the logic of realism could suggest that the protection of human rights was tied

[3] See Stephen Krasner, "Sovereignty, Regimes and Human Rights," in Volker Rittberger, ed., *Regime Theory and International Relations* (New York: Oxford University Press, 1993).
[4] The Organization of American States did approve an Inter-American Convention on Human Rights in 1948; however like the Universal Declaration, this was mostly a statement of normative principles. It would be inaccurate to characterize this as a regime, at least as I define it in chapter 1.
[5] See, for example, Kathryn Sikkink, "The Power of Principled Ideas"; Donnelly, "International Human Rights" and Keck and Sikkink, *Activists Beyond Borders*, ch. 2.

to security considerations brought about by the Cold War and the fear of Soviet power. From this perspective, the mutual protection of human rights helped to facilitate the cohesion of NATO and prevent the intrusion of Soviet influence within its member states. The development of a European human rights regime would then most likely be the result of American and British initiatives. As G. John Ikenberry argues, European and American leaders agreed after the war that their ability to establish binding ties with one another rested on a shared commitment to democratic institutions.[6] Human rights, then, had a strategic purpose.

Andrew Moravcsik takes a different tack. He argues that international institutional commitments are a self-interested means of "locking in" domestic preferences, in the face of future political uncertainty.[7] Thus, the primary purpose of human rights protection in Europe was for governments to consolidate their own democratic institutions by binding future governments to observe human rights norms. In this case, the uncertainty is the long-term stability of one's democratic institutions. The motivation for constructing the regime therefore derived from instrumental calculations about domestic politics. As a result, the interest of established democracies in the stability of neighboring less-established democracies was less intense than the domestic interest of new democracies.

In tracing the development of the Council of Europe's international protection regime for human rights, I offer a fourth explanation that views the regime as a means toward building a new European order based on the values of political liberalism. Specifically, I argue that political leaders created a human rights regime to facilitate the creation of a liberal European community in which the form of state greatly mattered. Their goal was to construct a political order by imposing a strict set of rules about constitutional government and civil liberties on its members. In doing so, they linked participation in the new European community to the maintenance of a liberal state. To ensure the stability of such states, the governments of Western Europe created a Council of Europe that would ultimately oversee the most extensive and intrusive international protection regime in history. The protection of European citizens was therefore undertaken to promote the common good of Western Europe: liberalism and democratic governance.

[6] Ikenberry, *After Victory*, p. 164.
[7] Andrew Moravcsik, "The Origins of Human Rights Regimes: Democratic Delegation in Postwar Europe," *International Organization*, vol. 54, no. 2 (Spring 2000).

In pursuing this approach I acknowledge the role that principled beliefs played in spreading human rights *norms*, however I do not view this as a primary factor in explaining human rights *protection*. Similarly, I share Moravcsik's position that the members of the Council of Europe were very concerned with preventing a return of tyranny and genocide within their countries by securing their own liberties through international treaty. However, I maintain that we can explain more about the regime by examining its development from a European rather than a national perspective. That is, members of the Council were interested in protecting not only their own liberties, but also those of citizens throughout Western Europe because they saw a direct link between their own interest in liberal governance and the progress of a cohesive liberal political order in Europe. Therefore it was the *European* interest that guided their policies.

The political and strategic environment

The period surrounding World War II (1933–45) was the most destructive in human history. During the war, 25 million soldiers and 30 million civilians were killed in Europe and the Pacific. Close to 15 million others perished in German concentration camps, Stalinist purges, and Italian and Spanish state terror campaigns.[8] Economists estimate that governments spent $1 trillion on the war effort, and countless billions were lost in material destruction. Millions were left homeless, starvation was rampant, and much of the industrial infrastructure of the world's most modern economies had been destroyed.

Yet aside from the terrible human cost, the most dramatic long-term impact was political. In particular, twelve years of terror, war, and occupation caused a crisis of legitimacy for the European nation-state and challenged the durability of the European state system. The inability of many governments to defend their societies and protect their populations during the Axis onslaught undermined the authority of states

---

[8] It is impossible to get exact statistics on the number of people killed as a result of the political activities during the 1933–45 period. However, according to the official estimates, in addition to the 55 million people killed during the war, about 10 million Jews, Slavs, Roma, gays, and communists were murdered in German concentration camps. In the Soviet Union, Stalin's purges and social policies are estimated to have killed between 2 and 10 million political opponents. These figures do not include the thousands who died during the Spanish civil war, and the subseqent efforts by Francisco Franco to consolidate his power. See Norman Davies, *Europe: A History* (New York: Oxford University Press, 1996).

throughout the continent.[9] The German occupation had not only led to the collapse of almost every government on the continent, it destroyed the sovereignty of the states themselves. Only Germany, Italy, Britain, Ireland, Sweden, Switzerland, and Spain survived the early war period as cohesive independent states. For many Europeans, state power was no longer viewed as a necessary means toward security and prosperity. The brutality of German Nazism, Italian fascism, and Soviet Stalinism suggested that the state could not be trusted to protect the security and well-being of its population; indeed, it demonstrated that states could also be the primary source of insecurity and abuse. Finally, national-ism – the legitimizing principle for sovereign statehood in Europe since the early part of the century – was discredited, raising questions about the viability of a continent of autonomous nation-states. All of this con-vinced many political leaders that a qualitatively new European order was needed to prevent another descent into nationalist rivalry, genocide, and warfare.

The idea of a new political order emerged among political leaders and resistance fighters during the course of the war. As the conflict dragged on, many Western leaders began to publicly define World War II as a battle between liberal and anti-liberal forces. Although the Atlantic Charter said little about the type of order that would emerge after the defeat of Germany (beyond a respect for territorial integrity and eco-nomic freedom), there were other indications that a liberal order was rapidly becoming a war aim of the alliance. Franklin Roosevelt's "Four Freedoms" speech and the subsequent release of the British White Paper on war aims (both in 1941) suggested that the allies viewed the denial of human rights by totalitarian states as the greatest threat to European security and stability. In his 1941 annual message to Congress, President Roosevelt called for a postwar international order in which all people were guaranteed freedom of expression, freedom of worship, freedom from want, and freedom from fear.[10] In a world based on these princi-ples, he argued, war and aggression would be replaced by the friendly cooperation of free countries. The speech was particularly significant

---

[9] See William Wallace, *The Transformation of Western Europe* (London: Royal Institute of International Affairs, 1990), p. 59 and Alan Milward, *The European Rescue of the Nation State* (London: Routledge, 2000), Introduction.

[10] See Franklin D. Roosevelt's Address to the 77th Congress, January 6, 1941 in Edward H. Kavinoky and Julian Park, eds., *My Friends: Twenty-Eight History Making Speeches* (Buffalo, NY: Foster & Stewart, 1945).

inasmuch as it occurred almost a year before the American entry into the war.

The British War Aims Committee endorsed this position, describing the war as a life and death struggle for the cause of human freedom, the rule of law, and individual liberty.[11] This became official policy when British Ambassador Halifax incorporated the report into a White Paper issued in March. Prime Minister Winston Churchill provided further support in a speech describing the war as one that was being waged to "establish on impregnable rocks the rights of the individual."[12] A year later the allied coalition adopted a similar principle in the United Nations Declaration (no relation to the future international organization of the same name) by linking peace and security to the preservation of human rights and fundamental freedoms.[13] The document was signed by twenty-six countries and governments-in-exile.

Similar principles were promoted by a variety of nongovernmental organizations in the United States and Britain, such as the American Jewish Conference, World Citizens Association, Catholic Association for International Peace, and the American Committee on Human Rights. More specifically, during the latter days of the war, a number of British NGOs (some of which included future leaders such as Prime Minister Clement Attlee) developed detailed proposals for a union of European democratic states based on the protection of human rights.[14] More important than the NGOs, however, was the growing activity of the Resistance, which was active in every country occupied by Germany. While the liberation of the occupied territories was the primary focus of these groups, resistance movements throughout Europe developed detailed proposals for reorganizing the continent after the war. For many in the Resistance, fascism was only an extreme form of nationalism and statism. Consequently, many within the Resistance movements came not only to oppose totalitarianism, but also state sovereignty itself.[15]

---

[11] Quoted in A. W. Brian Simpson, *Human Rights and the End of Empire* (Oxford: Oxford University Press, 2001), p. 174.
[12] Winston Churchill, *His Complete Speeches, vol. VII, 1943–1949*, ed., Robert Rhodes James (London: Chelsea House Publishers, 1974).
[13] "Declaration by United Nations," Pamphlet No. 4, *Pillars of Peace* (Carlisle Barracks, PA: Army Information School, May 1946).
[14] Simpson, *Human Rights and the End of Empire*, pp. 167–68.
[15] Walter Lipgens, *A History of European Integration*, vol. I, *1945–1947* (Oxford: Clarendon Press, 1982), pp. 47–48.

The Resistance literature from 1944 and 1945 is filled with proposals for building a supranational European authority that could "counter the absolutist, centralizing and bureaucratic power of the national sovereign state."[16] In 1944 the various groups began to coordinate their political activities, leading to a series of Europe-wide meetings. Between March and July of that year, about a dozen meetings were held bringing together representatives from nine Resistance movements. In both the deliberations and final document the conference drew a connection between preventing a recurrence of totalitarianism on the continent and building a European community that would act as a watchdog over the power of states. The final Draft Declaration, for example, called for the construction of a federal union that would be "responsible not to the governments of the various member states, but to their peoples."[17] A general consensus began to develop among these groups that such a federation should guarantee basic human rights, and that this guarantee should prevail over national law.[18] As the Declaration articulated it, the union would be "based on a declaration of civil, political and economic rights which would guarantee democratic institutions and the free development of the human personality."[19] This suggests that many of those in the Resistance had begun to view the security of their own populations as being tied to the maintenance of a broader political order that guaranteed human rights and democratic governance.

At the same time, while many of the European leaders clearly expressed a desire to build some type of liberal political order on the continent, there were several internal tensions that raised questions about what the postwar era would look like. In particular, at least three issues arose that would influence alternative outcomes. First was a tension between universalism and regionalism. The United States favored a universalist approach that would replace the old balance of power and spheres of influence system with a global security structure over which it would exert influence.[20] The United Nations would be the key political and security organization designed to fulfill this task. Many European leaders, however, argued that the wide differences in culture and governments existing in the world made it difficult for the United Nations

---

[16] Walter Lipgens, *A History of European Integration*, p. 48.
[17] Ibid., p. 47.
[18] See Peter Stirk, *A History of European Integration Since 1914* (London: Pinter, 1986), p. 67.
[19] Simpson, *Human Rights and the End of Empire*, p. 217.
[20] A. W. De Port, *Europe Between the Superpowers: The Enduring Balance* (New Haven: Yale University Press, 1979), pp. 79–85.

promote a liberal world order.[21] They proposed building a community of European democratic states through the creation of a "Western bloc" or federation. This would not be a rejection of the UN idea, but would create a parallel system based on Europeanism rather than globalism. This proposal *preceded* the division of Europe into two political blocs.

A second issue was how to consolidate relations among the traditional allies without alienating the Soviet Union. During the final days of the war and the early days of the postwar period, most Europeans assumed that the Soviet Union would remain active in European affairs and that this would facilitate cooperation within the continent. This would have precluded the formation of a West European order based on democratic governance. Political leaders in countries such as Britain and the Netherlands, where Labour and socialist parties had government majorities, were particularly eager to avoid alienating the Soviets.

Third, European leaders debated how they could maintain the autonomy and influence of Europe in a postwar world that clearly would be dominated by two non-European superpowers.[22] World War II destroyed the European balance of power system that had existed in various forms since at least the 1870s. It also marked the end of European dominance in world politics. The new reality was a non-Eurocentric system in which the continent would be under the military and economic influence of the United States and Soviet Union. Despite this reality, many European leaders hoped to avoid ceding their influence to the two great power giants.

Ultimately the resolution of these tensions and the determination of what kind of order would be created in Europe were influenced by both external events and political factors that were unique to the European experience. During the last years of the war, the "Big Three" (the United States, Soviet Union, and Britain and later France) held four major meetings and many smaller ones to discuss the organization of postwar Europe.[23] Most of the meetings dealt with practical matters such as facilitating the surrender of the Axis powers, the issue of reparations, possible border adjustments, and voting rules in the United States. The

[21] See, for example, the statement by Danish diplomat Rasmussen at the first session of the Council of Europe's Committee of Ministers, in Council of Europe, *Collected Edition of the "Travaux Préparatoires," Committee of Ministers*, vol. I, 11 May – 8 September, 1949 (The Hague, 1950), p. 24.
[22] See the discussions in de Port, *Europe Between the Superpowers*, p. 59.
[23] These included the Moscow Conference in October 1943, the Tehran Conference on month later, the Potsdam Conference in July 1945 and the Yalta summit in February 1945.

two most significant outcomes of these meetings for our purposes were first, the inability of the great powers to agree on a political order for the continent, and second, the informal understanding at Yalta that the allies would not interfere in each other's spheres of influence.[24] Both of these factors laid the groundwork for the development of two political orders on the continent. Consequently, rather than developing a coordinated approach toward state sovereignty and international order – as was done after World War I and the Napoleonic Wars – the leading powers pursued separate courses. The Soviets installed communist governments in those areas that had been liberated by the Red Army while the Western allies established liberal governments within territories under the control of the American and British military forces.

After the collapse of the four-power Paris Council of Foreign Ministers meeting on July 12, 1946, most European leaders realized that the universalist approach to international order would not be possible in the near future.[25] By 1947 relations between the United States/Britain and the Soviet Union had deteriorated to the point where one could consider Europe to be politically bifurcated (although the Cold War had not yet begun). By 1948 all countries in what had been traditionally considered to be "Eastern Europe" had various types of communist governments, while all of Western Europe except Spain and Portugal had liberal ones.[26] With these developments, the geography of Versailles Europe changed. The subsequent rise of the Cold War, for example, eliminated the traditional concept of central Europe (*Mitteleuropa*) and the boundaries of European international society fell along ideological and military lines. All of this created political barriers that enabled the leadership of the West to construct a relatively closed international society. Thus, the permissive condition for the development of a liberal West European order was the development of clear boundaries separating insiders from outsiders.

Building a liberal West European order

Carl Friedrich argues that the reorganization of Western Europe after World War II was not based so much on any positive enthusiasm for a

---

[24] See John Wheeler-Bennett, *The Semblance of Peace: The Political Settlement After the Second World War* (New York: St. Martin's Press, 1972).

[25] Wheeler-Bennett, *The Semblance of Peace*, p. 561.

[26] Spain remained a fascist state under the rule of General Francisco Franco. Franco was allowed to remain in power after the war because Spain did not enter the conflict and therefore was not a defeated enemy.

"wonderful future" but rather a "negative distaste" for a dismal past.[27] Many of those who lived through the occupation adopted the position that citizens needed to be protected from the state. Yet they also believed that such protections required creating a general guarantee that would provide basic rights to all citizens in Western Europe. This could best be accomplished by submerging the state into a broader political structure (that is, some type of federation) that would provide for the protection of all citizens from their governments.[28] Thus, from the beginning, the idea of an international protection regime for individuals in Western Europe was part of a broader effort to build a regional political order based on political unity, economic integration, and democratic governance.

In deciding how to reconstruct the state in Europe most political leaders agreed that any plan would have to be based on a broad political consensus and be highly responsive to the needs of a wide range of its citizens if its legitimacy was to be accepted. This, they believed, could only be accomplished through the construction and maintenance of parliamentary, democratic states.[29] At the same time, the strongest advocates for building a liberal European order were also the same ones promoting European unity and federation. For them, the protection of European citizens from the abuses of their governments was closely linked to the development of a formal cohesive association of liberal states. This idea of a non-military organization of democratic states was raised before the Cold War created new security concerns in the West. For example, British Ambassador Duff Cooper submitted a widely circulated memo to the Foreign Office in 1946 arguing that "the democracies of Europe should form close alliances with one another based on geographical proximity, community of interests, similarity of colonial problems and a mutually inherited tradition of civilization . . ."[30]

The concept of Euro-federalism based on liberal states was promoted by a wide variety of organizations and prominent individuals that included the leaders of the various resistance movements, governmental officials, and members of the various parliaments. During the early

---

[27] Carl Friedrich, "The Political Theory of the New Democratic Constitutions," in Arnold Zurcher, ed., *Constitutions and Constitutional Trends Since World War II* (New York: New York University Press, 1955), p. 15.

[28] See Simpson, *Human Rights and the End of Empire*, p. 602.

[29] Milward, *The European Rescue of the Nation-State*, p. 27.

[30] Quoted in Simpson, *Human Rights and the End of Empire*, p. 553.

postwar years the lines between governmental and nongovernmental organizations were often blurred. Many leaders of the Resistance become government leaders, others formed or participated in NGOs and European transnational networks, and still others were elected to their country's parliament. Such individuals often moved between these various organizations. Thus the construction of the European liberal order occurred on many different levels inside and outside of government.

Most of the Euro-federalist organizations were built by the leadership of the various Resistance movements, for example, the Italian Movimento Federalista Europeo (MFE), the Swiss Europa-Union, the French Comité Français pour la Fédération Européenne, and the Dutch Europeesche Actie. Many leaders of these organizations agreed with the sentiment expressed by Italian MFE founder, former Resistance leader, and future government official, Altiero Spinelli: "A healthy democracy can emerge today in Europe, only on a European scale through the creation of a federal European union."[31] The most prominent proponent of European unity was Winston Churchill, who gave this movement a public face after his party was defeated in national elections. In November 1945, Churchill spoke in Brussels and called for the creation of a European federation based on constituent states organized under the rule of law and democratic governance. Such states, he argued, could flourish only under a European system that protected individual rights.[32] This, and a subsequent speech given in Zurich several months later, created a momentum for a liberal federation that the nongovernmental organizations could not produce on their own.

In 1946 Churchill helped to found the United Europe Movement (UEM), an organization composed of delegates from thirteen countries that played a significant role in facilitating the creation of a Western political structure. The UEM was not an NGO in the traditional sense; it was more of a transnational European organization composed of both governmental and nongovernmental members. Many in the UEM leadership had very close connections with the reigning governments and ruling political parties in Europe.[33] Like the other organizations promoting unity, the UEM advocated a liberal European order among the

---

[31] Quoted in Lipgens, *A History of European Integration*, p. 112.

[32] See Churchill, *His Complete Speeches*, pp. 7251–52.

[33] For example, Paul-Henri Spaak was the prime minister of Belgium, Leon Blum was a former French prime minister and leader in the French Socialist Party, Alcide de Gasperi was a leader in the Italian Parliament, and Pieter Kerstens was a leader of the Upper Chamber of the Dutch Parliament.

Western states. In his inaugural address at the founding conference, Churchill proclaimed that the aim of the organization was to "bring about the unity of all nations of all Europe . . . which assures to its people those fundamental personal rights and liberties on which our democratic European civilization has been created."[34]

Despite this flurry of activity, the United States initially opposed plans for European unity, favoring instead a restoration of state sovereignty even in those countries where it had proved to be dysfunctional.[35] The American priority was the economic reconstruction of Europe rather than its political reorganization. The British took a more ambiguous position. They supported the idea of greater European unity in theory, but hesitated to become too entangled in continental politics, a continuation of traditional British policy. Moreover, the ruling Labour Party did not want to antagonize the Soviet Union by creating a "Western bloc." Even France – under the conservative leadership of Charles de Gaulle – gave only tepid support to European unity. An ardent nationalist, de Gaulle was more interested in rebuilding France's great power status and influence than in creating a united Europe.

Without strong support from these governments, the pro-union movements could not move their proposals forward. However, the inability of the United States and Soviet Union to secure a peace settlement – and the growing rift between them – soon spurred a revival of the European unity project. Many European leaders were frustrated at this growing political conflict and, as suggested above, chaffed at the development of a superpower-dominated world in which European influence was limited. Thus, the revival of the "European idea" represented an assertion of specifically "European" values and interests distinct from those of the United States and Soviet Union.[36] For many, this meant the construction of a united European community that would act as a third force in world politics. The resignation of De Gaulle and the election of a leftist, pro-European French government in 1946 bolstered this view. Ultimately, even the United States relaxed its position on European unity and began to view it as beneficial.

The first official support for the European ideal by ruling governments grew out of the Brussels Treaty in March of 1948. This agreement (signed by Belgium, France, Luxembourg, the Netherlands, and the

[34] Churchill, *His Complete Speeches*, p. 7486.
[35] Lipgens, *A History of European Integration*, p. 270.
[36] Wallace, *The Transformation of Western Europe*, p. 31.

United Kingdom) promoted economic, social, and cultural collaboration among European states and was the precursor to the West European Union (WEU). Included in the treaty was a pledge to "fortify and preserve the principles of democracy, personal freedom and political liberty, the constitutional traditions and the rule of law" in Western Europe, and to "reaffirm (our) faith in fundamental human rights, in the dignity and worth of the human person."[37]

The first significant collaboration between governmental and nongovernmental organizations in building a liberal order came with the opening of the Congress of Europe at the Hague in 1948. The Congress was organized by the Committee of the Movements for European Unity (a coalition of pro-federalist organizations) and brought together 663 delegates from sixteen countries, including twenty prime ministers and former prime ministers.[38] In its final declaration, the Congress called for the creation of a European Assembly, a charter of human rights to protect democracy and individual freedom in Europe and a European union open to all democratically governed European states. To facilitate this plan, the Congress formed the European Movement (EM), an umbrella organization that included all of the various national European unity organizations.

The EM gained momentum when Belgian Prime Minister Spaak invited the organization to submit its proposals to the Consultative Council of the Brussels Treaty association. The EM accepted the invitation and drafted a comprehensive proposal for a West European-wide organization representing democratic countries. In September the French and Belgian delegates officially presented the proposal to the Council, recommending the immediate creation of a European Parliamentary Assembly. After some discussion, the Council appointed a five-member Committee for the Study of European Unity to consider the question. The Committee met in Paris in November and submitted their recommendations to the Consultative Council a month later.

In January 1949, the Council debated various proposals for building a European organization of democratic states. France, Belgium, and Italy advocated the creation of a formal federation that included a parliamentary assembly, while Britain supported a less formal intergovernmental

---

[37] See West European Union, "Treaty of Economic, Social, and Cultural Collaboration and Collective Self-Defense," March 17, 1948 (http://www.weu.int).
[38] A. and F. Boyd, *European Movement and the Council of Europe* (London: Hutchinson and Company, 1950), p. 46.

council of ministers.[39] The Brussels treaty states ultimately agreed to create a Council of Europe to oversee the political organization of Western Europe. The final structure reflected a compromise between these two alternative positions. The highest decisionmaking body would be a Committee of (foreign) Ministers, which would represent the ruling governments. However, the Council would also consist of a Consultative Assembly (later renamed the Parliamentary Assembly), which would represent the various parliaments and, indirectly, the people of Europe. If the governments and political leaders were not ready for a federated Europe, they would at least create a loosely united Western Europe of liberal states that would provide for cooperation and democracy by protecting each others' citizens and democratic institutions.

The creation of the Assembly – a transnational parliamentary body rather than an intergovernmental one – ensured that national parliaments would be represented, thereby providing a supranational oversight of governments. In this sense, the Council of Europe represented the extension of the democratic process into international affairs by tying member states to the institution of European democracy.[40] In pursuit of this objective, members of the Assembly were seated alphabetically rather than by country, a structural feature that increased the transnational nature of the body. The addition of a Secretariat formalized the Council by creating a permanent administrative body to coordinate the organization's activities. Demonstrating their desire to create an inclusive community of democratic states, the members of the Council immediately extended an invitation to Ireland, Italy, Denmark, and Sweden to apply for membership.

The importance of the Council in building the postwar European liberal order cannot be overstated. Unlike most international organizations, the Council did not have defined functions of either a technical or diplomatic nature. Rather, it was created to promote the unity of European democracies and to oversee the development of a liberal democratic order in the western regions. For this reason, one of the early critics derided the Council as "an organization somewhat combining the

[39] See Marion Miller, "The Approaches to European Institution-Building of Carlo Sforza, Italian Foreign Minister, 1947–1951," in Ann Deighton, ed., *Building Postwar Europe: National Decisionmaking and European Institutions, 1948–1963* (New York: St. Martin's Press, 1995), p. 60.
[40] See A. H. Robertson, *The Council of Europe: Its Structure, Functions and Achievements* (London: Stevens and Sons, 1961), p. 251.

characteristics of an unending diplomatic conference and of a House of Lords."[41] However, the Council provided an important foundation for the maintenance of a liberal political order in Europe, as symbolized by its membership criteria. The protection of human rights and democratic governance was not only an objective of the Council; it was a condition of membership. According to Article 3 of the Statute, "every member of the Council of Europe must accept the principle of the rule of law and the enjoyment by all peoples within its jurisdiction of human rights and fundamental freedoms."[42]

This condition was enforced through Article 8, which provides for suspending or expelling any member who violated Article 3.[43] As the Scottish representative Ungoed-Thomas explained, "the Statute has wisely provided, by Article Eight, that anyone who seriously violates the ideals and aspirations to which we all subscribe may be ejected from this comity of nations."[44] This necessarily excluded loyal anti-Soviet allies such as Spain and Portugal from the new European community, a move that defied traditional alliance behavior.

From the beginning, then, the Council of Europe was the most political of the many European organizations that formed after the war. It acted more like a club of European democratic states than an organization concerned with the more practical aspects of integration such as trade and monetary cooperation. It was also the only organization that directly involved members of parliament (MPs) from its member states, ensuring that there would be a supranational check on the power of the executives.[45] Even as the functional tasks of European integration were soon assumed by other organizations such as the European Economic Community and the European Coal and Steel Community (ECSC), the Council remained as the guardian of a liberal European order. For this reason, it was far more inclusive than the other associations. For example, in 1953 there were six members of the ECSC but fourteen in the Council.[46] While Council plans to make itself into a "European political authority with limited functions but real powers" were dashed as early

[41] R. R. Baxter, quoted in Robertson, *The Council of Europe*, p. 246, fn. 1.
[42] Statute of the Council of Europe, *European Treaty Series*, no. 1, signed May 5, 1949.
[43] Since the Statute was approved, the Council never needed to exercise this provision. The only member country that overturned their democratic government – Greece in 1967 – withdrew from the Council just as its members were prepared to vote suspension.
[44] Council of Europe, *Collected Edition of the "Travaux Préparatoires,"* vol. I (The Hague: Martinus Nijhoff, 1975), p. 80.
[45] The European Union adopted this structural feature several decades later by creating a European Parliament as part of its decision-making apparatus.
[46] Robertson, *The Council of Europe*, ch. 1.

as 1951, it became the center of a human rights protection regime and the conscience of a democratic Europe.

Resolving the "German question"

The importance that Western leaders attached to the maintenance of a liberal state as the best guarantee of stability and cooperation is strongly indicated by the way it dealt with the "German question" during the immediate postwar decade. Unlike the aftermath of World War I, when the primary focus was on demilitarization and territorial contraction, European leaders chose domestic reorganization and democratization as their preferred method of taming potential German aggression. For many European leaders, the most effective way to resolve the German question was to integrate that country into a democratic system of European states.[47] At the Berlin Conference in July 1945, the victorious powers decided to reconstruct Germany as a democratic state under the rule of law, with guaranteed human rights protections.[48] The first stage of this effort was "de-Nazification," a broad campaign to purge Nazi sympathizers from all significant levels of German society. The Occupation Statute of 1949 allowed some level of self-government, however Article 3 gave the occupation authorities the right to reassert full authority over all levels of German society if they considered it essential to preserve democratic governance in Germany.

Germany became part of the Western liberal community even before the occupation ended after the Committee of Ministers voted to admit that country into the Council of Europe as an associate member in 1950. The Council did so in order to "associate Germany with those European countries which are determined to preserve the democratic way of life."[49] As Churchill stated at the time, "one of the most practical reasons for pressing forward with the creation of a European Assembly was that it provided an effective means . . . of associating a democratic and free Germany with the Western democracies."[50] This led to the Bonn

---

[47] Lipgens, *A History of European Integration*, p. 193.

[48] See the Report of the Berlin Conference, Potsdam, Germany, August 2, 1945 in Louise Holborn, ed., *War and Peace Aims of the United Nations, January 1, 1943 – September 1, 1945*, vol. II (Boston: World Peace Foundation, 1948), pp. 40–60.

[49] Council of Europe, "Letter from Secretary-General J. C. Paris to Konrad Adenauer, 31 March 1950," *Consultative Assembly, First Ordinary Session, 1950, Documents* (Strasbourg, 1950), p. 582.

[50] Council of Europe, *Consultative Assembly, First Session, 10 August – 8 September, 1949* (Strasbourg, 1949), Document U, p. 127.

Conventions, which ended the occupation in May 1952. According to the Convention, the Federal Republic of Germany was to "maintain a liberal democratic federal constitution which guarantees human rights." Moreover, Article 5 empowered the three occupying powers (the United States, France, and Britain) to take action "if the liberal democratic basic order" was subverted or disrupted.[51]

Building an international protection regime for human rights

From the beginning, European political leaders knew that the endurance of their political order rested on stabilizing the liberal democratic state. This required that they secure a basic set of rights for all West European citizens since such states are built on some degree of individual autonomy. The construction of an international protection regime was thus closely fused with the development of a liberal political order in Western Europe. This is clearly evident in the early work of the Council of Europe. At its inception, members of the Council (particularly those in the Consultative Assembly) sought to tie the two issues together. According to human rights historians A. H. Robertson and J. G. Merrills, the protection of human rights by the Council was undertaken to preserve the rule of law and the principles of democracy *both* within the Council member states and within the West European community as a whole.[52] This position is supported by both the process through which the regime was created and the justifications offered by members of the Consultative Assembly and the Committee of Ministers.

Much of the evidence can be found in the detailed minutes and transcripts of meetings held by both bodies, as well as the historical accounts from the participants themselves. The minutes of the Assembly clearly reflect the musings of a deliberative body, indicating that the debates were not tailored for public relations purposes. In fact, during the crucial period of the regime's formation (1949–51), the publics of the member states were not significantly involved or informed about the daily negotiations.

The idea of developing a European human rights charter and a mechanism for enforcement was one of the first items on the agenda of

---

[51] "Convention on Relations between the Three Powers and the Federal Republic of Germany."

[52] A. H. Robertson and J. G. Merrills, *Human Rights in Europe: A Study of the European Convention on Human Rights* (Manchester: Manchester University Press, 1993), p. 5.

the newly constituted Consultative Assembly. The initial push came from the European Movement, whose International Judicial Section produced a draft convention written by French political leader Pierre-Henri Teitgen, British MP David Maxwell Fyfe, and French Professor Fernand Dehousse. Although the Committee of Ministers initially wanted to postpone discussion of the draft, pressure from the Consultative Assembly forced the Committee to include it on the agenda of the first Assembly meeting. The deliberations occurred over a period of several weeks, focusing primarily on how the Council could maintain democracy and the rule of law within the European community. The purpose of the deliberations was well defined in an early Assembly resolution stating that in the political and legal field:

> The democratic basis of the European community shall be clearly defined during the Session, with a view to safeguarding and developing the fundamental rights of freedom which must be guaranteed in accordance with the provisions of the Statute (of the Council of Europe).[53]

The substance of the subsequent deliberations reveals the motives of those promoting the regime. Virtually all Assembly delegates spoke of the need to safeguard democracy and the rule of law in Europe as the primary means of preventing member states from descending into authoritarianism. Many of the founders of the Council had been either in the Resistance or in prison during the war and believed that the protection of human rights was vital for the maintenance of democracy and the prevention of war.[54] Ungoed-Thomas, for example, argued that the purpose of establishing a European human rights protection system was to "ensure that the states of the Members of the Council of Europe are democratic and remain democratic . . ."[55] Similarly, Italian representative Benvenuti stated that the goal was to "strengthen in all circumstances the democratic regimes of all Member countries of the Council of Europe, especially where the totalitarian menace is or could be more acute."[56] And as the British delegate Lord Layton added, a European protection system "provides a mechanism for a common defense of the rule of law, democracy and a common heritage by making acceptance a condition of membership in the West European community." We

---

[53] Council of Europe, *Consultative Assembly, First Session*, Document T, p. 125.
[54] Douglas Brinkley and David Facey-Crowther, *The Atlantic Charter* (New York: St. Martin's Press, 1994), p. 3.
[55] Council of Europe, *Collected Edition of the "Travaux Préparatoires,"* vol. II, p. 60.
[56] Ibid., vol. II, p. 136.

must therefore "accept joint responsibility for the preservation of those human rights among ourselves."[57]

The above quotes are only a small sample of statements contained in the minutes clearly suggesting that a primary motivating factor in the regime construction was to preserve the liberal European community by stabilizing the liberal state.

In addition, the delegates were also acutely aware that in order to maintain a cohesive political order composed of liberal states, there must be a collective guarantee for each other's populations. Teitgen put it thus:

> Experience has proved to us that the problems (of totalitarianism) are insoluble on the national plane. It can only be solved by means of a collective effort (and therefore the members of the Council have implicitly) accepted the principle of a collective guarantee of fundamental freedoms.[58]

The Secretary-General of the Council echoed this sentiment, arguing that the primary motivation for providing a collective guarantee of human rights was based on:

> the fundamental principle of collective responsibility for the observance of human rights in the territories of the Member States . . . The reason for making responsibility collective is the belief that without respect for human rights, the political basis for the European association postulated by the Council of Europe would be deprived of its essential elements.[59]

The European Human Rights Commission confirmed these principles several years later in a rather wordy ruling:

> The purpose of the High Contracting Parties in concluding the (Human Rights) Convention was not to concede to each other reciprocal rights and obligations in pursuance of their individual national interests, but to realize the aims and ideals of the Council of Europe, as expressed in its Statute, and to establish a common public order of the free democracies of Europe with the object of safeguarding their common heritage of political traditions, ideals, freedom and the rule of law.[60]

Still, justifications and lofty statements in and of themselves could not protect either the rights of citizens or the stability of their democratic institutions. Thus, after much deliberation, the Assembly unanimously

---

[57] Ibid., vol. V, p. 264.   [58] Ibid., vol. I, p. 45–6. Parenthetical, mine.
[59] Quoted in Stirk, *A History of European Integration Since 1914*, p. 4.
[60] Quoted in Robertson and Merrills, *Human Rights in Europe*, p. 28. Parenthetical, mine.

passed Recommendation 38, proposing that the Committee of Ministers draft a legally binding convention for the protection of human rights. They further proposed that they create an internal organization within the Council to "ensure the collective guarantee of human rights," and provide enforcement mechanisms to ensure that all states abided by these commitments. The ministers delegated the task of drafting such a convention to its Committee on Legal and Administrative Questions, (CLAQ) headed by Teitgen. The resulting "Teitgen Report," issued in September 1949, became the foundation for the most extensive international protection regime to date.

The report began by drawing a direct link between the protection of human rights and the maintenance of a liberal order in Europe. In the preamble the Report stated that a collective guarantee was essential because it would:

> demonstrate clearly the common desire of the Member States to build a European Union in accordance with the principles of natural law, of humanism and of democracy; it would contribute to the development of their solidarity and would fulfil the longing for security among their peoples.[61]

These rights are "the common denominator of our political institutions, the first triumph of democracy, but also the necessary condition under which it operates."[62]

The Report then developed a detailed proposal for what should be included in a human rights charter, and recommended the establishment of a Human Rights Commission and a European Court of Human Rights. The former had three main tasks: (1) to accept, process, and investigate specific complaints of human rights violations; (2) if the complaint is deemed valid, to attempt to resolve the conflicts stipulated in the complaints; and (3) if unsuccessful, to issue a public report and/or refer the complaint to an adjudication body. The Court would have legal authority to consider specific complaints of violations and issue binding rulings against offending states.

The basic framework of the European Convention on Human Rights and Fundamental Freedoms was non-controversial. All agreed that the Convention should outline the obligations of the signatories in terms of protecting human rights domestically and within the community

---

[61] Council of Europe, *Consultative Assembly, First Ordinary Session, 1950*, "Measures for the Fulfillment of the Declared Aim of the Council of Europe," Document 77, p. 197.
[62] Council of Europe, *Collected Edition of the "Travaux Préparatoires,"* vol. I, p. 194.

represented by the Council of Europe. There were, however, some fundamental splits influenced by different interests. How states and political leaders were divided can help us to understand the motivations of the various parties in pursuing a human rights protection regime.

First, there was a split between the Committee of Ministers (representing the European governments) and the Consultative Assembly (representing the European parliaments). The empirical record suggests that this division was the most acute and generally more significant than those that arose between various countries. The foreign ministers were clearly more reluctant to surrender their sovereignty than were the parliamentary representatives. Consequently, the more popular-based Assembly promoted stronger legal mechanisms for enforcing the Convention and placed greater weight on the supranational institutions. This suggests that the more democratic bodies (the parliaments) saw a greater need to place European-wide checks on the power of the nation-state.

A second division developed between those states that strongly supported greater European integration/federation, and those that favored a weaker association. Those who were more pro-Europe also tended to support stronger enforcement mechanisms and greater guarantees of democratic institutions. Conversely, those states which were less pro-Europe sought a weaker regime. For example, according to a poll of members of parliament taken in 1946, 62 percent of Italian, 49 percent of Belgian, and 50 percent of French MPs supported the creation of a European federation.[63] The representatives from these countries also supported a strong regime, according to the criteria developed by Moravcsik.[64] At the same time, Britain (23 percent), Norway (8 percent), Sweden (8 percent), and Denmark (10 percent) voted in the Committee of Ministers for a weaker regime.[65] This tends to support the thesis advanced in this book, since it suggests a close correlation between one's commitment toward the political order and one's willlingness to make greater sacrifices to ensure the cohesion of the order.

[63] H. Gisch, "The European Parliamentary Union (EPU)," in W. Lopgens and W. Loth, eds., *Documents on the History of European Integration*, vol. IV (New York: De Bruyter, 1991), p. 114.
[64] Moravcsik cited as indicative of weak and strong regime a state's position on whether the Human Rights Commission would allow individual citizens to petition the body and whether the Court would have voluntary or compulsory jurisdiction. Andrew Moravcsik, "The Origins of Human Rights Regimes," p. 231.
[65] The correlation is not perfect. Greece (58 percent) and the Netherlands (53 percent) also voted against the stronger provisions of the regime.

Finally, as Andrew Moravcsik demonstrates, there was also a division between what he terms "new democracies" (those who established democratic institutions after 1920) and "established democracies."[66] Moravcsik's statistical analysis suggests that new democracies were more likely to support stronger enforcement mechanisms than established ones. While his statistical evidence certainly supports his thesis (see above), when taken in context with the other divisions it suggests that there may be other explanations as well.

The divisions took on a practical form over four key issues that would determine the shape of the regime. The positions taken by the various parties provide some additional evidence on motivation: first, should the list of rights be limited to civil and political liberties or should they also include economic and social protections? The resolution of this issue by the Assembly and Council suggests that their priority was to support the basic foundation of the liberal state over more ambitious efforts to create a social charter. During the debate in the Assembly, for example, the members overwhelmingly agreed that the fundamental requirements for a democratic society would be the standard from which the list of rights would be developed.[67] In particular, the Teitgen committee decided to focus only on those rights that were "defined and accepted after long usage by democratic states" and those that "are the common denominator of our political (liberal) institutions."[68] While the committee (and other representatives within the Council of Europe) also strongly supported the concept of social and economic rights (most were from social democratic governments), they agreed that "it is necessary to begin at the beginning and to guarantee political democracy in the European Union" before pursuing social protections.[69]

Second, in addition to outlining human rights guarantees, should the Convention also include a guarantee of each state's democratic institutions? Article Three of the draft Convention stipulated that all signatories must "respect the fundamental principles of democracy in all good faith and in particular . . . to hold free elections at reasonable intervals, with universal suffrage and secret ballot so as to ensure that Government action and legislation is, in fact, the expression of the will of the peoples . . ." The primary purpose of this provision was the preserve

---

[66] Moravcsik, "The Origins of Human Rights Regimes," p. 231.
[67] Robertson and Merrills, *Human Rights in Europe*, p. 8.
[68] Council of Europe, *Consultative Assembly, First Ordinary Session, 1950,* Document 77, p. 198. Parenthetical, mine.
[69] Ibid., p. 198.

the integrity of the democratic state.[70] This would have been a more significant guarantee than the Council of Europe's membership criteria, since the Convention was to be a legally-binding treaty. The provision as worded was unanimously approved by the Consultative Assembly, but it ran into some opposition in the Committee of Foreign Ministers. The Committee sent the question to a "committee of experts" and then discussed it during the Meeting of Senior Officials (also an intergovernmental body). During the deliberations, all but the British representatives supported the provision.[71] Ultimately, however, other states such as Greece and the Netherlands voted against the democratic guarantee at the Council, and it was thus eliminated.[72] Once again, the popular-based Assembly was more concerned with creating European-wide oversight to protect democracy while some on the intergovernmental committee wanted greater freedom of maneuver.

Third, should individuals and groups have a right to petition the Commission or could only states file such complaints? The former would have reduced the power of the states at the European level by allowing individual citizens and domestic organizations to directly challenge their own governments. This issue was closely related to the fourth issue: should complaints ultimately be forwarded to an independent court or to the Committee of Ministers? If the court did receive the complaints, should its jurisdiction be compulsory or rely on voluntary participation by the signatory states? In short, should the process be a legal proceeding or a political one? Again, the Assembly voted for the stronger regime (right to petition and an independent court), while the Committee was split. As Moravscik demonstrates, there was a rough correlation between the positions taken at the Committee and whether the representative was from a new or old democracy. Yet I found the division between the Assembly and Committee to be more significant, since the breakdown between old and new democracies did not appear within the parliamentary body. This suggests that there was a rough consensus among the popular-based representatives that was not shared by some of their executive counterparts.

At the same time (as discussed above) there was also a correlation between those supporting deeper integration/federation and those favoring greater independence for the European-wide human rights bodies.

[70] Ralph Beddard, *Human Rights and Europe: A Study of the Machinery of Human Rights Protection of the Council of Europe* (London: Sweet and Maxwell, 1973).
[71] Simpson, *Human Rights and the End of Empire*, pp. 697 and 705.
[72] Council of Europe, *Collected Edition of the "Travaux Préparatoires,"* vol. IV, p. 136.

For example, Britain not only opposed the creation of a court (and compulsory jurisdiction for the court if one were created), if also opposed giving the Consultative Assembly any substantive authority. They were therefore consistently pushing a strong intergovernmentalist (as opposed to a European) position at all levels. Similarly, the Dutch argued at the Conference of Senior Officials meeting that greater independence for the supranational legal bodies would decrease state sovereignty. The establishment of the mandatory court, they argued, could only be the last chapter of European integration.[73] Conversely, Belgium, Italy, and France were among the strongest advocates of both Euro-federalism and stronger enforcement mechanisms for the Convention.[74]

Ultimately, a compromise was reached. The Committee created enforcement mechanisms that reflected a combination of legal and political procedures. Initially the functions of the Commission were limited to hearing complaints by one state against another, however after six states accepted the right of individual petition in 1955 (one year after the first meeting of the Commission), individuals and groups gained legal standing. The court was established as proposed, with cases able to be referred by either the Commission or a Contracting Party to the Convention. The court could only act when there was a breach of the Convention and only after domestic remedies had been exhausted. Thus, while the court had jurisdiction in cases of violations that resulted from legislative, judicial, or executive acts of state, the Committee of Ministers was charged with supervising the implementation of the court's decisions. Although the court could issue a binding ruling, if that ruling was violated, the Council of Europe would consider what, if any, action would be taken.

Unlike the minority rights treaties and the minority protection regime created after World War I, the human rights system after World War II remained cohesive for half a century. This paralleled the continued strength of the liberal political order in Western Europe.

Conclusion

The historical record suggests that the creation of an international protection regime for European citizens after World War II was part of an

[73] Ibid., p. 128.
[74] See the statements made at the Committee in ibid., vol. IV.

effort to build a cohesive regional order based on the liberal state. Since the foundation of the liberal state was the semi-autonomous citizen, the supranational protection of individuals was deemed the best method for preventing the rise of authoritarianism in Western Europe. As one of the prime architects of the regime, Pierre-Henri Teitgen argued that a collective guarantee was essential for the stability of a democratic Europe because in the event of a threat to democracy "it is necessary to intervene before it is too late. A conscience must exist somewhere which will sound the alarm to the minds of a nation menaced by this progressive corruption."[75] After more than a decade of tyranny, genocide, aggression, and war, many European leaders realized that they would have to take a European – rather than a national – approach to the problem of reconstruction. The maintenance of a liberal order in which states would guarantee each other's liberties became the common good for the European community. Thus the European interest became the national interest, and political leaders recognized a structural interdependence among themselves.

For this reason, the international regime for the protection of human rights was closely tied to the European integrationist movement. The strongest advocates of European unity and federation were also the strongest proponents of the most intrusive type of human rights protection regime possible. While European economic integration was soon split off from political unity, efforts to protect human rights moved forward in the name of building a democratic community of states. British representative Lord Layton explained the connection as follows:

> If we had decided upon federation, with a rigid constitution, these things (human rights guarantees) would have been defined in the constitution. But we have not got to that point . . . In the meantime, we wanted to lay down the rules of the club, so we drew up this Convention as a symbolic, clear declaration which marks us as free Western Europe; and as a joint undertaking recognizing the right of each Member to pull another up if the rules are not observed.[76]

This indicates that there was a close connection between the protection of human rights and efforts to build a new European order. The best evidence for this is the Council of Europe, the organization

---

[75] Council of Europe, *Consultative Assembly Official Reports, August* (Strasbourg, 1949), p. 1158.
[76] Council of Europe, *Collected Edition of the "Travaux Préparatoires,"* vol. V, p. 264.

through which the protection regime developed and operated. The Council was formed as a club of liberal states with no security or economic functions. Its approach to European integration was not a common market or a security community but rather a closed international society in which only democracies which guaranteed human rights could participate.

While nongovernmental organizations and norm entrepreneurs had a strong influence on the movements for federation and human rights protection, ultimately the regime was created by political leaders who were less concerned with the welfare of individuals than with the stability and cohesion of Western Europe. NGOs and prominent individuals greatly helped to make human rights into an international issue in Europe, however they were not as influential in efforts to create a regime for human rights protection. Moreover, both the Euro-federalist and human rights movements were led not by domestic groups or transnational policy networks, but by former Resistance fighters and political leaders who moved in and out of government. Their base of influence was not civil society but national parliaments and political parties which were very much part of political society.

At the same time, it was clear that the parliamentary representatives in the Consultative Assembly were much more willing to cede some of their state sovereignty to supranational human rights bodies than the intergovernmental Committee of Ministers. The evidence suggests that without pressure from the Assembly the Council of Europe would have moved much more slowly and less decisively in creating an international protection regime for human rights. This should not be surprising, given the propensity of governments to jealously guard their sovereignty.

This chapter also clearly demonstrated that security considerations and power concerns did not play a significant role in the creation of the regime. The extensive record of deliberations (as well as the first-hand accounts by participants and historians) show virtually no discussion of the Cold War, NATO, or even European security in general. Certainly the Council of Europe helped facilitate greater solidarity among West European states and this increased the cohesion of the "Western bloc." Yet this was at best a by-product, not a cause. In fact the human rights protection regime and the membership requirements of the Council of Europe harmed the anti-Soviet alliance in several ways. First, it excluded loyal non-democratic allies such as Spain and Portugal. Second, the Convention and its enforcement mechanisms raised the possibility that the Council would have to sanction an ally during the height of the Cold War, should one of them violate human rights commitments. Finally, it empowered those who sought to create a "third way" independent of the superpowers, thus threatening the unity of the Western alliance.

The process through which the regime was created also showed the limits of power in the context of an international society or community. The regime was not initiated by either the United States or Britain, the two strongest Western states, both of which emerged from the war largely intact. In fact Britain's "power" was largely its ability to manipulate the decision rules (consensus) in its favor, thus pushing a "lowest common denominator" result. Moreover, according to a British historian of the period, the explanation for Britain's interest in protecting human rights could not be found in the history of English constitutional thought, but rather as a product of British foreign policy.[77] Its domestic interest was guided by its European interest.

Finally, as suggested in the introductory chapters, the success of the regime was directly related to the level of state commitment toward the cohesion of the West European community. All states were strongly committed to the progress of European international society and as a result were more willing to act on its behalf even when it was inconvenient. The willingness of the Europeans to cede much of their sovereignty in the treatment of their populations is evidence of this. Certainly the fact that all of the states were democracies made them more willing to subject themselves to international scrutiny, since they had less to fear from a supranational human rights body than an authoritarian state. Yet many of the states also recognized that a such oversight could interfere with state interest and domestic policy.

For example, the British, Norwegian, and Dutch governments wanted the option of banning their Communist Parties or even arresting their leaders should they believe it to be necessary. This, of course, would have violated the principles of the Convention. As British representative Le Quenne stated, "taking the world as it is, political considerations may well justify restrictions on the enjoyment of these rights, which are not strictly justifiable under the terms of the Convention."[78] Still, in the end, they all accepted a Convention that would not allow such exceptions. In

---

[77] Brian Simpson, *Human Rights and the End of Empire*, p. 18.
[78] Ibid., pp. 702, 719.

fact, over time – as the Cold War became increasingly acute – the regime became even stronger to the point, where the Court of Human Rights could overturn domestic legislation.

The strength of Western Europe's commitment to human rights protection never faltered. This is a testament to the strength of European international society after World War II.

5   The multicultural state and the protection of ethnic communities

As we saw in Chapter 4, the political order that was established after World War II enabled West European leaders to build a cohesive community of liberal democratic states in which citizenship was defined in secular terms. The end of the Cold War raised expectations among political leaders that this community could be expanded to include the former communist states of Eastern Europe and Eurasia. This expansion would involve extending Western institutions eastward and building a shared commitment to the values underlying these institutions. It was the prevailing belief that democratization, economic cooperation, and a commitment to protect human rights within the new and reorganized states of Eastern Europe would facilitate the integration of the continent. In short, the initial goal of the post-Cold War leadership was to build a new integrated European order based on the liberal state.

However, soon after initiating this strategy, European and North American leaders realized that the integration of Europe would require the resolution of internal tensions that stemmed from competing definitions of "state," "nation," and "citizenry." In this effort, the adoption of democratic institutions alone would be insufficient. The political geography of Eastern Europe had been established at Versailles seventy years earlier. Since both blocs agreed not to allow any significant border changes after World War II, the Versailles settlement remained frozen in time.[1] As a result, the external borders and internal administrative

---

[1] The principle that borders should not be altered even to facilitate self-determination was confirmed in the 1975 Final Act of Helsinki, which declared the "inviolability of frontiers of all States in Europe." See Conference on Security and Cooperation in Europe, "Final Act of Helsinki, 1 August 1975," Section 1 (III) in Arie Bloed, ed., *The Conference on Security and Cooperation in Europe: Analysis and Basic Documents, 1972–1993* (London: Kluwer Academic Publishers, 1993).

boundaries of most East European and Eurasian states reflected the values and priorities of the post-World War I era.

Yet, as we saw in chapter 4, the values and priorities of the European community changed dramatically after World War II. Self-government replaced self-determination. Human rights – based on the autonomy of the individual – replaced minority rights – which are rooted in the autonomy of the nation. The national state was discredited in favor of the liberal one. While the end of the Cold War offered an opportunity to extend these values throughout the continent, European leaders knew that reopening the question of borders would breed instability and conflict. The key problem, then, was how to harmonize the values of New Europe with the borders of Versailles Europe without changing either. In this quest, neither the liberal nor national state would suffice.

This chapter traces the process through which European and North American leaders attempted to create a new European order after the end of the Cold War, and examines how the protection of ethnic communities was critical to achieving this goal. It will argue that the decision by European leaders to build a united Europe from "Vancouver to Vladivostok" created strong tensions and contradictions that ultimately required direct intervention by the Organization for Security and Cooperation in Europe (OSCE) in the relationship between the nationalizing governments and the various ethnic communities that constituted the reorganized states of Europe.[2] This meant not only transforming the political order created at Yalta and Strasbourg, but undermining the legacy of Versailles as well. In practical terms it also meant undermining the national state in favor of the multicultural one by protecting the collective identities and political rights of national minorities throughout the continent. In pursuing this goal, the OSCE built an international protection regime aimed at ethnic communities. The protection of national minorities would only occur within the broader context of protecting ethnic *groups* by providing for cultural pluralism and cultural autonomy.

In making this argument, this chapter will consider how security concerns and considerations of stability influenced the decisions of European leaders. As in the other empirical chapters, I will consider also potential humanitarian motives promoted by nongovernmental organizations and transnational advocacy networks. The first section will explore the political and strategic environment that the leaders of the OSCE

---

[2] In 1993 the *Conference* on Security and Cooperation in Europe (CSCE) was transformed into the *Organization* for Security and Cooperation in Europe (OSCE). In this chapter I use both names interchangeably, depending upon the time period I am explaining.

found itself in after the Cold War. Specifically, it will discuss the cultural and political divisions that had long separated the eastern, southern and western regions of Europe. I will show how these divisions contributed to the difficulties in building a united political order after the Cold War. The next section will examine the efforts of the OSCE to overcome these difficulties. Following this, I will examine how the creation of an international protection regime centered in the Office of the High Commissioner on National Minorities contributed toward this effort. The last section will examine the Bosnian Peace Agreement as a case study in how European institutions attempted to create a multicultural state.

Although several organizations were involved in promoting the rights of national minorities during this period – for example, the Council of Europe and the United Nations – the OSCE was the only institution to build a coherent international protection regime. Therefore this chapter will focus almost exclusively on this organization.

The political and strategic environment

In the years following World War II, the states of Western Europe built the most cohesive and highly institutionalized international society in its history. This community was maintained by a complex network of institutions through which member states committed themselves to unprecedented levels of cooperation and integration in the political, economic, cultural, security, and even judicial arenas. Such cooperation stemmed from a variety of factors: increased economic interdependence, a desire to avoid major war, a perception of a common security threat from the Soviet Union, and skilled efforts from political entrepreneurs.[3] Toward this end, European states signed a number of legally binding treaties that ceded (or pooled) a portion of their sovereignty to supranational institutions such as the European Community/European Union, NATO, and the European Court of Human Rights.[4]

---

[3] There is a vast literature that seeks to explain European integration and organization. For a sampling of the major theoretical approaches, see *inter alia*, Moravcsik, *The Choice for Europe*, particularly the introduction and ch. 1; Milward, *The European Rescue of the Nation-State*, particularly ch. 1; Dinan, *Ever Closer Union?*, ch. 1.

[4] See, *inter alia*, John Pinder, *European Community: The Building of a Union* (Oxford: Oxford University Press, 1991); Robert O. Keohane and Stanley Hoffmann, "Institutional Change in Europe in the 1980s," in Robert O. Keohane and Stanley Hoffmann, eds., *The New European Community: Decisionmaking and Institutional Change* (Boulder: Westview Press, 1991); and Wayne Sandholtz and John Zysman, "1992: Recasting the European Bargain," *World Politics*, vol. 42, no. 1 (October 1989).

At the same time, the cohesion of the Western political order was not only the product of complex interdependence, domestic politics, security concerns, and a commitment to institution-building. It was also facilitated by the creation of political and geographic boundaries separating the West from Eastern Europe and Eurasia. This separation helped to facilitate a sense of exclusiveness and solidarity among the Western democracies.[5] These boundaries were in part ideological; however, the division of Europe into East and West predated the ideological cleavage of the Cold War. Historically, many in the West had long considered Russia, Eastern Europe, and the Mediterranean states as being on the periphery of Europe.[6] The division between the Catholic/Protestant societies of the West and those adhering to the Eastern Orthodox and Moslem faiths in the East emerged long before the rise of the nation-state.[7] The layers of differentiation became embedded in European history and left imagined boundaries which persisted well into the late twentieth century.[8] These boundaries grew stronger over time, particularly when they were linked with ideologies of nationalism. This cultural division was starkly evident in the way the 1919 Paris Peace Conference dealt with the break-up of the Ottoman Empire compared with how it treated the territories of the Hapsburg empire.[9]

In addition, Western and Eastern Europe evolved from different political traditions. Many of the Western states had a liberal tradition that dated back to the late eighteenth and early nineteenth centuries, while most of the eastern regions remained under monarchic rule until after World War I. This had a significant influence on the way nationalism developed in the two regions, a factor that would play an important role in the construction of the new European order.

---

[5] In his study of the relationships between the members of the Western alliance, Thomas Risse-Kappen suggests that associations comprised solely of liberal democracies are most likely to form pluralistic security communities. Thus, he attributes the cohesion of the alliance to the liberal community that was its foundation. See his *Cooperation among Democracies: The European Influence on US Foreign Policy* (Princeton: Princeton University Press, 1997).

[6] See, for example, Denys Hay, *Europe: The Emergence of an Idea* (Edinburgh: Edinburgh University Press, 1968).

[7] With the founding of Constantinople in 324 and the subsequent rise of the Byzantine empire, "Western" society was divided between the eastern and western regions. Moscow assumed control over what was left of the Byzantine Empire in the fifteenth century. The division between the Christian and Moslem societies grew into an ongoing conflict between the eleventh and sixteenth centuries.

[8] See Wallace, *The Transformation of Western Europe*, p. 17.

[9] All of the former Hapsburg territories became recognized nation-states while most of the Ottoman ones were held in trust as "mandates" through the League of Nations.

Western liberalism was built on the assumption of a common citizenry, and therefore ethnicity and religion had little to do with the definition of either the state or the nation. John Stuart Mill, for example, argued that "free institutions are next to impossible in a country made up of different nationalities. Among a people without a fellow-feeling . . . the united public opinion, necessary for the working of representative government, cannot exist."[10] For this reason, until the late nineteenth century, nationalism and liberalism were considered to be compatible ideologies. Since the nation was viewed as synonymous with the people (a legacy of the French revolution), popular sovereignty and self-determination were two sides of the same coin. In this context, nationalist movements could also be movements for democracy and liberty.[11] Contemporary liberal theorists continued to hold this view even into the late twentieth century.[12]

At the same time, the respective cultural difference between east and west also reflected dissimilar historical political developments and migration patterns. States such as Britain, France, and Spain existed as centralized political units long before the development of popular ideologies such as nationalism gave ethnicity or religion political meaning.[13] Moreover, there had been relative stability in the composition of the populations within the territories of Western Europe ever since the end of the "great migrations" of the early Middle Ages.[14] Thus, when these territories became states – and later developed a concept of "nationality" – the populations were relatively homogenous and ethnicity was not an important factor in the definition of the state.

On the other hand, as we saw in chapter 3, nationalist ideology took a different turn as it began to spread throughout Eastern and Central Europe in the late nineteenth century. The nationalist consciousness that swept the region occurred within the context of widespread diversity in culture, religion, and ethnicity that existed within the great central and southern European empires. So long as the state was built upon loyalty to the emperor, this did not have political meaning. However,

[10] John Stuart Mill, *Three Essays: Consideration on Representative Government, on Liberty, and the Subjugation of Women* (Oxford: Oxford University Press, 1975), p. 382.

[11] See Hobsbawm, *Nations and Nationalism Since 1780*, ch. 1.

[12] See, for example, the work of liberal political theorist Robert Dahl, who argues that ethnic homogeneity is a precondition for the maintenance of a stable democracy. Robert Dahl, *Dilemmas of Pluralist Democracy: Autonomy vs. Control* (New Haven: Yale University Press, 1982).

[13] See Hugh Seton-Watson, *Nations and States: An Enquiry into the Origins of Nations and the Politics of Nationalism* (Boulder: Westview Press, 1977).

[14] Bagley, *International Protection of National Minorities*, p. 10.

as anti-monarchic movements grew, the leaders adopted the position that a people could not be truly free if they were ruled by governments composed of different nationalities. For this reason, many nineteenth-century opposition movements in Eastern and Central Europe promoted ethnic nationalism as a dissident ideology.

Thus, within the Hapsburg and Ottoman empires (which encompassed virtually all of central, southern and eastern Europe), political liberation also meant cultural autonomy. The nation was no longer viewed by nationalists as the protector of citizenship and political rights (as it had been in France), but rather it was seen as a mechanism for asserting and protecting one's ethnic identity in a Darwinian world of competing nationalities.[15] The experience of World War I and the Versailles settlement solidified these beliefs. Virtually all of the states in Eastern and Central Europe owed their existence to the principle of nationality, however imperfectly it was applied. While this was greatly downplayed after World War II, the political and geographic map of the region remained as the legacy of Versailles.

From 1945 until the mid-1980s, the national state virtually disappeared from the international scene. Decolonization was facilitated through a transfer of authority from the colonial powers to indigenous leaders within the old colonial administrative units. Consequently, nationality and ethnicity had little to do with the creation of new states in Africa and Asia. Both the liberal societies of the West and the communist ones of the East minimized the role of ethnicity and nationality as a foundation for statehood. Yet the national idea never completely disappeared. Within the Soviet Union and Yugoslavia a new concept of nationality emerged. While nationalist ideologies were marginalized and nationalist movements discouraged, both the Soviets and the Yugoslavs institutionalized nationhood as a fundamental social category within their societies.

The Soviet state was divided into eighty-nine "national territories" in which each was defined as a homeland for a particular group. Nationality (*natsional' nost'*) was not only a social and statistical category, but also a legal one that was registered in internal passports and recorded in official transactions.[16] Complicating this situation was the fact that the Soviet Union was also legally a federation of fifteen semi-sovereign republics, each of whom was given the status of titular statehood. Thus,

---

[15] John Hall, *International Orders* (Cambridge: Polity Press, 1996), p. 90.
[16] See Rogers Brubaker, *Nationalism Reframed: Nationhood and the National Question in the New Europe* (Cambridge: Cambridge University Press, 1996), p. 18.

while individuals could carry their own nationality with them, this did not necessarily match the territorial division of the federation. Successive Soviet governments had further complicated this situation by encouraging population transfers and large-scale migration of people from different nationalities to the various republics.[17]

In Yugoslavia the question of nationality was even more complex. The post-World War II regime of Josip Tito transformed the state from one that had represented the South Slavs (see chapter 3) to a multinational polity by recognizing ethnic distinctions and creating internal borders that were defined in national terms.[18] Its constitution made an important distinction between the "nations" and the "republics" of Yugoslavia. The nations had no specific territorial connection while the six republics had no specific ethnic connection. By 1974, with the exception of defense, foreign trade, and labor policy, most authority rested with the constituent republics. Thus, in both the Soviet and Yugoslav cases, nationality became institutionalized even as it was officially rejected as the foundation for sovereignty and statehood.

So long as the Cold War divisions remained, there was no need to reconcile the divergent approaches between East and West toward the ideas of statehood and nationality. The Yalta agreement – subsequently confirmed by the 1975 Helsinki Final Act – provided for the development of multiple political orders in Europe by allowing each state to "choose and develop its political, social, economic and cultural systems . . ."[19] Thus, within Western Europe, a liberal political order could flourish among states sharing similar state structures and ideologies without having to address any of the political or cultural differences with the East. However, the 1989 revolutions in Eastern Europe and the subsequent break-up of the Soviet Union posed fundamental challenges for the states of Western Europe, not the least to their self-image as a cohesive community of liberal states.

The rapid collapse of the political order that had been established at Yalta raised immediate questions about how Europe would be politically

[17] See, for example, John Jaworsky, "Nationalities Policy and Potential for Inter-Ethnic Conflict in Ukraine," in Magda Opalski, ed., *Managing Diversity in Plural Societies: Minorities, Migration and Nation-Building in Post-Communist Europe* (Ontario: Forum Eastern Europe, 1998), p. 105.

[18] Susan L. Woodward, "Diaspora, or the Dangers of Disunification? Putting the 'Serbian Model' into Perspective," in Michael Mandelbaum, ed., *The New European Diasporas: National Minorities and Conflict in Eastern Europe* (New York: Council on Foreign Relations Press, 2000), p. 170.

[19] Conference on Security and Cooperation in Europe, "Final Act of Helsinki, 1 August 1975," Section 1 (I) in Arie Bloed, ed., *The Conference on Security and Cooperation in Europe.*

organized. Aside from the practical security questions, the architects of the "new European order" had to decide how far they would go in expanding their previously insular community into eastern and southeastern Europe. Any type of expansion would have political consequences for their identities as Europeans. While many Western leaders expected a relatively smooth transition to liberal democratic governance, the historic legacies of Versailles made this difficult. This produced internal tensions that eventually required the construction of an international protection regime.

A new political order for Europe

The rapid transformation of Eastern Europe and the former Soviet Union caught political leaders of both blocs by surprise. Rhetoric aside, neither side had given much thought to what Europe would look like if and when the Cold War were to end. As late as 1991, most Western leaders continued to support the political and territorial unity of the Soviet Union. They assumed that the process of reconciliation between East and West would be measured and gradual. Indeed, when President George Bush visited Kiev on July 31, he argued that freedom was not the same as national independence and urged the republics to remain within a reformed Soviet Union.[20] The United States and other Western governments took a similar position toward other potential secessions in Yugoslavia and Czechoslovakia up until the breakups began to occur.[21]

Moreover, while Western leaders were committed to promoting political and economic liberalism in Eastern Europe, it was not clear at the beginning how far they were willing to go toward politically integrating the continent. Indeed, there were at least three alternative possibilities for a new geopolitical architecture for European society: one that would be limited primarily to the core of Western Europe (essentially encompassing the European Union and NATO countries); an "OSCE Europe"

[20] Stefan Lehne, *The CSCE in the 1990s: Common European House or Potemkin Village?* (Laxenburg, Austria: Austrian Institute for International Affairs, 1991), p. 78.

[21] In May of 1991, Jacques Delors, then president of the European Commission (of the European Community) announced on a trip to Belgrade that the European Community would refuse to recognize any breakaway republics or offer them benefits. Similarly, US Secretary of State James Baker announced US support for "the preservation of the unity of Yugoslavia." See James B. Steinberg, "International Involvement in the Yugoslav Conflict," in Lori Fisler Damrosch, ed., *Enforcing Restraint: Collective Intervention in Internal Conflicts* (New York: Council on Foreign Relations Press, 1993), p. 34.

(which would include all states from "Vancouver to Vladivostok"); or a "Common European House" (which would extend from the Atlantic to the Urals).[22]

These alternative conceptions of the New Europe not only reflected security and economic considerations, but also regional identities that were rooted in historical geographic, cultural, religious, and political affiliations. For many years Europe had been a problematic concept. It was not only a geographic region but also a set of common values and a common culture bound together by a common history. In a geographic sense, there has long been disagreement among Europeans over where it began and where it ended.[23] Underlying this debate was the wide variety of regional histories and cultures, which at times did not coincide with one another.

Thus, although the end of the Cold War ended the political division of the continent, there were still many "Europes" to contend with: Western Europe (centered around France, Britain, Spain, Belgium, Italy, and the Benelux countries); East Central Europe (Poland, Hungary, Czech Republic, and Slovakia); West Central Europe (Germany and Austria); South-East Europe (the Balkans, Romania, Bulgaria, Slovenia, Albania, and Greece); and the Soviet Union's European successor states (Russia, Ukraine, Belarus, and the Baltics).[24] Even after the breakup of the Soviet Union, political leaders had to consider which of these regions would be part of the new European architecture and what this would mean for their traditional identity as a cohesive community of "Western" liberal and social democratic states.

Consequently, beyond the practical security and economic questions that arose with the end of the Cold War, the leaders of Western Europe had to decide whether to expand the boundaries of their community to include the traditionally peripheral states of Eastern Europe, the Baltics, and Eurasia. This would mean not only establishing closer diplomatic ties with the new states of the east and south, but also including them in their economic, political, and security institutions. In the alternative view, some believed (and advocated) that a multitiered system would develop on the continent between the relatively prosperous liberal democracies of the west and the less developed "nationalizing

---

[22] See Stephen Iwan Griffiths, *Nationalism and Ethnic Conflict: Threats to European Security*, SIPRI Research Report 5 (Oxford: Oxford University Press, 1993), pp. 7–8.

[23] Hay, *Europe*.

[24] See Adrian Hyde-Price, *The International Politics of East Central Europe* (Manchester: Manchester University Press, 1996), pp. 6–7.

states" of the east.[25] In that case, the western region would continue to consolidate while the peripheral areas would be treated with benign neglect. These alternative visions were debated among both policymakers and academics.[26]

Ultimately, the Western states settled on a strategy of total integration between east and west. The NATO summit meeting held in London on July 5 and 6 of 1990 was the turning point in determining the future of the new European order. In its concluding declaration, NATO indicated its preference for an "OSCE Europe" by advocating a significant expansion of the organization (then named the Conference on Security and Cooperation in Europe or CSCE). Specifically, NATO called for creating a set of permanent decisionmaking structures and agencies within the CSCE, transforming the institution from a series of periodic meetings into a formal organization.[27] Since the CSCE was the only institution that encompassed all states "from Vancouver to Vladivostok," the decision to expand the scope of this Cold War organizational relic was an indication that Western states wished to build a new European community that was highly inclusive. This meant that all of Europe would have to become involved in deciding how the new and reorganized states would resolve the internal tensions brought about by the events of 1989–91.

While the NATO summit was crucial in articulating the position of the Western alliance, the most important event in determining the future of Europe occurred several months later in Paris. For fifteen years, the Conference on Security and Cooperation in Europe (CSCE) had been the only European institution through which countries from the East and West cooperated on a regular basis. Dubbed a "process" rather than an organization, the CSCE acted as a forum through which the two sides could initiate confidence-building measures, negotiate military force reductions, and conclude minimal agreements concerning human rights

---

[25] Rogers Brubaker defines a nationalizing state as one in which the political elites believe that the core nationality is not flourishing sufficiently and therefore specific action is needed to promote the language, culture, and political hegemony of the core nation. See Brubaker, *Nationalism Reframed*, p. 84.

[26] See, for example, Robert Kaplan, *The Coming Anarchy: Shattering the Dreams of the Post Cold War* (New York: Random House, 2000); Max Singer and Aaron Wildavsky, *The Real World Order: Zones of Peace, Zones of Turmoil* (Chatham, NJ: Chatham House Publishers, 1996); Benjamin Barber, *Jihad vs. McWorld* (New York: Times Books, 1996); Samuel Huntington, *The Clash of Civilizations and the Remaking of World Order* (New York: Simon & Schuster, 1996).

[27] See the North Atlantic Council, "London Declaration on a Transformed North Atlantic Alliance," London, July 5–6, 1990.

127

and the mutual recognition of sovereignty. The Soviets were particularly interested in the CSCE inasmuch as it legitimized the spheres of influence that had existed *de facto* since Yalta.[28] Building from the mutual commitment to CSCE diplomacy, Soviet President Gorbachev had proposed holding a CSCE summit to evaluate the changes that had occurred in Eastern Europe. NATO's London Declaration endorsed this idea, setting into motion a process that would create the foundation for a new European order.

The CSCE summit in Paris was attended by virtually all states in Europe as well as Canada and the United States. The resulting Charter of Paris for a New Europe was notable not only for officially ending the Cold War, but also for establishing new standards on internal governance and domestic politics. In particular, the Charter's declaration that the CSCE would "undertake to build, consolidate and strengthen democracy as the only system of government of our nations" suggested a consensus around principles of state organization unseen since the Congress of Vienna in 1815.[29]

Based on this consensus, many Western leaders assumed that the liberal state would provide the foundation for the new European order. For almost fifty years, this form of state had been successful in providing for economic prosperity, international cooperation, and social peace in Western Europe. Thus, most European and North American leaders assumed that the liberal state – with its concern for the rights of the individual citizen – would also provide for the protection of the various religious and national groups within Eastern Europe. This position is clearly suggested by both the internal activities and declarations issued by the CSCE during the period surrounding the Paris summit.[30] Thus, for example, the 1991 meeting of "experts on national minorities" concluded in part that "human rights and fundamental freedoms are the basis for the protection of rights of persons belonging to national minorities," and that "questions relating to national minorities can only

[28] Arie Bloed, "Two Decades of the CSCE Process: From Confrontation to Cooperation," in Arie Bloed, ed., *The Conference on Security and Cooperation in Europe: Analysis and Basic Documents, 1972–1993* (London: Kluwer Academic Publishers, 1993), p. 5.
[29] See Conference on Security and Cooperation in Europe, Charter of Paris for a New Europe, Paris, November 19–21, 1990, "A New Era of Democracy, Peace and Unity," paragraph 5.
[30] This was also confirmed during the dozen interviews I conducted at the Office of the High Commissioner on National Minorities at the Hague, May 28–June 1, 2001. For a comprehensive set of documents issued by the CSCE during this period, see Bloed, ed., *The Conference on Security and Cooperation in Europe.*

be satisfactorily resolved in a democratic political framework based on the rule of law . . ."[31]

Building on what was known previously as the "Third Basket" of the 1975 Helsinki Final Act, the Charter of Paris articulated a standard of governance that had come to define the liberal state: the rule of law, universal civil and political rights, religious toleration, and sovereignty of the citizen.[32] The Charter referred to this area as the "human dimension" of the CSCE. In order to help states to implement these provisions, the Charter created an Office for Free Elections (later transformed into the Office of Democratic Institutions and Human Rights). The purpose of this institution was to facilitate democratization within the states undergoing transition. This involved monitoring the implementation of commitments within the OSCE regarding the "human dimension"; acting as a clearinghouse for information; monitoring the fairness of elections; and assisting member states in building democratic institutions. In pursuing the latter function, the office was to provide legal, technical, administrative, and academic experts to states needing assistance in these efforts.

This suggested that membership in Europe's emerging international society would require states to go beyond traditional security commitments such as non-aggression. Domestic political relationships between governments and their populations would be linked to international legitimacy.

Problems in the new order

Despite this newly developed consensus, the integration of East and West did not proceed as easily as originally envisioned. Fundamental differences in culture and politics began to emerge, challenging what many had hoped would be a smooth transition.

In 1991 the Soviet Union and Yugoslavia began to break up into their constituent republics, resulting in the creation of sixteen new European and Eurasian states. The borders of these states largely reflected the internal administrative boundaries that had existed under the old

[31] The Charter of Paris called for the CSCE to convene a meeting of experts to address issues of national minorities. This meeting was held in Geneva in mid-July. Its final report, "Report of the CSCE Meeting of Experts on National Minorities," can be found in Arie Bloed, *The Conference on Security and Cooperation in Europe*. The quoted passage is in Section II, paragraph 2.

[32] See Conference on Security and Cooperation in Europe, *Charter of Paris for a New Europe*, Paris, November 19–21, 1990, "Human Rights, Democracy and Rule of Law."

regimes – the legacies of the Soviet and Yugoslav nationality policies. Such policies had created "national" elites and political institutions within the republics, providing them with a political base. Yet to the extent that the newly empowered elites considered the republics to be institutional manifestations of national self-determination, they represented a legacy of Versailles that had been explicitly rejected by the Western powers since the end of World War II. This made their existence somewhat contradictory to the principles of New Europe.

At the same time, the administrative boundaries that defined the republics did not necessarily match the ethnic distribution of the population. In post-World War I Yugoslavia, for example, it was more important *where* one was from (that is, which region or republic) rather than what one's ethnic background was.[33] Thus, migration patterns did not necessarily match the composition of ethnic communities. As a result, territorial problems emerged when the boundaries of the republics, which previously had little meaning in ethnic terms, became national borders. The West European governments legitimized (and in some cases encouraged) these divisions by offering to recognize any of the Yugoslav republics that wished to secede, provided that they met a set of minimal conditions established by the European Community's Arbitration Commission.[34]

Moreover, throughout the region, the former communist countries of Eastern Europe began to relegitimize themselves as national states by adopting the principle that they did not represent the citizenry *per se*, but rather the ethnocultural nation for which their state was named.[35] Thus, for example, the new Croatian and Macedonian constitutions specifically stipulated that they were states of, by, and for the Croatian and Macedonian nations, respectively.[36] In some cases – for example, Serbia and Croatia – this was the result of conscious state-building projects initiated by political entrepreneurs and newly empowered elites.[37] In other

---

[33] Interview with legal advisor to the high commissioner on national minorities, Dženana Hadžiomerovic, June 1, 2001.

[34] See Misha Glenny, *The Fall of Yugoslavia: The Third Balkan War* (London: Penguin, 1992), pp. 142–3.

[35] George Schöpflin, "Nationalism and Ethnic Minorities in Post-Communist Europe," in Richard Caplan and John Feffer, eds., *Europe's New Nationalism: States and Minorities in Conflict* (Oxford: Oxford University Press, 1996), p. 153.

[36] The new Croatian constitution claimed their sovereignty as the "historical right of the Croatian nation," while Macedonia's 1989 constitution defined the republic as "the national state of the Macedonian people." See Glenny, *The Fall of Yugoslavia*, pp. 81–3.

[37] For a discussion of nationalism as a form of political entrepreneurship, see John Breuilly, *Nationalism and the State* (Chicago: University of Chicago Press, 1994).

cases, such as Hungary and Albania, political elites used the opportunity of systemic change to raise national territorial issues that stemmed from the Versailles settlement. In each case, as civic bonds began to unravel, social, ethnic, and economic differences became the basis for group cohesion on the one hand, and "outgroup" discrimination on the other.[38]

The emergence of this institutional form of ethnic nationalism challenged the liberal principles that underlay the Charter of Paris, and more fundamentally the principles upon which the West European community had been built. Over the previous few decades, Western Europe not only had developed a multilateral commitment to democracy, human rights and economic cooperation. It had become a culturally diverse, pluralistic, cosmopolitan society that transcended national borders. As the Council of Europe stated in one of its parliamentary reports, "History has transformed the continent of Europe into a Mosaic of peoples . . . The mixing and overlapping of these people is such that it is impossible to define their geographic boundaries fully and exclusively."[39] Subsidiarity and devolution of authority had become the creed of the European Union countries, and the trend was moving toward multilevel rather than majoritarian democracy. Thus, the rise of nationalist democracy in the East placed political roadblocks to continental integration.

The leaders of the CSCE member states realized this as they gathered for what turned out to be the organization's most important historic meeting, the 1992 4th CSCE Follow-Up Meeting in Helsinki (commonly referred to as Helsinki II). While Helsinki II is most noted for transforming the CSCE into a formal organization (specifically, a "regional security arrangement" in accordance with Chapter VIII of the United Nations charter), its most important political legacy was how it responded to the challenges that had come to haunt the new European order since the conclusion of the Charter of Paris. This was articulated in the final document issued by the conference, *The Challenges of Change*.

While the Charter of Paris had been drafted within an atmosphere of euphoria brought about by the end of the Cold War, the *Challenges of Change* reflected a more sober approach. Within a few months after

[38] See Lee Walker, "Nationalism and Ethnic Conflict in the Post-Soviet Transition," in Leokadia Drobizheva *et al.*, eds., *Ethnic Conflict in the Post-Soviet World: Case Studies and Analysis* (London: M. E. Sharpe, 1996), p. 11.

[39] Council of Europe, Recommendation No. 1177 on the Rights of Minorities, adopted by the Parliamentary Assembly of the Council of Europe, February 5, 1992.

the Charter had been signed, ethnic/political conflicts broke out in Nagorno-Karabakh, Croatia, and Moldova. The violent breakup of Yugoslavia and the spread of war throughout the Balkans and parts of the former Soviet Union caught the great powers by surprise.[40] There was a growing perception that democratization and peace were being threatened by ideologies of nationalism and the potential for majorities to use their numbers to suppress minorities.

The problem, many Europeans believed, was rooted in the nature of the new states that had emerged from the transformations of the previous few years. In his opening statement at Helsinki, Hungarian Foreign Minister Geza Jeszenszky warned of a growing number of the new national states that had "established democracy only for their own kin, excluding fellow citizens having different national or ethnic background."[41] This was indeed a significant problem, because despite efforts to create unified national states throughout the region, ethnic populations within Eastern Europe and the former Soviet Union were so intertwined that virtually all countries had significant minority populations within them.[42] As suggested in chapter 3, the existence of ethnic minorities as organized political communities threatens the cohesion of a national state. This raised a particular set of problems for the OSCE, because the solutions to the minority dilemma were incompatible with the principles of New Europe.

Governments generally have four alternative strategies for reconciling the existence of a national state with the presence of ethnic minorities: assimilation, autonomy, repression, and elimination. Many governments first attempt to assimilate minorities into the majority culture by granting them citizenship and trying to absorb them into the national culture. Turkey and Greece are examples of the assimilationist approach. This strategy, however, often leaves the minorities dissatisfied, since it denies them their identity as a community. Some members of national minority groups wish to retain their ties to their kin state, while others want to preserve their own language and control their own

---

[40] See Griffiths, *Nationalism and Ethnic Conflict*, p. 90.
[41] Alexis Heraclides, *Helsinki – II and its Aftermath: The Making of the CSCE into an International Organization* (New York: Pinter Publishers, 1993), p. 55. Hungary, of course, had a direct interest in the treatment of minorities inasmuch as 3.5 million ethnic Hungarians lived in neighboring countries.
[42] For example, twenty-two East European states had national minorities that accounted for more than 10 percent of the population. See Hugh Miall, ed., Minority Rights in Europe: Prospects for a Transnational Regime (London: Royal Institute of International Affairs, 1994).

charitable, religious, educational, and social institutions. The only policy that would completely satisfy these aspirations within the context of a national state is territorial autonomy. Governments are extremely reluctant to grant this, since it tends to result in a political partition of the state. This leaves a policy of repression or, in the extreme, elimination through ethnic cleansing (mass eviction) and genocide. All of these solutions were incompatible with the cosmopolitan, liberal character of New Europe.

It was the Versailles problem all over again, however two important differences created an entirely new set of problems for the European powers. First, unlike the post-World War I era, the assimilationist solution, even if workable, was explicitly rejected by the CSCE states. Any resolution in post-Cold War Europe would have to provide some form of legal recognition and public space for minority communities.

Second, the new national states were adapting democratic institutions that enabled the "core" nationalities to legally dominate minorities using the rules of democracy. For example, in Latvia and Estonia, the new governments created highly restrictive language and residency requirements for citizenship. This was done primarily to assert Latvian and Estonian nationhood in the face of the large Russian minorities who were living there.[43] The right of any government to set its own conditions for citizenship has long been recognized under international law as an absolute sovereign prerogative of a state. Thus, the Estonian language laws – which were legally passed by the democratically elected parliaments – were consistent with the requirements of the rule of law. This, however, disenfranchised hundreds of thousands of Russians who had lived in Estonia for decades when it was part of the Soviet federation.

Under these conditions, majoritarian democracy was an elitist institution, undermining the political values so recently accepted by European society.[44] From the perspective of many minorities within Eastern Europe, then, the problem went beyond those that could be

---

[43] See Konrad Huber, *Averting Inter-Ethnic Conflict: An Analysis of the CSCE High Commissioner on National Minorities in Estonia, January–July 1993*, Working Paper Series of the Conflict Resolution Program of the Carter Center of Emory University, April, 1994, pp. 11–12.

[44] Vello Pettai refers to such regimes as "ethnic democracies," which he defines as a system of majoritarian rule in multiethnic states in which a given ethnic group uses the mechanisms of the state to promote its own values and power within society. See his "Emerging Ethnic Democracy in Estonia and Latvia," in Magda Opalski, ed., *Managing Diversity in Plural Societies: Minorities, Migration and Nation-Building in Post-Communist Europe* (Ontario: Forum Eastern Europe, 1998), p. 18.

resolved within the context of a liberal state. Many of the tensions that arose within the democratizing national states – in the areas of language, education and representation – could not be adequately addressed through the rule of law or human rights. There was no recognized "human right" for an ethnic community to have its own secondary school or university or for multiple languages to be spoken in public agencies.[45] Nor did the principle of democratic governance guarantee adequate (proportional) representation of said communities within governmental bodies. Lacking a political mechanism to advance minority identities, ethnic tensions rapidly escalated into social conflicts.

This raised the fear that domestic conflicts within the new and reorganized states in Eastern, Central, and Southern Europe could pose a threat to the security and principles of New Europe in several ways.

First, it could spark external intervention by an outside state, particularly a kin-state seeking to protect its ethnic brethren. This threat was particularly acute in states with Hungarian, Russian, and Albanian minorities. The Russian government had officially claimed responsibility for protecting its nearly 20 million kin in the "near abroad" (the former Soviet republics). Similarly, in 1994 Hungarian Prime Minister Jozsef Antall announced that he was the prime minister not only for the 10 million Hungarians living in Hungary, but also for the 5 million ethnic Hungarians living in neighboring states.[46] Albania also adopted this position regarding the 40 percent of ethnic Albanians who lived outside the borders of Albania, mostly in Kosovo and Macedonia.

Second, it could undermine the West's policy of "European consolidation" by creating new divisions within the continent. A new European order could not remain cohesive if a two-tiered system developed between a pluralistic, cosmopolitan West and a exclusionary, intolerant East. Third, it could produce massive refugee flows into neighboring states, particularly Germany and Austria. Fourth, it could lead to an illicit market in international arms trafficking (as suggested by the situation in the former Yugoslavia). Fifth, it could undermine the democratization process that was central to the expansion of European international society, by sparking authoritarian mobilizations and repression. Finally, it could threaten the concept of cultural pluralism that had come to define European society. It had been a central aspect of

---

[45] Language and education issues tended to be the greatest sources of tension and conflict in many East European states, particularly Moldova, Romania, Slovakia, and Macedonia.

[46] Mark Shields, "Hungary Backs its Exiles," *The Independent*, August 20, 1992, p. 8.

Western Europe's identity and self-image that it was immune from the ethnic conflicts and wars that had plagued other regions of the world.

For these reasons, policy analysts and political leaders began to link international security with the promotion of diversity and tolerance throughout Europe. Thus, a 1993 RAND study reflected the growing perceptions of North American and European leaders, that "the main threat to European security comes not from a possible military threat from Russia or a reconstituted Soviet Union, but from a proliferation of ethnic conflicts and territorial disputes in Eastern Europe and the former Soviet Union."[47] Similarly, another report argued that "although the conflicts (in the OSCE area) have . . . never threatened the national security of the principal powers, they have raised important questions about the enforcement of the values embodied in the Charter of Paris for a New Europe."[48]

In this spirit, many CSCE members believed that it was necessary to move beyond the human rights guarantees provided for in a liberal state. The CSCE had already come out in favor of extending the liberal concept of "rights" to national minorities.[49] Sensing an impending crisis, the Dutch delegation at Helsinki II tried to extend this even further by proposing that the CSCE create a formal institutional mechanism to protect national minorities. This mechanism would be a CSCE high commissioner on national minorities. The Dutch proposal immediately sparked a debate over whether national minorities should be protected collectively as political communities or whether they should be protected as individuals under the human rights provisions of existing agreements.[50] This debate reflected a deeper question over whether ethnic conflicts could be addressed within the context of liberal democratic states or whether they required the construction of multicultural states in which ethnic communities were officially recognized.

---

[47] F. Stephen Larrabee, *Eastern European Security After the Cold War* (Santa Monica: RAND, 1993), p. 4.

[48] Griffiths, *Nationalism and Ethnic Conflict*, p. 63.

[49] See, for example, paragraph 8 in the "Human Rights, Democracy and the Rule of Law" section of Charter of Paris; the Document of the Copenhagen Meeting of the Conference on the Human Dimension of the CSCE, June 29, 1990, Section IV; and the Report of the CSCE Meeting of Experts on National Minorities, July 19, 1991.

[50] According to Hannie Zaal, a member of the Dutch delegation to Helsinki, the United States, France, and Greece opposed creating "special rights" for minorities as a group. All three countries, however, eventually supported the Dutch proposal. See her "The CSCE High Commissioner," *Helsinki Monitor*, no. 4 (1992), pp. 33–37.

Some states, such as Turkey, Greece, and France, did not officially recognize national minorities as a legal category and thus did not want to extend legitimacy to them. They also argued that this could escalate tensions by encouraging irredentism among kin states.[51] Others feared that a high commissioner would act as an independent advocate for minorities, rather than as a mediator. Still others worried that raising the profile of national minorities could undermine the cohesion and unity of the new states.[52] Ultimately, however, the proposal was unanimously approved with several alterations. The organization asked the former Dutch foreign minister Max Van der Stoel to assume the position as the first commissioner.

Former HCNM advisor Konrad Huber argues that the creation of this office represented a broad consensus within the CSCE that there is a close triadic link between the internal structure of states, conflict prevention, and European security.[53] Yet the original mandate of the HCNM was limited. As conceived at Helsinki, the job of the commissioner and his staff was to identify and seek early resolution of ethnic tensions that might endanger peace, stability, or friendly relations between participating states. As such, the high commissioner's task was to provide "early warning" and, as appropriate, "early action" at the earliest possible stage "in regard to tensions involving national minority issues which have not yet developed beyond an early warning stage, but, in the judgment of the High Commissioner, have the potential to develop into a conflict within the OSCE area."[54] Toward this end, the HCNM was empowered to conduct on-site missions in areas of potential ethnic tension and permitted to contract with outside "experts" to assist him. If the commissioner and his staff determined that OSCE mandates were being violated, she would attempt to induce the government to initiate new policies and then report his progress to the OSCE decisionmaking bodies. The OSCE could then take "appropriate action" to rectify the situation. In this sense, the HCNM was not originally conceived as

---

[51] Irredentism is an effort to detach neighboring territories in which ethnic or national kin live and annex them to the kin state.

[52] Rob Zaagman and Hannic Zaal, "The CSCE High Commissioner on National Minorities: Prehistory and Negotiations," in Arie Bloed, ed., *The Challenges of Change: The Helsinki Summit of the CSCE and its Aftermath* (Dordrecht: Martinus Nijhoff, 1994), pp. 95–111.

[53] Konrad Huber, "The CSCE HCNM," in Ian Cuthbertson and Jane Leibowitz, *Minorities: The New Europe's Old Issue* (New York: Institute for East–West Studies, 1993), pp. 290–91.

[54] Conference on Security and Cooperation in Europe, Summit of Heads of State or Government, Helsinki; Helsinki Document 1992 "The Challenges of Change," July 9–10, 1992, Section 2.

part of the OSCE's human dimension program, but rather of its conflict prevention apparatus.

Over time, however, the role of the HCNM expanded from being a diplomatic watchdog that identified potential conflicts to the center of an international regime focused on protecting both the identities of and public space for national minorities. This reflected both a change in mission and a change in policy among many within the CSCE.

Promoting the multicultural state through a protection regime

As I suggested above, European and North American leaders originally believed that the liberal state would be the most stable and desirable foundation for the new political order. For this, the establishment of the CSCE's Office of Democratic Institutions and the adoption of widespread human rights commitments would have been sufficient institutional mechanisms. Yet it soon became apparent that this order could not be easily built simply by expanding Western Europe's liberal community eastward. The evolution of nationalizing states in Eastern and Southern Europe were leading to societies that were inherently unstable and contrary to the principles upon which New Europe was built. In particular, the experiences with the former Yugoslavia and the Baltics suggested that liberal states might not be able to resolve the tensions that arose within multinational societies.

As a result, European leaders began to draw from another model of Western European statehood that had emerged during the postwar era: civic multiculturalism. This model was based on the legal recognition of various nationalities as constituent units of the state, and the creation of political structures that would provide for these nationalities a set of cultural, language, and educational rights. Such structures had varied from constitutional guarantees to a system of multicultural federalism.[55] Within the West, various forms of civic multiculturalism had already been created in Belgium (focused on the Flemish and Walloons), Spain (the Basques), Italy (Germans in South Tyrol), Britain (Scots and Welsh), and Canada (Québecois).[56] Yet the OSCE understood the tensions that

---

[55] Wil Kymlicka defines European multicultural federalism as a model of the state as a territorial federation of regionally concentrated nations in which boundaries are drawn to ensure that each national group is able to maintain its own culture. See his "Ethnic Relations and Western Political Theory," in Opalski, ed., *Managing Diversity*.

[56] István Íjgyártó, "Codification of Minority Rights," in Cuthbertson and Leibowitz, eds., *Minorities*, p. 276.

would arise in trying to change the relationship between the governments and the populations of the new and reorganized states while at the same time respecting their sovereignty. It would require a delicate balance.

The international protection regime in Europe developed out of this dilemma. While several organizations were involved in promoting the norm of minority rights (for example, the Council of Europe), the focus began to rest with the changing role of the HCNM. This change was not the result of a grand plan by the OSCE; it was initiated largely by the high commissioner himself, working closely with key OSCE officials and diplomats from member states. Over time, the office of the HCNM began to evolve from a passive instrument of "early warning" to a more proactive "teacher" that would assist target states in the process of transition. In effect, a key part of the high commissioner's job became socializing the leaders of new states in how to act as leaders of a twenty-first-century European state, and providing direct assistance in helping them to make the political changes necessary for achieving legitimacy in the New Europe. Among these changes was "integrating diversity," an institutional mechanism that would undermine the foundation of the national state.[57]

In this sense, the HCNM became a major part of the OSCE's mechanism for promoting OSCE norms and implementing the organization's vision of a New Europe.[58] According to Van der Stoel, "OSCE principles and commitments – as well as international legal norms and standards – are the foundation of my work and provide the blueprint for my actions."[59] Since the OSCE operates by consensus, his office was able to hold states to principles that they themselves had already accepted. Van der Stoel clearly appeared to view the adoption of diversity principles as central to being a member of the international society of the New Europe. For example, in a speech before the OSCE Parliamentary Assembly, the commissioner argued that the protection of minorities by member states is: "an expression of the fundamental values of European

[57] The theme of "integrating diversity" became dominant in the work of the HCNM. Their office defined it as an "official acknowledgment of the existence of minorities and therefore of diversity within the state"; in effect, recognition of the plurality of national communities. Walter Kemp, ed., *Quiet Diplomacy in Action: The OSCE High Commissioner on National Minorities* (The Hague: Kluwer Law International, 2001), p. 104.
[58] See Maria Amor Martin Estebanez, "The High Commissioner on National Minorities: Development of the Mandate," in Michal Bothe, Natalino Ronzitu, and Allan Rosas, eds., *The OSCE in the Maintenance of Peace and Security* (The Hague: Kluwer Law International, 1997), pp. 123–4.
[59] Interview with HCNM Max Van der Stoel, June 2, 2001.

morality . . . (they) are pillars of contemporary European social and political order. For a state to be European in this sense, it is simply expected
and required that it respect these standards."[60]

Over time, the OSCE member states, the HCNM staff, and the high
commissioner himself began to view the job of the commissioner as
being more of an "advisor" who would address the "root causes" of
ethnic conflict and help the leaders of target states to adopt policies
that would be more consistent with OSCE values. These root causes,
according to another one of Van der Stoel's top advisors, stemmed from
the attempt by leaders of many societies in transition to build unified
national states. This, HCNM Director John Packer argued, had become
incompatible with democratization and human rights.

> The nation-state is a nineteenth century idea that is clearly falling away
> in recent times, but it still has a lot of resonance among many popula-
> tions and politicians. We are trying to get all states to follow the trend
> that has existed in Western Europe over the past decade, which has been
> moving away from the idea of the unitary national state and toward
> a more decentralized system based on diversity and distinctiveness at
> the local levels.[61]

For this reason, it became one of the unofficial goals of the office of the
high commissioner to help ensure that the structures of the states reflect
the pluralistic, diverse nature of their societies. As senior advisor Walter
Kemp argued, "it is far easier to maintain the multinational character of a
state than to rebuild a multinational society after a crisis has erupted and
that society has collapsed."[62] In pursuing this goal, the OSCE leadership
began to shift its focus away from purely crisis management toward the
internal reorganization of new member states.

The commissioner's office helped to guide the transition process in
the new and reorganized states of Europe by trying to get these states
to incorporate specific multicultural standards into their domestic legal
and constitutional systems. In effect, then, the office of the high commissioner became a mechanism for the OSCE to socialize states and institutionalize the values of the New Europe. "By declaring the legitimacy
of international concern for human rights and minority questions," Van

[60] Max Van der Stoel, "The Protection of Minorities in the OSCE Region," speech given at
a meeting of the OSCE Parliamentary Assembly, Antalya, April 12, 2000.
[61] Interview with John Packer, director of the Office of the High Commissioner on National
Minorities, 1 June, 2001.
[62] Interview with HCNM Senior Advisor Walter Kemp, May 31, 2001.

der Stoel stated, "the CSCE community has assumed as its responsibility the burden of supporting individual CSCE states which cannot by themselves solve the problems which are confronting them."[63] Thus, according to one of Van der Stoel's senior advisors, the high commissioner turned his mandate on its head: rather than issuing an "early warning" as a prelude to taking "early action," he took early action *first* in the hopes of avoiding having to issue an early warning.[64]

Subsequent activities of the HCNM support the view that the mission of the HCNM expanded from promoting harmony and minority rights to the protection of ethnic communities and social diversity. Using in part what Emanuel Adler has termed "seminar diplomacy" and what Frank Schimmelfennig calls "rhetorical action," the high commissioner began to work with governments directly to change the internal structure and constitution of the target states.[65] His various methods were clearly aimed at sparking a reorganization of the domestic political institutions and processes. The national minorities the regime was theoretically designed to protect were not directly involved. Unlike the highly legalistic approach initiated by the international protection regime during the post-World War I period, the OSCE used a variety of political and diplomatic means to pressure target governments to make the necessary changes.

First and foremost were the direct contacts between the commissioner and his staff and the various political leaders of target states. Between 1993 and 2001, Van der Stoel (the only commissioner until his second term ended in July 2001) conducted more than one hundred field visits in fourteen states experiencing ethnic tensions. The high commissioner was empowered to initiate these visits without prior approval from the OSCE decision-making bodies or any of the member states (including the state that he decided to visit). This enabled the office to separate its

---

[63] Max Van der Stoel, speech given at the Netherlands Institute of International Relations, March 24, 1994.

[64] Interview with HCNM Senior Advisor Walter Kemp, May 31, 2001.

[65] Adler defines seminar diplomacy as a form of multilateral diplomacy "aimed at promoting political dialogue and international cooperation . . . by means of consensual technical and normative knowledge." Schimmelfennig conceptualizes rhetorical action as the strategic use of norm-based arguments. See Adler's "Seeds of Peaceful Change: The OSCE's Security Community-Building Model," in Emanuel Adler and Michael Barnett, eds., *Security Communities* (Cambridge: Cambridge University Press, 1998), p. 138 and Frank Schimmelfennig, "The Community Trap: Liberal Norms, Rhetorical Action, and the Eastern Enlargement of the European Union," *International Organization*, vol. 55, no. 1 (Winter 2001), p. 76.

missions from the particularistic interests of one or more OSCE members. Since the high commissioner answered to the OSCE's chairman-in-office rather than any member state, he was somewhat insulated from the political pressures that can emerge from a self-interested use of the institution.[66]

On each visit the commissioner and his contracted "experts" met with the foreign minister, representatives of national minority organizations (except those engaged in terrorism), and officials from nongovernmental organizations.[67] During these visits, the commissioner and his advisors attempted to convince public officials that the principle of integrating diversity was not only a core principle of the OSCE, but also in the interest of internal stability within their own states. Jeffrey Checkel refers to this process of social learning through interaction as "argumentative persuasion."[68] As part of this process, the commissioner and his advisors also closely monitored the various stages of new legislation as it related to the relationship between the government and national minorities. While governments were technically free to refuse to meet with the commissioner, such a refusal would likely have had serious political repercussions within the OSCE. For this reason, no state prohibited a visit by the high commissioner.

Second, after each visit the commissioners made specific recommendations to the target government on adopting new legislation, altering pending legislation that might violate OSCE principles, amending constitutional provisions, and/or developing domestic institutions that would provide for increased minority representation, inter-ethnic dialog, legal equality, and a "public space" for multiple languages and minority schools.[69] In doing so, the commissioner translated general standards into specific applications and attempted to make them part

[66] The chairman-in-office is the foreign minister of a participating state who is chosen annually by the OSCE members. He or she has overall responsibility for executive action and coordination of OSCE activities and missions.

[67] The provision against meeting with organizations engaged in terrorism was added at the insistence of Britain, Spain, Turkey, and France. Most insiders acknowledge that this was included largely to keep the OSCE from becoming involved in their conflicts with the Irish Catholics, the Basques, the Kurds, and the Corsicans, respectively.

[68] Checkel defines argumentative persuasion as a social process of interaction that involves changing attitudes about cause and effect in the absence of overt coercion. See his "Why Comply? Social Learning and European Identity Change," *International Organization*, vol. 55, no. 3 (Summer 2001), p. 562.

[69] Interview with HCNM Personal Advisor Carl Salicath, May 30, 2001. See also Diana Chigas, "Bridging the Gap Between Theory and Practice: The CSCE High Commissioner on National Minorities," *Helsinki Monitor*, vol. 3, no. 4 (1993).

of the state's domestic laws.[70] For example, the commissioner developed a proposal for Ukraine to confer official recognition on the Crimean Tatars as a constituent group by providing them with a guaranteed quota of seats in the parliament. Similarly, he helped to draft (and amend) Latvia's law on languages and Lithuania's laws on citizenship. These laws helped to "de-ethnicize" the state.

An analysis of the high commissioner's recommendations reveals a consistent problem-solving, assistance-oriented approach toward resolving tensions in target countries, particularly those in transition. This approach was geared largely toward getting states to adopt the widely accepted norms and standards as articulated in various OSCE and Council of Europe agreements.[71] Thus, while the implementation of European norms was not part of the high commissioner's original mandate, norm compliance in the area of interethnic relations in fact was at the heart of his approach. As a result, beginning in 1995 the commissioner started to rely increasingly on the advice of legal (as opposed to technical) experts. These experts assessed the compatibility of domestic policy and law with specific European and international standards and reported on their conclusions to all interested parties.[72] All recommendations were then submitted to the OSCE Permanent Council. Finally, the commissioner writes a confidential report (usually blunt and devoid of diplomatic language) to the OSCE's chairman-in-office and often discusses the situation with him or her.

The commissioner's recommendations were often accepted, at least in part, by most states with whom he has developed an ongoing presence. For example, Estonia implemented twenty-eight out of thirty HCNM recommendations in 1997 and Latvia made significant changes to its laws regarding citizenship and language in 1995.[73] At the same time, as the office staff acknowledged, they had far greater success with the smaller states wishing to integrate into European society (particularly the European Union) than with larger states such as Russia which were less susceptible to the subtle pressure of the OSCE.[74] In this sense power differentials were a significant factor in influencing compliance.

[70] Stephen Ratner, "Does International Law Matter in Preventing Ethnic Conflict?" *NYU Journal of International Law and Politics*, vol. 32, no. 3 (2000); John Packer, "Making International Law Matter in Preventing Ethnic Conflict: A Practitioner's Perspective," *NYU Journal of International Law and Politics*, vol. 32, no. 3 (2000).
[71] The full text of all of Van der Stoel's recommendations can be found on the OSCE's website at www.osce.org/hcnm/documents/recommendations.
[72] Kemp, ed., *Quiet Diplomacy in Action,* p. 74.   [73] Ibid., p. 158.
[74] HCNM Personal Advisor Carl Salicath, May 30, 2001.

Third, the office of the high commissioner had come to act as a "gate-keeper" *vis-à-vis* entry into the European Union (EU) and other European institutions. In the course of its work, the office of the high commissioner helped government officials to adapt constitutional changes necessary for them to join these various organizations. This was indeed a powerful tool, since virtually all of the new states in Eastern Europe and the Baltics had expressed a strong interest in joining the EU. The close links between OSCE, the EU, and the Council of Europe (as well as the close personal ties between Van der Stoel and many European leaders) provided strong leverage for the high commissioner in his negotiations with government officials. In fact, on a number of occasions the HCNM, the Council, and the EU initiated joint missions to states in order to provide advice on legislation. Thus, one of the high commissioner's tools was his ability to mobilize support from European institutions and member states. This leverage was crucial in affecting changes in Croatia, Slovakia, Latvia, and Estonia.[75]

Fourth, on occasion the commissioner's office developed new standards concerning national minorities when they believed that current ones did not adequately provide a guide for promoting cultural pluralism within multiethnic states. Specifically, through the HCNM's research arm, the Foundation for Interethnic Relations (later changed to the Project Unit), they developed detailed standards in the areas of education (Hague Recommendations), language (Oslo Recommendations), and political participation by minority communities (Lund Recommendations).[76] These recommendations constituted a form of "soft law" (not legally binding under treaty law but accepted as obligations by a wide range of states) that was intended to influence political leaders in adopting new policies and domestic institutions.[77] They further suggested what was expected of a European state in its internal relations among various national communities.

Finally, the office of the high commissioner held seminars, roundtables and conferences in states and regions that experienced ethnic conflict or tension. These meetings brought together government officials and representatives of minorities to discuss policy and structural issues that

[75] The commissioner's criticism of Slovakia's treatment of minorities played a major role in keeping that country out of the first group of accession countries to the European Union in 1997. See Kemp, ed., *Quiet Diplomacy in Action*, p. 71.

[76] According to the high commissioner and several staff members, disputes over education, language, and political participation tend to the three primary sources of tension in states experiencing conflict between national minorities and majorities.

[77] Ratner, "Does International Law Matter in Preventing Ethnic Conflict?"

would enable target states to better develop multicultural institutions and relations among various national groups. This, in turn, would improve the relationship between majorities and minorities. For example, in 1996 the Foundation for Interethnic Relations brought together members of the Macedonian Parliament, the governing administration, and Albanian political parties for a two-day conference to discuss (among other things) the role of local self-government in a multiethnic society and the use of minority education to preserve minority ethnic identities and increase their role in public affairs.[78] Emanuel Adler argues that seminars of this type are socialization mechanisms that promote the development of common meanings and the dissemination of new ideas, making the office of the HCNM a "community of epistemic communities."[79]

In sum, through the office of the HCNM, the OSCE sought to influence the internal development of target states in Eastern and Central Europe. Despite its name, the HCNM was designed neither as an ombudsman or an advocate for national minorities. Rather, he worked to protect all national communities – including majority ones – and in the process helped to facilitate the development of multicultural institutions.

The Bosnian Peace Plan as a model of multiculturalism

Perhaps the best indication of European intentions in attempting to influence the international structure of states is how it addressed the "Bosnian problem." Bosnia is a good case because it is the one area in which the European powers were able to become directly involved in reorganizing a target state. In this sense, it reveals the preferences of the Europeans and Americans, much as the reorganization of Germany and Japan into liberal states did so after World War II.

The violent breakup of Yugoslavia posed a unique challenge to European leaders in their efforts to construct a new European order. While the revolutions in Eastern Europe and the dissolution of the Soviet Union proceeded without the direct involvement of European institutions, the rapid spread of violence in the region forced the West Europeans to become intimately involved in the transformation of the Balkans. As mentioned above, the West had a long-standing position supporting

[78] Kemp, *Quiet Diplomacy in Action*, p. 180.
[79] Adler, "Seeds of Peaceful Change," p. 139.

the continued unity of the Yugoslav Federation. This changed when Croatia and Slovenia declared their independence in June 1991. Immediately following these declarations, war broke out between the armed forces of the Yugoslav National Army (JNA) and Slovenian militias. The three major European organizations – CSCE, European Community, and North Atlantic Treaty Organization (NATO) – and later the United Nations and the West European Union, reacted quickly, trying to contain the violence and stabilize the region.

In September, the Committee of Ministers of the EC held a Peace Conference on Yugoslavia to develop a program that would keep the federation together. They proposed a devolution of authority not only to the republics but also to ethnic communities within them. Specifically, the draft treaty suggested granting national minorities within the republics a special status of autonomy and the creation of independent legislative, administrative, and educational institutions.[80] When this failed to stop the conflict, Germany threatened to unilaterally recognize Croatian independence. Wishing to maintain unity during the Maastricht negotiations (which were aimed at developing a European Union treaty), the other EC members reluctantly agreed to establish criteria for the recognition of independence for the republics.[81] In addition to these general criteria that would apply throughout Europe, the Arbitration Commission of the EC (dubbed the Badinter Commission) issued a set of opinions in January 1992 that related specifically to the former Yugoslav republics. This paved the way for European (and later United Nations) recognition of four new states – Slovenia, Croatia, Bosnia, Macedonia. It also led to the outbreak of war in Bosnia-Herzegovina.[82]

---

[80] See Paul Szasz, "Protecting Human and Minority Rights in Bosnia: A Documentary Survey of International Proposals," *California Western International Law Journal*, vol. 25, no. 2 (1994), p. 261.

[81] On December 17, 1991 the EC foreign ministers issued a declaration on the Guidelines on the Recognition of the New States in Eastern Europe and the Soviet Union. This included the following: adherence to the UN Charter, the Helsinki Final Act, and the Charter of Paris; guarantees for the rights of ethnic communities and national minorities; respect for the inviolability of frontiers; and respect for human rights. See Roland Rich, "Recognition of States: The Collapse of Yugoslavia and the Soviet Union," *European Journal of International Relations*, vol. 4, no. 1 (1993).

[82] This is obviously a very brief synopsis of a much longer and more complicated process. For an excellent discussion of the break-up of Yugoslavia, see Susan Woodward, *Balkan Tragedy: Chaos and Dissolution After the Cold War* (Washington, DC: The Brookings Institution, 1995). For a good collection of essays on the role played by international institutions and European and North American states in the conflict, see Richard H. Ullman, ed., *The World and Yugoslavia's Wars* (Washington, DC: Council on Foreign Relations, 1996).

Although the war in Bosnia was one of four that accompanied (and precipitated) the break-up of Yugoslavia, it was the only one in which the Europeans were able to exercise direct influence on the outcome.[83] In many ways the "Bosnian question" was symbolic of the problem that had developed in many of the new and reorganized states of Eastern and Central Europe: how to balance the interests of politically conscious ethnic minorities with the desire of political leaders to construct a national state. The republic of Bosnia was a multiethnic society, consisting of approximately 44 percent Muslims, 31 percent Serbs, and 17 percent Croats.[84] The constitutional order of Yugoslavia had provided for self-determination of *nations* not *republics*, and thus Bosnia as such did not specifically represent a national community. This was compounded by the efforts of the leadership within each of the communities to retain their positions by politicizing the ethnic differences that had previously had little meaning.[85]

The Serbian solution to this problem was to redraw the borders of the republics. Refusing to live in a Bosnian state in which the Muslims held a majority, the Bosnian-Serb leadership began to consolidate control over those territories in which they held a majority. They declared their intention to construct a Republika Srpska as a prelude to annexing these regions to Serbia proper. The government of Serbia encouraged these efforts as part of its project to build a "Greater Serbia" that would include those portions of the former Yugoslavia in which Serbian communities were dominant. Backed by support from the JNA, Bosnian-Serb militias began to wage war against the Muslim and Croat populations of Bosnia. In prosecuting the war, the Serbian militias engaged in practices that Europeans had long denounced as crimes against humanity: ethnic cleansing, military attacks on densely populated civilian areas, and, ultimately, attempted genocide.

The war raged for several years, while European and international institutions initiated a variety of ineffective mechanisms to stem and control the violence. After many feeble attempts by the OSCE and the United Nations to broker a settlement and regulate the conflict, NATO eventually intervened through a massive aerial bombing campaign against the Bosnian-Serb positions. This was accompanied by an all-out offensive

---

[83] The other three wars were between Slovenia and Yugoslavia, Croatia and Yugoslavia, and the Krajinan Serbs (within Croatia) and the central government of Croatia.
[84] Richard H. Ullman, ed., *The World and Yugoslavia's Wars*, Introduction, p. 2.
[85] See Woodward, *Balkan Tragedy*, p. 233.

by Muslim and Croat armies. Both of these actions turned the tide of the war against Serbia. The result was an agreement by all sides to negotiate under the mediation of the United States.

The negotiations – held at a military base in Dayton, Ohio in 1995 – were aimed not only at ending the war, but also reorganizing the Bosnian state according to the principles established by European institutions. This was difficult inasmuch as the talks did not involve representatives from Bosnia's ethnic communities, but rather the two kin states, Serbia and Croatia, and nominal Bosnian officials. The original plans offered by the European–American "Contact Group" and by Cyrus Vance and David Owen in 1993 sought to partition the country into ten regions that reflected a balance between ethnic and nonethnic representation. The Bosnian Serbs would control three cantons and two enclaves, accounting for just under 43 percent of the country.

In contrast, the guiding principle at Dayton was the construction of a multicultural state, which was supposed not only to provide regional stability, but also effective democratization.[86] At the heart of the Dayton multiethnic policy was the decentralization of political power and the guarantee of security for all ethnic communities. The goal was to guarantee a level of self-government for each constituent nationality and prevent any policies that would favor one over the others. Thus, the political foundation for the state would be three constituent nationalities – Bosnians, Croats, and Serbs – which would provide the basis for citizenship.[87] In this version of a multicultural state, Bosnia consisted of two separate entities, a Bosniak Federation (of Croats and Muslims) and a Republika Srpska. The central government was responsible for foreign policy, trade, transportation, and law enforcement between the entities, while education and social policy were placed in the hands of the local communities. All central state institutions were organized on the basis of ethnic representation.[88]

According to the agreement, these structures of governance were to be supervised by a variety of judicial, administrative, and regulatory institutions directed by the OSCE, NATO, and the United Nations. The

[86] See David Chandler, *Bosnia: Faking Democracy After Dayton* (London: Pluto Press, 1999), p. 66.
[87] See Office of the High Representative, "The General Framework Agreement for Peace in Bosnia and Herzegovina," initiated in Dayton on November 21, 1995 and signed in Paris on December 14, 1995, Annex 4, preamble.
[88] Ibid., Annex 4, Article 1.

extent of external involvement in the daily governance of Bosnia was unprecedented within a sovereign state.[89] While these external oversight bodies were designed to be temporary (part of a transition process) they have remained longer than originally anticipated. This was a clear indication that the transition process would be very slow. According to one of the former legal advisors to the International Conference on the Former Yugoslavia, Paul Szasz, this high level of intervention reflects the widespread human rights violations that characterized the conflict; the inability of the various parties to secure an agreement on their own; and the belief by European leaders that the future of the new European order would rest on their ability to stabilize the region.[90]

Certainly the construction of a multicultural state in Bosnia by European leaders did indeed reflect the special challenges posed by the war in the Balkans. At the same time, it also demonstrates a commitment by these leaders to prevent the rise of national states without assuming that liberal democracy would resolve the problems of multiethnic societies. In fact, much thinking on the democratization of Eastern Europe downplayed the importance of government institutions and procedures in favor of a more rigorous development of civil societies. This was largely a recognition that the political organization of the state needed to reflect the distribution of populations and the identities of the domestic communities.[91] In this sense, the Bosnian peace plan reflected the determination of Western leaders to build multicultural states by guaranteeing the security and interests of the various ethnic communities that comprise them.

Conclusion

The evidence offered above suggests that the goal of the OSCE's international protection regime was to undermine the political foundation

[89] See Susan Woodward, "Compromised Sovereignty to Create Sovereignty: Is Dayton Bosnia a Futile Exercise or an Emerging Model?" in Stephen Krasner, ed., *Problematic Sovereignty: Contested Rules and Political Possibilities* (New York: Columbia University Press, 2001).

[90] Paul Szasz, "Current Developments: The Protection of Human Rights Through the Dayton/Paris Agreement on Bosnia," *American Journal of International Law*, vol. 90 (1996), p. 314.

[91] See, for example, Bruce Parrott, "Perspectives on Postcommunist Democratization," in Karen Dawisha and Bruce Parrott, eds., *Politics, Power, and the Struggle for Democracy in South-East Europe* (Cambridge: Cambridge University Press, 1997); M. Krol, "Where East Meets West," *Journal of Democracy*, vol. 6, no. 1 (1985); and Larry Diamond, "Rethinking Civil Society: Toward Democratic Consolidation," *Journal of Democracy*, vol. 5, no. 3 (1984).

of the national state in favor of a multicultural one. Unlike in the post-World War I era, European leaders did not try to integrate national minorities into the majority culture, but rather they sought to expand the national culture to include those of the minority communities. Like the regime of the interwar period, its purpose was not aimed primarily at "protecting" minorities, but rather promoting the norms and principles of the new European order. The goals of this regime reflected both the principles of the new order and the tensions that arose when European and North American leaders attempted to expand this order to include all of Europe. While the liberal state was successful in providing for stability, cooperation, democratic governance, and the rule of law in the West, the OSCE realized that this could not be imposed on the East. As a result, they used their experiences in multicultural statehood from some of their members to promote similar structures in the new and reorganized states of Eastern, Southern, and Central Europe.

While security considerations were undoubtedly present in the OSCE's decision to become involved in the internal politics of some of its member states, it was the decision to expand West European society that convinced their leadership that conflicts in Eastern Europe were in fact a security concern. Few if any of the major powers viewed themselves as having any vital interests in Eastern Europe, beyond preventing conflicts and refugee flows from expanding.[92] Had the NATO countries decided to pursue a policy of benign neglect toward Eastern Europe and the Baltics, there would have been little need to help democratize and stabilize the new and reorganized states in the region. So long as conflicts in the region could be isolated (and refugees kept out), they would not directly affect the security of the Western states.

As with the previous cases in chapters 3 and 4, there was no evidence that strategic calculation, power balancing, or economic or military advantage were significant motivations in creating the protection regime. Rather, the motives appear to be centered on a desire to expand European international society and ensure that the internal organization of the emerging states reflects the principles of that society. This is consistent with Schimmelfennig's finding regarding EU expansion: that the goals of international organizations are determined more strongly by

---

[92] This appears to be the general consensus among many academics and political leaders. See Richard Ullman, "The Wars in Yugoslavia and the International System After the Cold War," in Ullman, ed., *The World and Yugoslavia's Wars*.

the standards of legitimacy and appropriateness of the new European order to which they belong, than by the utilitarian demand for efficient problem solving.[93] Thus, the protection regime organized through the office of the HCNM fits the definition of an institution for the common good, as defined in chapter 1.

At the same time, I found little to demonstrate that humanitarian motives were significant, or that transnational organizations played much of a role in either the development or the expansion of the regime. While there were clear demands from various populations within OSCE member states for increased European involvement in the protection of national minorities,[94] nongovernmental organizations were not a major force. The cautious approach taken by the OSCE and its member states highlights this fact. While the organization did devote significant resources toward protecting ethnic communities within target states, the OSCE members also showed the limits to this commitment. They were most effective when they were able to employ "seminar diplomacy" and "rhetorical action" but were less effective in dealing with the most egregious cases that could have threatened their own citizens (for example, Bosnia and Chechnya).

This above narrative also demonstrates that the members of the OSCE did not make the fine distinctions between stability and justice or security and order that are often made by political realists. Underlying the OSCE's vision of conflict prevention was the concept of "comprehensive security," an approach that links military/security issues with the spread of human rights, the rule of law, ethnic pluralism, and democratization.[95] Thus, the OSCE's conflict management approach was to rely heavily on the promotion of OSCE values and principles as a critical part of the political solutions to crises. In the OSCE world, legitimation would be a key aspect of stability and order.[96] Domestic relationships and international behavior would therefore be linked. Thus, the CSCE Parliamentary Assembly declared in 1992: "Intervention to help national

---

[93] Schimmelfennig, "The Community Trap," p. 58.
[94] For data on domestic attitudes toward involvement in the former Yugoslavia, see Richard Sobel, "US and European Attitudes Toward Intervention in the Former Yugoslavia: *Mourir pour la Bosnie?*," in Ullman, ed., *The World and Yugoslavia's Wars*.
[95] See Bloed, ed., *The Conference on Security and Cooperation in Europe*, p. 40.
[96] Kari Möttölä, "The OSCE: Institutional and Functional Developments in an Evolving European Security Order," in Michal Bothe, Natalino Ronzitu, and Allan Rosas, eds., *The OSCE in the Maintenance of Peace and Security: Conflict Prevention, Crisis Management and Peaceful Settlement of Disputes* (The Hague: Kluwer Law International, 1997), pp. 26–7.

minorities is no longer considered an interference in the internal affairs of the State in question."[97]

As Flynn and Farrell argue, the normative framework of the OSCE emerged from the participating states' collective attempts to develop standards that would underlie a new security order.[98] Thus, according to Finland's special advisor on security policy for the Ministry of Foreign Affairs, Kari Möttölä, the new OSCE became "a community of values and a security-policy institute that (codifies) standards and norms for intra-state and inter-state behavior in all the dimensions of security."[99] From this perspective, the European order was created to preserve stability based on a specific set of values advocated by the United States and European leaders.

---

[97] Budapest Declaration of the CSCE Parliamentary Assembly, 5 July 1992, ch. III, B, paragraphs 2 and 3.

[98] Gregory Flynn and Henry Farrell, "Piecing Together the Democratic Peace: The CSCE, Norms and the Construction of Security in Post-Cold War Europe," *International Organization*, vol. 53, no. 3 (Summer 1999), p. 510.

[99] Möttölä, "The OSCE," p. 2.

6   The nation-state and the protection of refugees

Refugees, Jacques Vernant laments, are symbols of instability, the curse weighing upon those whose homeland is nowhere. They do not enjoy the legal guarantees accorded by every state to its own nationals. They come to earn their daily bread in places where no one invited them and which they cannot leave at will.[1] "Once they leave their homeland," Hannah Arendt adds, "they remain homeless. Once they leave their state, they become stateless. Once they have been deprived of their human rights, they are rightless, the scum of the earth."[2] Refugees can only leave their country if they have somewhere to go; however, the availability of such a place is determined by the willingness of a foreign state to accept them. Yet unlike the other vulnerable population groups discussed in the previous three chapters, refugees do not have co-ethnics, fellow citizens, or kin states to advocate on their behalf. In a world in which one's international status is tied to one's citizenship, they are nomads without an identity.

Compounding this problem, the international system is not equipped to deal with individuals or groups who are not under the authority or protection of a state. Refugees are not recognized under customary international law and lack travel documents that would enable them to move freely between countries. They have no embassies to represent them and no government from which they can demand security protection. Refugees are therefore an anomaly in a world of sovereign states. They are not, however, a passive anomaly. In large numbers they can disrupt the ethnic balance in their country of refuge, create tensions

---

[1] Jacques Vernant, *The Refugee in the Post-War World* (New Haven: Yale University Press, 1953), pp. 13, 14.
[2] Hannah Arendt, *Origins of Totalitarianism* (New York: Harcourt Brace Jovanovich, 1973 [1951]), p. 267.

between the host state and the state of origin, and impose prohibitive costs on those forced to provide for their material care.

Yet the refugee problem does not lend itself easily to international cooperation. Refugees are *ipso facto* at best an embarrassment, and at worst traitors to countries with whom other states carry on diplomatic and political relations.[3] Even in the best of circumstances, the institution of sovereignty precludes the international community from addressing the root causes of their situation, since this would inevitably involve facilitating some type of political change within the country of origin. Within the context of domestic politics governments rarely find any political advantage in caring for refugees or integrating them into their societies. Indeed, they are often more valuable as pawns in the pursuit of a state's foreign policy objectives, and are therefore better dealt with through unilateral action. While a system of burden-sharing may help to alleviate a particular refugee flow, the easiest way for a state to avoid these problems is to close its borders, as Jewish refugees from the Nazi genocide quickly discovered. It is no wonder that refugees have been the most helpless and vulnerable victims of the nation-state system.

Despite these obstacles, states have developed extensive systems to protect and assist refugees over the past eighty years. These regimes were not designed to protect all who were involuntarily forced to flee their homelands, but rather were limited to certain classes of displaced persons. Others in similar situations were deliberately excluded. This chapter explains how and why political leaders designated political migrants as a distinct category of victims in the twentieth century, and why states collectively assumed the responsibility for their protection and care. It also explains how political leaders chose which of the international homeless they would consider to be refugees.

While the refugee regime has evolved and expanded extensively over the past half century, the principles established in the early days of the League of Nations and United Nations remain the foundation upon which all refugee protection systems have operated at both the international and regional levels. Therefore, this chapter focuses on the evolution of the IPRs for refugees from the creation of the "Nansen office" in 1921 through the birth of the Office of the United Nations High Commissioner on Refugees (UNHCR) in 1950 and the Convention Relating to the Status of Refugees in 1951. My primary focus is on the negotiations

---

[3] John Stoessinger, *The Refugee and the World Community* (Minneapolis: University of Minnesota Press, 1956), p. 32.

and debates that occurred within the United Nations over how to define a refugee, the types of obligations states should assume for their welfare, and whether the protection regime should be universal or particular in character. By focusing on the "original intent" of the creators at the beginning of these processes, we can better determine how and why states have chosen to protect the most helpless and unwanted populations in international society.

Explaining refugee protection

Refugees are neither an inevitable nor a universal part of the human condition. The concept of "refugee" is primarily a twentieth-century one, and the notion of international responsibility for their protection is tied directly to changes in the international order and the domination of the nation-state. While people have been forced to flee their homes in the face of violence, persecution, and natural disasters since the beginning of human society, the idea that certain types of migrants constitute a defined legal and political category did not emerge until after World War I. Until that time, governments did not make a legal distinction between individuals leaving their country for personal reasons and those forced out for political ones. Political leaders did not view those fleeing an intolerable situation as victims in need of protection, but rather they treated them as regular immigrants on a case-by-case basis. In the nineteenth century, for example, revolutionaries who took refuge in England or France were not considered to be refugees but rather political "exiles."[4]

Moreover, until the twentieth century, international movement was relatively unfettered and therefore there was almost always some place one could go. Although the idea of providing official documents to travelers dates back to Louis XIV, the modern system of immigration controls and passport verification only emerged after World War I.[5] Prior to that, there was little need for an individual to certify his or her nationality when entering a new country, and with few exceptions (for example, during times of war) states were not particularly concerned with the citizenship of those entering their borders. The pre-nineteenth-century

[4] Aristide Zolberg, "The Formation of New States as a Refugee-Generating Process," in *Annals of the American Academy of Political and Social Science*, special issue 467, *The Global Refugee Problem: US and World Response* (Beverly Hills: Sage Publications, 1983).
[5] Louise Holborn, *Refugees: A Problem of Our Time: The Work of the United Nations High Commissioner for Refugees 1951–1972* (Netuchen, NJ: The Scarecrow Press, 1975), vol. I, ch. 1.

mercantilist state actually encouraged immigration, viewing new inhabitants as potential generators of wealth and power.[6] The tie between a
state and its citizens was an opportunistic one and the government had
few obligations toward its population other than providing for basic
security.

This changed with the emergence of nationalism and citizenship as
the foundational concepts of the state. The status of individuals became
increasingly tied to a defined territory and nationality, leading to the notion of fixed political identities, which were by definition exclusive. As
many scholars have pointed out, the growth and development of the
centralized "nation"-state was facilitated in large part by the expulsion
of specific groups of people for whom the state would not assume responsibility.[7] State-building strategies began to define which categories
of people were to be nationals and which were to be considered aliens.
As a result, the consolidation of the nation-state in the twentieth century (facilitated by the collapse of the last four great European empires)
forced large-scale dislocation of populations. It also forced the members
of international society to consider what constituted a legitimate state
and what to do with those who were excluded from these states. In
this sense, the complete control of the globe by sovereign nation-states
made possible the expulsion of people from society, and immigration
controls turned certain types of "migrants" into "stateless persons."[8]
Under these circumstances, individuals fleeing an intolerable situation
could no longer simply relocate at will.

Yet although these changes can explain the political alienation of those
forced to flee their countries without a preapproved destination, it does
not explain why certain types of migrants became conceptualized as
"refugees" while others in identical circumstances were denied such
categorization. This is important, because refugee status is an entitle-
ment given to those who qualify for access to certain international legal
protections and resources outside of their home country.[9] International
efforts to protect such individuals have been tied to very specific definitions of who counts as a political migrant. For example, during the
interwar period refugees were defined in terms of membership in a

---

[6] Michael Marrus, *The Unwanted: European Refugees in the Twentieth Century* (New York:
Oxford University Press, 1985), p. 6.
[7] See, for example, Marrus, *The Unwanted*, p. 51 and Zolberg, "The Formation of New
States as a Refugee-Generating Process."
[8] See Arendt, *Origins of Totalitarianism*, ch. 9 and Stoessinger, *The Refugee and the World
Community*, p. 3.
[9] Vernant, *The Refugee in the PostWar World*, p. 3.

designated ethnic group such as Armenians, Russians, and Germans. Yet after World War II the criteria shifted toward individual victims having a "well-founded fear of persecution." This suggests that refugee status reflects the political values of the time, and in this case, the political values of the international order.

While the modern image of the refugee is often one who is forced to flee his or her home in the midst of a devastating war or other forms of violence, the IPR for refugees was not created to assist those displaced from war. Rather states constructed the system to address post-war political developments that were related to the construction of new states and new political orders. The definitions of refugee articulated in both the interwar and the post-World War II regimes specifically excluded those whose situation was related to the violence of warfare. This is largely because governments correctly understood that large movements of refugees – as defined within the regimes – have tended to accompany new state formations. More specifically, it became clear that refugees were the outcome of particular state-integration strategies.[10] The decision by international political leaders on who to protect has thus been tied directly to the types of states that constituted the countries of origin, and the values of the international order. The key component in the conceptualization of a refugee has been thus the belief that the root cause of his or her status was the relationship between the state and its citizens.[11] In this sense, the protection of refugees has served to regulate these relations.

Changes in the migration patterns also do not explain why states decided to become involved in refugee protection. While both world wars displaced millions of people from their homes, in both cases most of those uprooted by the wars themselves returned within a few years after the end of hostilities. Prior to 1921, efforts to aid displaced persons and political migrants were initiated and overseen almost exclusively by nongovernmental organizations, in particular humanitarian and religious groups. Such assistance took the form mostly of relief. No significant efforts were made to facilitate repatriation or resettlement, and the approach to the problems was *ad hoc* rather than systematic. No attempts were made to grant such persons legal recognition. On the other hand, state-organized refugee protection regimes have sought to substitute for the protection of a state a set of principles providing for humane

---

[10] This is essentially the thesis advanced by Aristide Zolberg ("The Formation of New States as a Refugee-Generating Process") and Hannah Arendt (*Origins of Totalitarianism*).
[11] Vernant, *The Refugee in the Post War World*, p. 5.

treatment of nonsanctioned migrants within another state's territory. The regimes also have provided a form of international supervision for ensuring that these principles were observed, and developed plans for facilitating repatriation or resettlement.

Historians and political scientists have tried to explain international efforts to protect refugees by referring to strategic interest, humanitarian concern, and international necessity. Reflecting a realist position, Gil Loescher and John A. Scanlan argue that government policies toward refugees have been based primarily on foreign policy objectives.[12] International refugee regimes are simply an extension of those objectives. For example, refugees are viewed as a means of destabilizing adversaries and occasionally an opportunity to create an opposition-in-exile for possible future action. More specifically, Loescher argues that the international protection of refugees emerged after World War II as a political tool by Western countries to help fight the Cold War. The United States, in particular, considered its policy toward refugees as part of its broader strategy to wage ideological war against the Soviet Union and to undermine the legitimacy of communism in Eastern Europe.[13] In this effort, the United States sought not to *protect* refugees, but to *create* them, by encouraging flight from within the Soviet sphere.

Jack Garvey and Louise Holborn take a different approach. They argue that the protection of refugees was largely (though not exclusively) the result of humanitarian motivations by both political leaders and non-governmental organizations after World War II. This reflected a genuine concern for those who had nowhere to go and who faced grave exploitation and misery as a result of World War II and its aftermath.[14] In the course of developing postwar reconstruction policies, state leaders believed that they had a responsibility to cooperate in "cleaning up" the mess that all had helped to create during and after the war. While there may have been some political or ideological value in helping East European refugees, the primary concern was with their welfare.

The institutionalist approach holds that the protection of refugees is an attempt at burden-sharing among states facing a common predicament. Kim Salomon, for example, holds that states created the postwar

---

[12] Gil Loescher and John A. Scanlan, *Calculated Kindness: Refugees and America's Half-Open Door, 1945 to the Present* (New York: Free Press, 1986).

[13] Gil Loescher, *The UNHCR and World Politics: A Perilous Path* (Oxford: Oxford University Press, 2001) and *Beyond Charity: International Cooperation and the Global Refugee Crisis* (Oxford: Oxford University Press, 1993).

[14] Jack Garvey, "Toward a Reformulation of International Refugee Law," *Harvard International Law Journal*, vol. 26, no. 2 (1985) and Holborn, *Refugees*.

regime in order to address a potentially explosive international problem that was beyond the ability of any single state to resolve. As mentioned above, refugees can create regional instability and become economic burdens. The refugees had to go somewhere and no one wanted to shoulder the entire responsibility. In the course of dealing with the many postwar problems that were raised on the UN agenda, the leading members of the organization believed that the refugee issue could be resolved only through multilateral cooperation. This led to a series of agreements between states and the creation of several international organizations to handle the functional tasks. This institutional cooperation also reflected the interests of the West in challenging Soviet influence in Eastern Europe.[15]

I offer a fourth approach. I argue that an international protection regime for refugees emerged after World Wars I and II as part of broader efforts to stabilize the nation-state system and build coherent international orders centered around the League of Nations and United Nations, respectively. During both periods, political leaders recognized refugees to be the by-products of a transformation from an old political order into a new one. The interwar regime reflected the belief in ethnicity and nationality as the foundation of the nation-state, while the post-World War II system was based on the rights of the individual and the protection of basic human rights (see chapters 3 and 4). Both regimes also reflected an attempt to reconcile two contradictory principles in the creation of new political orders: (1) the sovereign right of states to control their borders; (2) the need to protect those forced to flee their countries in the wake of postwar state-building activities. On a deeper level, I argue that the protection of refugees was a method of trying to deal with "unaffiliated" individuals in a world of nation-states. In this sense, the protection of refugees helped to stabilize the territorial nation-state by absorbing those who did not fit within this system.

The protection of refugees after World War I

The protection of refugees after World War I was an extension of allied efforts to protect the national state and build a new international order based on law and interstate cooperation. While the violence of World War I forced millions of people to flee their homes, the allied powers did

[15] Kim Salomon, *Refugees in the Cold War: Toward a New International Refugee Regime in the Early Postwar* (Lund: Lund University Press, 1991).

not consider them to be refugees. Rather, the leadership expected those displaced by the war to return to their homes after the end of hostilities, and therefore did not believe that they required any special protection or assistance. Based this belief, the League of Nations only classified those displaced by postwar political developments as refugees.

As we saw in chapter 3, the allies redrew the political and geographic map of Europe extensively after the war by creating and reorganizing states based on the ethnic composition of the population. The transformation of the last remaining European empires into nation-states produced violent social changes throughout central and eastern Europe. The border changes and new state formations led to massive population displacements, many of which consisted of individuals who could not integrate into new territories ruled by alien nationalities. While the national minority protection system established a set of rights for defined ethnic groups, it could not provide for those who could not become citizens of a particular state. The allies were not concerned with the political persecution of these individuals *per se*, but rather with the inability of the League's minority protection system to secure citizenship rights for those who did not fit into the legal categories established under the system.[16]

For example, the transformation of the Romanov Empire into the Soviet state produced large numbers of refugees, particularly after the defeat of the Western-supported counter-revolution against the Bolsheviks. While some of the White Russians left out of fear, many others were "denationalized" (had their citizenship revoked) by the new government on the theory that tsarists could not become loyal citizens of the new socialist state. In either case, there were more than 1 million people who could not be integrated into the new state, and they thus became stateless at a time when citizenship had increasingly become the sole foundation for legal recognition.

At the same time, the creation of a Turkish state from the remnants of the Ottoman Empire was facilitated at least in part by the expulsion and elimination of the Armenian population from Asia Minor. Beginning in 1915, the Committee of Union and Progress (commonly known as the Young Turks) sought to build a Turkish state based on the principle of Pan-Turanism by creating an exclusively Turkic polity. While most of the genocide occurred between 1915 and 1918, the postwar nationalist government renewed the massacres and expulsions in 1920,

[16] See Arendt, *Origins of Totalitarianism*, p. 289 and Marrus, *The Unwanted*, p. 71.

forcing thousands of Armenians to flee the newly created national state of Turkey. Even with a minority rights protection regime overseen by the victorious allies, no one expected the surviving Armenians to return to the country that tried to eliminate them as a people. As a result, it was not immediately clear where they would go.

While these were the most dramatic cases, other efforts to build national states also produced large numbers of refugees. More than 1 million Turkish Greeks and 360,000 Greek Turks were "exchanged" between the two countries, leading to massive displacements of populations.[17] A similar exchange between Greece and Bulgaria resulted in nearly 100,000 displaced people.[18] Various treaties signed after the war reduced this particular problem by allowing members of the transferred populations to relocate to their kin state; however, in some cases this proved to be impractical. For example, Turkey expelled thousands of its citizens who had Greek-sounding names or who used Greek characters when writing Turkish. Yet they were not ethnic Greeks and could not simply move to Greece after they were expelled, since they neither spoke the language nor understood the customs.[19]

The most vulnerable victims of these new state formations, the *Heimat-losen* or stateless people (for example, Jews and Roma), had even fewer options, since no matter how the borders were drawn they had no kin state to which they could emigrate.[20]

Compounding these problems was the unprecedented institution of new travel restrictions and immigration rules enacted by states throughout Europe and North America. For the first time, *émigrés* were required to produce passports and provide evidence that they could live in their new country without being a burden on the state or its native population. Such restrictions were the result of an increased nativism, rising unemployment, and newly accepted responsibility by governments for providing social welfare to their populations.

Yet despite this growing continental problem, during the immediate postwar period attempts to deal with displaced and stateless persons were highly politicized and parochial. States tended to assist only those individuals fleeing adversaries, and government decisions as to which refugees to assist were made on a case-by-case basis. For example, most East European governments helped refugees from the Soviet Union

---

[17] See John H. Simpson, *The Refugee Problem: Report of a Survey* (London, 1939), p. 14.
[18] Stephen Ladas, *The Exchange of Minorities: Bulgaria, Greece, Turkey* (New York, 1932), p. 722.
[19] Marrus, *The Unwanted*, pp. 100–01.   [20] Arendt, *Origins of Totalitarianism*, p. 271.

but refused to assist Germans. Similarly, the British helped Greece and Bulgaria with the refugee problems (both were considered strategic allies), but not other countries in Eastern Europe.[21]

While these *ad hoc* efforts provided some relief for those displaced by political circumstances, it soon became clear to many political leaders that a stable European order of national states required a more systematic approach. In addition to the practical problems raised by large numbers of people trying to gain residency in an alien country, the idea of a "stateless person" was a new one in international relations. As suggested above, the collapse of the great European empires and the domination of the citizen-based state after the war created fixed national identities for the European populace. The existence of millions of individuals without a defined citizenship was a challenge to the new European political order in which sovereignty was now based on a direct tie between individual and territory. Moreover, for the first time – as suggested in the Soviet case – governments in newly constituted states began to denationalize those they did not consider to be legitimate citizens, a practice that was inconsistent with the concept of a state-based system. For example, in addition to actions taken by the Soviet government against its counter-revolutionaries, Romania stripped 100,000 Jewish residents of their citizenship.[22]

In addition to the political problems raised by these practices, a humanitarian crisis was growing. In an era that promised a new international order of peace, justice, and cooperation, the problem could no longer be ignored. In 1921, under pressure from a coalition of NGOs led by the International Committee of the Red Cross, the League of Nations Council agreed to appoint a high commissioner for refugees. The job of the newly created office was to deal specifically with Russians who were not allowed to return home, at the time the biggest group of stateless persons.[23] The International Labor Organization followed their lead by agreeing to help find employment for those designated as refugees. For the first time in history, refugees were granted an international legal status and were distinguished from other types of migrants and exiles. While the high commissioner's functions were limited initially to providing administrative assistance, the first international protection system for refugees was born.

---

[21] Loescher, *Beyond Charity*, p. 39.   [22] Vernant, *The Refugee in the Post War World*.
[23] The United States, France, and Britain also had a special interest in the fate of Russian refugees inasmuch as they had armed and supported the White Russian armies.

Consistent with its commitment to nationality as the foundation of the new international order, the League defined refugees exclusively in terms of ethnic group. While the Russian problem was the primary concern in the early years of the regime, the League soon expanded the list of protected displaced nationalities to include Armenians, Turks, Assyrians and – on the eve of World War II – Austrians, Czechs, and Germans. In each case, the decision to include a new nationality was made on the basis of which ethnic groups could not be absorbed into the interwar national states. Thus, according to the Arrangement of 1926, a refugee was defined as anyone of a specified national group who "does not enjoy . . . the protection of the Government . . . and who has not acquired another nationality."[24]

The key component of the interwar regime was the creation of an international travel document established by the Arrangement of 5 July 1922. Informally dubbed "Nansen Passports" (in reference to the first High Commissioner, Fritjof Nansen), these documents served as substitutes for official passports or other identity papers that were universally being required by states upon admission to their territory. Nansen's office thereby assumed the task of certifying the identities and status of those the League designated as refugees. This certificate was accepted in principle by fifty-three states, although forty actually signed the Arrangement.[25] The High Commissioner's mandate was further expanded in the 1928 Arrangement Concerning the Extension to Other Categories of Refugees, which authorized him to act as a *de facto* international embassy for legal refugees. Thus the first protection of refugees was diplomatic.[26]

Although the office was woefully underfunded, it soon expanded its functions to include repatriation and – when this proved to be impractical in the Soviet case – resettlement or integration into the country of refuge. For the first time, large refugee camps were created as an interim measure pending final dispensation. In this area, the League received considerable assistance from nongovernmental organizations such as the International Committee of the Red Cross, the Armenian Refugee Fund, and the Russian Relief and Reconstruction Fund.

---

[24] Claudena Skran, *Refugees in Inter-War Europe* (New York: Oxford University, Press, 1995), p. 109.

[25] Stoessinger, *The Refugee and the World Community*, p. 18.

[26] Diplomatic protection refers to activities by states that seek to ensure that their citizens receive the rights considered universal according to customary practice and international law. Such rights include the protection of their life, property, and security when outside their countries. See Guy Goodwin-Gill, *The Refugee in International Law* (Oxford: Oxford University Press, 1996).

In addition to creating an office responsible for diplomatic protection, the League of Nations also attempted to develop the first comprehensive set of state obligations toward refugees by drafting a legally binding Convention in 1933. By this time, many advocates realized that it would not be enough to provide refugees with diplomatic protection. Many of the Nansen refugees refused to be repatriated to their countries of origin, raising the difficult question of what to do with them. The 1933 Convention attempted to facilitate a smooth resolution of this problem by providing refugees with a set of international legal rights concerning education, movement, and basic liberties. The most important of these rights was the freedom from expulsion, the precursor to the postwar principle of *nonrefoulement*. Like the functional activities through the high commissioner's office, the Convention applied only to those ethnic/national groups who were already under the League's protection. Although only eight countries signed the Convention – and eight more agreed to adhere to its provisions without ratification – it established a set of norms and rules for protecting and caring for refugees that would provide the foundation for the far more extensive postwar regime.[27]

Despite the progress in establishing a protection system for those who could not adapt to the new political order, the regime broke down as state commitments to the international order receded. The true test of the regime came when thousands of people fled fascism in Germany, Italy, Spain, and Portugal. Although the League expanded the scope of its refugee protection activities by appointing a high commissioner for refugees coming from Germany in 1933, the refusal of the member states to accept the victims of fascism into their territories undermined the foundation of the system.[28] Certainly, increased nativism, isolationism, and economic uncertainty were partly to blame for this shameful behavior, but one can attribute it also to the collective failure of political leaders to uphold the principles of the international order they had created less than two decades earlier.[29]

---

[27] Skran, *Refugees in Inter-War Europe*, p. 125.

[28] This refusal was not universal. Despite the breakdown of the regime, France upheld its commitments to the 1933 Convention by admitting 400,000 refugees from Spain in 1939. Goodwin-Gill, *The Refugee in International Law*, p. 119, fn. 9.

[29] There were some small attempts to address this problem. In 1938 US President Franklin Roosevelt called a conference in Évian, France to discuss the resettlement of Jewish refugees from Germany and Austria. The conference established an Intergovernmental Committee on Refugees on the eve of World War II. The Committee, however, only had a marginal impact, as most European states were more concerned with the depression and the emerging conflict that was brewing in Eastern and Central Europe.

By design the regime was politically neutral *vis-à-vis* the conditions that produced the refugees, thus the League was unable to guarantee that future refugee flows could be stemmed. For example, even when the League agreed to assist German refugees in 1933, its members specifically decided not to discuss the policies that produced them. At the time Germany was a member of the League, and the priority of the organization was on maintaining international peace and security rather than justice. Thus, as the Dutch minister of foreign affairs explained, "we have no wish to examine the reasons why these people have left their country . . . we are not called upon to judge (this). For us, it is a purely technical problem."[30] Of course, as most people would later agree, the League's failure to uphold its commitment to guarantee the protection of national minorities *within* national borders was not a technical problem but a political and moral one.

The political and strategic environment after World War II

With the onset of global war, the plight of refugees became a sideshow. However as the military tide began to turn in favor of the allies, the leading states realized that the international homelessness problem would inhibit their ability to reconstruct Europe and Asia after the expected defeat of the Axis powers. The destructive effects of World War II had not only manifested themselves in an unprecedented loss of lives, property, and infrastructure. The war displaced more than 65 million people in Europe alone.[31] Yet despite the magnitude of this displacement, these people were not considered "refugees," and their dispensation did not pose any significant political problems for the allied powers. In most cases, the countries of origin welcomed the return of their brethren to assist with reconstruction, and most displaced persons were anxious to return home. While repatriation would involve considerable logistical coordination and a commitment of significant funds,

---

[30] Quoted in Skran, *Refugees in Inter-War Europe*, p. 230.

[31] This figure includes 40 million individuals displaced by the violence; 13 million ethnic Germans (*Volksdeutsch*) who were expelled from the Soviet Union and Eastern Europe after liberation; 11 million forced laborers and prisoners of war released from Germany after the fall of the Nazi regime; and approximately 1 million Estonians, Latvians, and Lithuanians who fled the Soviet takeover of the former Baltic republics. See Holborn, *Refugees*, vol. I, p. 23 and UNHCR, *The State of the World's Refugees: Fifty Years of Humanitarian Action* (Oxford: Oxford University Press, 2000).

most political leaders presumed that the situation was a temporary one that could be resolved through national action and international cooperation.[32]

Working on the assumption, representatives from forty-four allied countries met in 1943 to establish the United Nations Relief and Rehabilitation Agency (UNRRA).[33] It was not the purpose of the organization to deal with refugees *per se*, but rather to assist displaced persons who were "victims of war in any area under the control of any of the United Nations."[34] The primary tasks of the organization were twofold: to provide food, clothing, and medical supplies to displaced persons living in areas liberated by the allies; and to facilitate the repatriation of such persons to their countries of origin. This included not only those displaced during the war and its immediate aftermath, but the small number of stateless people left over from the interwar period. In order to facilitate this process, the UNRRA set up and operated a series of assembly centers and temporary camps for those waiting to be repatriated.

From a logistical perspective, the UNRRA was highly successful. By the beginning of 1946, the organization had repatriated more than three-quarters of those forced to leave their homes during the war, about 7 million people.[35] Few of those displaced by the war itself required diplomatic or legal protection, and there was little need for a regime to deal with this aspect of postwar reconstruction. It was not the war that made refugees into an international issue, but rather developments related to the construction of the postwar order, in particular the state-building strategies of the European powers. Many of these strategies contradicted allied efforts to construct a new international order, raising unexpected problems with the repatriation program.

The first indication that there could be a conflict between the smooth repatriation of the displaced and the principles of the new postwar order arose when UNRRA officials discovered that at least 1 million of their clients did not want to return to their countries of origin. This group was highly diverse. It included approximately 200,000 Jewish people not wishing to return to the communities that cooperated in sending their

---

[32] Holborn, *Refugees*, vol. I, p. 36.

[33] The term "United Nations" referred to the anti-Axis coalition; it had no relation to the international organization of the same name that would be created after the war.

[34] Agreement for the UNRRA, Article 1, paragraph 2.

[35] Leon Gordenker, *Refugees in International Politics* (New York: Columbia University Press, 1987), p. 24; Marrus, *The Unwanted*, p. 320.

brethren to their deaths; 200,000 Spanish loyalists fearing for their safety under Francisco Franco; thousands of Ukrainians and other Soviet citizens who feared reprisals by the Stalin regime; 175,000 Poles not wishing to live under the new communist-dominated government; and former residents of the Baltic states who did not recognize the 1939 Soviet annexation of the three republics.[36] It also soon became clear to many allied leaders that the UNRRA had already repatriated thousands of people against their wishes. As a result, mass repatriations were halted in mid-1946.

This raised a difficult political problem. The Yalta agreement had provided for the repatriation of Soviet prisoners of war and other Soviet nationals living in the former German-occupied territories.[37] Millions of Soviet citizens had already been sent back to the Soviet Union following the end of the war, as called for in this agreement. The principle of state sovereignty and the commitment toward building a postwar political order based on multilateral cooperation and international law mandated that this policy be continued. Unlike the post-World War I era, the allies were committed to protecting the sovereignty of the state over the sovereignty of the nation. Individuals were not given the right to choose their own nationality or form their own political communities as they were under the Versailles system.[38]

At the same time, many people had come to believe that the Holocaust was at least partially facilitated by the refusal of states to accept Jewish refugees from Nazi Germany. When the Nazis were unable to expel the Jewish populations from Germany and Eastern Europe, they resorted to elimination through genocide.[39] As we saw in chapter 4, the Western states had already committed themselves to building a new international order based on individual freedom and human rights. While it may have been in the interests of international security and peace to proceed with the repatriations and avoid a political conflict with the Soviet Union, this policy would have contradicted the Western approach to international order. The dilemma needed to be resolved. The presence of large numbers of refugees inhibited the UN member states from building their postwar international order under the auspices of the world

[36] Vernant, *The Refugee in the Post War World*, p. 31 and Holborn, *Refugees*, vol. I, p. 56.
[37] Gil Loescher, *Beyond Charity*, p. 47.
[38] See J. Samuel Barkin and Bruce Cronin, "The State and the Nation: Changing Norms in the Rules of Sovereignty in International Relations," *International Organization*, vol. 48, no. 1 (Winter 1994).
[39] Arendt, *Origins of Totalitarianism*, p. 269.

organization. As US delegate Eleanor Roosevelt argued, "As long as a million persons remain with refugee status, they delay the restoration of peace and order in the world . . . Collectively they present a sore on the body of mankind which it is not safe to ignore."[40]

This much everyone agreed. However, how political leaders would seek to resolve this "sore on the body" would be heavily influenced by the type of political order they wished to create. The Western states favored a liberal approach, viewing the issue as a political and social problem that should be resolved on the basis of individual choice. In the aftermath of the Holocaust, West European leaders believed that the situation of the stateless and displaced constituted a denial of human rights, as it would soon be proclaimed in the Universal Declaration.[41] Conversely, the Eastern states promoted the primacy of state sovereignty, and viewed the issue as a technical problem requiring more concerted efforts to facilitate repatriation. It was the Soviet position that the majority of those refusing repatriation were traitors, quislings, and war criminals who feared being held accountable for their offenses. They demanded that the United Nations uphold the Yalta agreement and the principles of the UNRRA.

The construction of the refugee in the postwar political order

It was obvious that the issue of displaced persons would not go away as quickly as most had thought. While the UNRRA had successfully dealt with most of the wartime homeless, the organization lost its political support over the issue of forced repatriations. A longer-term approach was necessary. In late 1945, Norway proposed that a new international organization be created to address the issue of refugees and stateless persons. Britain forwarded this proposal to the Preparatory Committee of the newly formed United Nations, which then referred the question to its Economic and Social Council (ECOSOC). For the first time, the international community agreed to address the issue of displaced persons on the basis of individual choice. In establishing the basic principle of UN involvement, General Assembly Resolution 45 stated, in part, that: "No refugee or displaced person who has fully . . . expressed valid

---

[40] United Nations General Assembly, *Official Records*, first session, second part, p. 1421.
[41] Holborn, *Refugees*, vol. I, p. 33.

objections to returning to their country of origin . . . shall be compelled to return . . ."[42]

Of course, what would constitute a "valid objection" would be the key question in defining a refugee and the type of international regime that would protect them. Realizing the enormity of the task, the General Assembly resolution also called for the creation of an international organization that would deal with the future of refugees and displaced persons. The task of developing proposals for this organization fell to the General Assembly's Third Committee (which deals with social, cultural, and humanitarian questions) and a Special Committee on Refugees and Displaced Persons that was created by ECOSOC to work out the details of an organizational charter. The debate within these bodies reveals much about the motivations and political approaches of the various states. Although the discussion was focused on the immediate problem of the "last million" people not repatriated by the UNRRA, two controversial issues emerged that would define future attempts to build an international protection regime for refugees.

First, who should be eligible for protection? That is, who should be counted as a refugee? The resolution of this question was the most important factor in determining the type of international refugee regime that would evolve. British representative Rendel was probably correct when he stated at an early meeting of the Special Committee that one's definition of "refugee" was rooted in his or her conception of the rights of the individual verses the rights of the state.[43] The Soviet approach toward economic development, domestic security, and social cohesion was highly state-centric, and the Soviets favored an international order in which state sovereignty took precedence over other values. From this perspective, the tie between a state and its citizens was an exclusive one, and individuals could not simply "opt out" and choose a new nationality. The Soviet Union, Poland, Yugoslavia, and Byelorussia all viewed an international protection regime that "resettled" rather than repatriated refugees to be at best an affront to state sovereignty and at worst a deliberate attempt to undermine the authority of the state within the refugees' countries of origin.[44]

---

[42] The text of the resolution can be found in Louise Holborn, *The International Refugee Organization: its History and Work, 1946–52* (Oxford: Oxford University Press, 1956), p. 598.

[43] Holborn, *Refugees*, vol. I, p. 36.

[44] See statements made by the Polish and Byelorussian representatives in UN Document A/C.3/SR.323 and 325.

From the Western perspective, the purpose of an international regime for refugees was to protect individuals who were forced to flee persecution by the state, which in liberal social contract theory is supposed to be the protector of last resort.[45] Yet while the Western states promoted the rights of the individual over those of the state, they also faced a liberal paradox that a refugee regime would be needed to help resolve. Liberal states support the protection of human rights, including the right to emigrate and seek asylum when those rights are denied. However, few of these states wished to absorb large numbers of people fleeing such situations, nor were they willing to surrender their sovereign right to establish immigration criteria. Trying to harmonize human rights principles with those of social and economic stability was a challenge to the construction of an international order based on law and freedom.

The second major issue to arise concerned the kind of organization that should be created. Specifically, what should be its mission and scope of authority? In creating ECOSOC and the many specialized agencies under its authority, the founding states had developed a UN order that would address a wide variety of social and humanitarian problems around the world. In doing so, the international community had assumed an unprecedented degree of responsibility for the welfare of the world's population, even though the primary task of development and prosperity would remain state-based. Thus, the discussion of refugee protection – which was one of the first items on the General Assembly's agenda – occurred within the context of a new concept of collective responsibility.

The records of the deliberations that occurred within the various UN bodies over the five years following the creation of the United Nations clearly suggest that those states that were most committed to the new UN-based international order were far more likely to support a stronger, more intrusive, and broader regime than those with a weak commitment to the organization.[46] Largely for that reason, American support for the refugee regime varied with its wavering support for multilateralism and international organization, while West European and Latin American support remained relatively strong and constant during this period.

At the early meetings of both the Third Committee and Special Committee, the West European states expressed support for a UN-based

---

[45] See Ronald Scheinman, "Refugees: Goodbye to the Good Old Days," *Annals of the American Academy of Political and Social Science*, special issue 467, *The Global Refugee Problem: US and World Response* (Beverly Hills: Sage Publications, 1983), p. 82.
[46] See, for example, the discussions in UN Document A/C.3/SR, p. 53.

organization that would exist on a semi-permanent basis. At the first meeting of the Third Committee, for example, British delegate P. J. Noel-Baker proposed that the United Nations assume the responsibility for protecting and determining the fate of those who had not been repatriated. He suggested that a UN special agency be created to facilitate this task. The United States supported the idea of a new organization to replace UNRRA, however it favored a temporary agency that would exist independently of the United Nations.[47] While the United States was a key founder of the world organization, it viewed it as a deliberative body rather than an operational agency and favored functional specificity rather than universalism as the organizing concept for the UN's activities.[48] The Soviet Union and Yugoslavia opposed both approaches, arguing that the future of the displaced was not an international issue and should be addressed through bilateral agreements between the countries of origin and the countries of refuge.[49]

In the end, the committees struck a compromise between the three approaches. The Special Committee drafted a constitution for a nonpermanent semi-independent specialized agency with a formal relationship to the United Nations. The newly created International Refugee Organization (IRO) would have a limited mandate: it would only work with the "last million" people whose status the UNRRA could not resolve and would have a nonrenewable life of only three years.

The IRO was the first international organization to make a sharp distinction between a "refugee" and a "displaced person." It was also the first to focus on the individuals seeking refuge rather than the group or category to which they belonged. Its constitution described a displaced person as one who was forced to leave his or her home due to conditions brought about by war or natural disaster. Although they lived outside of their country of citizenship, they still retained their nationality and were considered to be under the protection of their state of origin. Refugees, on the other hand, were considered to be victims or potential victims of political persecution and as such could neither return home nor rely on their states to provide diplomatic protection. In deference to the Soviet and Yugoslav position, the IRO constitution limited this definition to victims of Nazi, fascist, or quisling regimes; Spanish republicans; and those who were already outside of their country of origin

[47] UN Document E/REF/60, May 2, 1946.
[48] See Robert W. Gregg, *About Face?: The United States and the United Nations* (Boulder, CO: Lynne Rienner Publishers, 1993), ch. 1.
[49] UN document A/C.3/VR 28, June 28, 1946, p. 9.

and were unwilling or unable to avail themselves of their governments' protection.[50]

This definition clearly reflected the desire of the liberal states and their allies (including India and the Latin American countries) to place the protection of refugees within the context of an international order based on international law and collective responsibility. In particular, the West European states viewed refugees as possessors of human rights who were entitled to protection from the tyranny of state action. Louise Holborn, for example, argues that the creation of the IRO was designed specifically to uphold the purpose and principles of the United Nations, particularly those sections of the Charter that focused on promoting human rights and the dignity of the individual.[51] For this reason, the IRO mandate did not extend to displaced persons or economic migrants, even though in large numbers they could also constitute a threat to stability. The records of the deliberations within the two committees supports this contention. The Western delegates argued that all refugees should be given a right to seek asylum and freedom of movement, and that pending this determination, they should be under the protection of international law and the UN agencies administering the refugee camps.[52] As the Dutch delegate Sassen argued, "a person who has expressed his desire not to return to his country of origin is entitled to resettlement elsewhere as a basic human right."[53]

The delegates agreed that the IRO should protect all those awaiting a final resolution of their situations. As such, the organization maintained a network of camps to provide food, shelter, and medical care, and provided legal protection for those individuals certified as refugees.[54] Consistent with the emphasis on individual determination, the IRO registered and classified those requesting certification to ascertain whether they fell within the mandate of the organization.[55] Its main task, however, was the re-establishment of refugees through repatriation to the country of origin, integration into the country of refuge, or resettlement in a third country. In deference to the Soviet Union, the UN agreed to

---

[50] *Constitution of the International Refugee Organization*, part 1, section A in Holborn, *The International Refugee Organization*, appendix.

[51] Holborn, *The International Refugee Organization*, pp. 45–46.

[52] See, for example, UN document E/REF/73.

[53] UN Document A/C.3/VR, February 4, 1946, p. 24.

[54] The organization issued a "document in lieu of passport" that was recognized by thirty-two governments and allowed the refugees to travel freely and work in their country of refuge. Stoessinger, *The Refugee and the World Community*, p. 100.

[55] The IRO established a board of specialists comprising representatives from various countries to evaluate each case.

171

include in the IRO constitution a provision stipulating that repatriation would be the primary and preferred (although not exclusive) means for resolving the refugee issue.[56] However, by 1947 it was apparent that the border and regime changes that occurred after the war had created a new situation in which many of the refugees feared persecution should they return home. The IRO therefore began to switch its efforts from repatriation to resettlement, prompting the Soviet Union and East European states to withdraw from the organization.

Building an international protection regime for refugees

The creation of a refugee protection regime after World War II occurred within the context of plans to build an international order that promoted human rights and international law. In 1947, the UN Commission on Human Rights adopted a resolution calling on the General Assembly to assist those who lack the protection of a state to which they can assert their claims for human rights. They called on the Assembly to give: "early consideration . . . to the legal status of persons who do not enjoy the protection of any government, in particular, pending their acquisition of nationality as regards their legal and social protection and their documentation."[57]

With the impending end of the IRO approaching, France and Belgium proposed to the Third Committee that the United Nations create a new refugee organization with a broader mandate than that which was given to the IRO. The proposal sought to provide for the protection of refugees in a more open-ended and general way by adopting a universal definition of refugee and creating a high commissioner modeled after the Nansen office.[58] The majority of the members of the Third Committee agreed that the United Nations needed to move well beyond the limited work of the IRO in designing such an organization, and passed its recommendation on to the UN General Assembly. At its Fourth Session, the Assembly decided that the United Nations should create an office of high commission whose mandate would be broader and more comprehensive than that of the IRO.

The IGCR, the IRO, and the UNRRA all had been designed to work with refugees who had been displaced during and in the immediate

---

[56] See *Constitution of the International Refugee Organization*, Article II, paragraph I(a) in Holborn, *The International Refugee Organization*, appendix.
[57] UN Document E/600, paragraph 46.   [58] See UN Document A/C.3/529.

aftermath of World War II. In all three organizations, the preferred method of resolution was repatriation. The French and Belgian proposal was a radical departure from this approach in that it viewed the protection of refugees as an ongoing effort and did not prejudge the resolution of massive refugee flows. This provided the launching point for two years of deliberations that led to the most comprehensive refugee protection system to date. Most of the negotiations leading to the creation of the regime occurred with the Third Committee. As designed, the regime would consist of both a functional and a legal aspect: (1) an Office of High Commissioner on Refugees (UNHCR) to provide diplomatic protection and mobilize international resources to settle and/or repatriate its clients, and (2) a Convention Relating to the Status of Refugees that would impose legal obligations on states parties concerning their treatment of refugees.[59] It would be based on three fundamental principles: universality (establishing a general definition of refugees that would apply to all nationalities and political systems), legal protection, and *nonrefoulement* (prohibiting states from sending refugees back to their countries of origin).

From the beginning, the debate over the scope and principles of the regime reflected competing visions of the new international UN order. The Soviet Union and its East European allies (excluding Yugoslavia) boycotted those UN sessions in which the regime was being discussed, so the negotiations occurred among states with a relatively common view of international relations. The first and least controversial issue was that of defining a refugee. Drawing from their commitment toward building a liberal international order based on international law and human rights, the members of the committees quickly reached a consensus that refugees should be defined as those in need of international protection due to a "well-founded fear of persecution" from their states of origin. As the French representative Rochefort argued: "[This definition is] the very embodiment of the liberalism of the European countries. The hospitality offered by the countries of Europe was a service they rendered on behalf of all the United Nations to the cause of freedom and civilization."[60]

This reflected the prevailing belief that the problem of refugees was directly related to the actions of illiberal and autocratic governments. Former League of Nations official, John Simpson, for example, argued

[59] This distinction between functional and legal obligations is suggested by Goodwin-Gill, *The Refugee in International Law*, pp. 25–28.
[60] UN Document E/AC.32/SR.33, p. 8.

that "the cause of every refugee movement is tyranny . . ."[61] Similarly, historian Louise Holborn wrote in 1956 that "the chief causes of permanent refugee movements are intolerant nationalisms and the violence of dictatorial regimes," while John Stoessinger mused, the same year, that it is a "truism that refugees are produced as a result of the abuse of fundamental human rights."[62] Turkish representative Savut echoed this by arguing that refugees were by definition victims of persecution; that was all they had to demonstrate.[63] Dutch representative Beaufort also held that the problem of refugees was above all one of human rights and human dignity.[64]

In developing this definition, the Statute of the UNHCR created a universal protection system that applied without regard to particular nationalities or political systems. The principle of legal equality and nondiscrimination that is embedded in this definition essentially mirrored the concept of "citizen" that was the foundation for the liberal state. The inclusion of this "universal clause" in the UNHCR Statute would raise the number of refugees that fell within the competence of the office to 20 million people over the following decades.[65] Significantly, however, by specifically using the term "persecution" rather than "repression" the negotiators distinguished between those who only lived under an authoritarian regime and those who were specifically singled out as targets for the willful exercise of "extraordinary malevolence."[66] The delegates did not view fleeing persecution as the same as fleeing totalitarianism, nor did they include in their definition of refugee those who simply disagreed with or opposed a governing political system. In this way, the regime was designed to protect the human rights of those who were able to flee their oppressors, but did not make a judgment as to the nature of the political system that produced the refugees. This suggests that the creation of the regime was not, as some have argued, aimed at undermining the communist systems of Eastern Europe.

Equally significant is who this definition left out. Those fleeing other types of life-threatening situations such as war or natural disasters were not eligible for international protection. While there was much discussion within the Third and *Ad Hoc* Committees on whether to include

---

[61] Simpson, *The Refugee Problem*, p. 5.
[62] Holborn, *The International Refugee Organization*, p. 1; Stoessinger, *The Refugee and the World Community*, p. 180.
[63] UN Document A/C.3/SR.329, p. 362.　　[64] UN Document A/C.3/SR.325, p. 337.
[65] Stoessinger, *The Refugee and the World Community*, p. 165.
[66] I borrow this term from Zolberg, "The Formation of New States as a Refugee-Generating Process," p. 26.

"stateless" and "displaced" persons as refugees, a consensus quickly developed to give priority to victims or potential victims of human rights abuses and to leave the question of statelessness to a future time.[67] This suggests that the creators of the regime were not so much concerned with international security or instability *per se*, as much as they were concerned with the connection between security and the principles of human rights and international law.

The more controversial issue concerned the scope and mandate of the regime. Here the differences between the United States and its Western allies were most pronounced, reflecting their varying commitments to multilateralism, international law, and the UN political order. France, Belgium, Denmark, Britain, and Brazil proposed creating a permanent UNHCR with broad authority, a high degree of administrative autonomy, and a mandate that would include all present and future refugees throughout the world.[68] As the Belgian representative argued at a meeting of the *Ad Hoc* Committee, "the time has come to impose (the political responsibilities for protecting refugees) on states." By establishing a UNHCR as a watchdog, facilitator, and coordinator, states would be prodded into accepting this responsibility.[69] For the French the existence of the High Commissioner's office would provide a material confirmation of the universal rights of refugees and the "sacredness of the rights of asylum." It would also ensure that refugees were protected, not for political or partisan reasons, but in the name of the "international community."[70]

On the other hand, the United States and Australia favored a temporary organization with narrow authority, and a mandate that was strictly limited to assisting the IRO refugees, without taking in any new clients.[71] They proposed that the UNHCR mandate last only three years. The United States also wanted the High Commissioner's office to be small and that he or she not be permitted to raise or disperse funds for refugee projects. Finally, it was the American position that the UNHCR not take a comprehensive approach toward refugee protection, but rather respond to each situation on an *ad hoc* basis.[72]

The American position was consistent with its approach to the postwar international order and the role of international organizations in facilitating that order. As suggested above, the United States favored

[67] For the deliberations on this question, see UN Document E/SR.283–343, pp. 630–48.
[68] See UN Document E/SR.283–343, p. 625.   [69] UN Document E/SR.283–343, p. 621.
[70] UN Document A/C.3/SR.230–269, p. 103.   [71] Loescher, *Beyond Charity*.
[72] Holborn, *Refugees*, vol. I, p. 70.

functional specificity rather than universalism and an *ad hoc* rather than a comprehensive approach to those international issues that did not directly affect its foreign policy priorities. By 1950, the United States had substantially abandoned the UN's universalist approach toward international order in favor of regional and bilateral alliances.[73] For that reason, it created or helped to create several issue-specific refugee organizations that operated outside the UNHCR regime, for example the Intergovernmental Committee for European Migration (aimed at resettling economic migrants from European countries with a population surplus to those with labor shortages), the US Escapee Program (which encouraged defections from Eastern Europe), the UN Relief and Works Agency (for Palestinian refugees), and the UN Korean Reconstruction Agency.

US refugee policy after 1949 was focused exclusively on encouraging and supporting those fleeing communist countries.[74] Thus, throughout the early years of the organization, the United States refused to give the UNHCR any substantive support and actively tried to inhibit its ability to raise funds. Its position only changed when its leaders realized that many East European refugees considered returning to their countries of origin rather than languishing in underfunded refugee camps.[75]

While the large majority of European and Latin American states supported the more comprehensive and universalist position, the Third Committee and General Assembly agreed to a compromise. The UNHCR would have a broad mandate, accepting as refugees anyone who fitted the definition as stipulated in the Statute; however the high commissioner would have to seek the approval of the General Assembly prior to raising any funds. The Assembly voted against the US proposal to prevent the UNHCR from becoming involved in resettlement or repatriation activities, however it did agree to limit its mandate to an initial three-year period, with a review by the United Nations in 1953. The European and Latin American states agreed to this compromise with the understanding that it would in fact be renewed at that time, and that it would eventually become permanent.[76]

Although the UN members demonstrated a clear commitment toward protecting and resettling refugees, they were reluctant to provide the necessary funds for direct material aid. They also did not surrender

[73] Salomon, *Refugees in the Cold War*, p. 230.
[74] Loescher, *The UNHCR and World Politics*, pp. 54–56.
[75] Ibid., p. 74.
[76] Salomon, *Refugees in the Cold War*, p. 221; Holborn, *Refugees*, vol. I, p. 68.

sovereignty over their borders. The decision on whether to grant political asylum or allow refugees to remain in their countries for an extended period of time remained in the hands of the state of refuge.

Despite its early limitations, the UNHCR was revolutionary in that it provided a universal definition of refugees that could be applied in a wide variety of cases. The effect of the Statute was to authorize the high commissioner to protect those fleeing persecution on behalf of the international community.[77] Previous attempts to deal with refugee problems focused on selected national groups and specific categories of refugees. The office was charged with protecting refugees from forced repatriation, attacks by police or military from their home countries and exploitation by host countries. This protection would continue even after a refugee had been resettled or integrated into a new state and would only end when the refugee became a permanent resident or citizen. Its mandate also included securing identity and travel documents for its clients, assisting refugees in asylum cases, and working with states to secure access to a procedure for determining refugee status.[78] The high commissioner was authorized to undertake these protection efforts independently of state approval or cooperation.

Imposing legal obligations on states

Even as the UN states were negotiating the creation of a UNHCR, they simultaneously worked to develop a legally binding convention that would impose specific obligations on states in their treatment of refugees. From the beginning the UNHCR and the Convention were directly linked. To facilitate this process, ECOSOC established an *Ad Hoc* Committee on Refugees and Statelessness to draft a convention and examine the means of eliminating statelessness. Like the negotiations surrounding the UNHCR, the states decided to give priority to the question of refugees and leave the stateless question to a future committee.

There was a strong early consensus that the convention should adopt the UNHCR's persecution criteria in defining refugee, and that the heart of the Convention should be the principle of *nonrefoulement*, an obligation that would prevent states from returning refugees to their home states even if they entered their country illegally. In addition to establishing the same persecution criteria as the UNHCR, the Committee

---

[77] Holborn, *Refugees*, vol. I, p. 83.
[78] Goodwin-Gill, *The Refugee in International Law*, pp. 230–31.

also quickly agreed that a refugee also had to lack those rights that are normally embedded in one's citizenship status. The postwar political order was still rooted in the primacy of state sovereignty, and liberal theory viewed human rights as being derived from citizenship. As US delegate Eleanor Roosevelt argued, "a refugee who has the same rights and obligations as the nationals of the host country does not need protection."[79]

The main controversy concerned whether the Convention would be open ended and apply to future situations, or whether it would include only those whose refugee status was already determined. Again, the position taken by states was directly related to their commitments to promoting international human rights through multilateral action. The large majority of delegates supported the broader, open-ended definition, suggesting their commitment to an international order over the long term. Britain, France, and the Benelux and Scandinavian countries all favored a universal treaty that would include future, unknown, and unforeseen refugees.[80] In particular, France argued that it was necessary to include future refugees who might come into existence when current democracies come under the control of an authoritarian regime and whose persecution would provoke refugee flight.[81] Its representative to the *Ad Hoc* Committee further held that an individual does not cease holding basic human rights and fundamental freedoms simply because he or she is deprived of government protection.[82]

The United States favored a more limited definition of refugee that would be only apply to the pre-war, wartime, and immediate postwar period. Its representative, Louis Henkin, stated that the United States needed to know in advance the extent of its responsibilities in protecting refugees, that is, precisely to whom the convention would apply.[83] He proposed that the Convention only apply to refugees who were created by "events occurring prior to" the signing of the Convention in 1951. He argued that if new categories of refugees appeared in the future, they could be added through protocols to the Convention.

The other major controversy concerned whether the Convention should cover only European refugees or those who appeared anywhere

---

[79] UN Document A/C.3/SR.334, p. 389.
[80] Paul Weiss, ed., *Travaux Préparatories of the Convention Relating to the Status of Refugees, July 28, 1951*, pp. 64–67, 314–15, and 278–79.
[81] UN Document E/AC.32/SR.3, p. 11.
[82] Weiss, ed., *Travaux Préparatoires of the Convention Relating to the Status of Refugees*, p. 24
[83] UN Document E/AC.32/SR.3, p. 9.

in the world. Positions on this issue fell along the same lines as the time question.

In the end, a compromise was struck. At the Conference of Plenipotentiaries called by the United Nations to draft the final version of the Convention, the delegates agreed to the 1951 limit and to leave the interpretation of the geographic boundaries up to individual states. This compromise did not indicate a change in the position of the majority; they voted with the United States for practical reasons. The Venezuelan delegate, for example, supported the broader definitions, however he also said that such a definition would prevent the largest possible number of states from signing the Convention, particularly the United States.[84] France also agreed to the compromise, fearing that without it the Convention would never move forward. Britain, however, sought to remove both restrictions at the Conference, arguing that they were contrary to the universal principle of human rights.[85] It received strong majority support for including in the preamble a paragraph expressing the will of the states that the Convention apply beyond the limits set in the text. Opposition by the United States prevented this from being included in the body of the Convention, however the British were successful in securing an addendum to the Convention in the form of the Final Act. This stated, in part, that:

> the Convention would have value as an example exceeding its contractual scope that all nations would be guided by it in granting as far as possible to persons in their territory as refugees, and who would not be covered by the terms of the Convention the treatment for which it provides.[86]

While the Final Act was not legally binding, it enabled the UNHCR and many of the states parties to the Convention to apply the broader concept of refugee protection in practice until all limitations were eventually removed in the 1967 Protocol to the Convention. Until that time, there was a disjuncture between UNHCR "Statute refugees" (who could emerge from any part of the world at any time) and "Convention refugees" (who were subject to the time and geographical limits).

It is clear from following the deliberations that the treaty was designed to protect the basic human rights that would exist in a liberal

---

[84] UN Document E/AC.32/SR.5, p. 12.
[85] Statement by Lord Macdonald, UN Document A/C.3/SR.323, p. 330.
[86] Weiss, ed., *Travaux Préparatoires of the Convention Relating to the Status of Refugees*, Preamble.

international order. The preamble makes specific reference to Articles 6, 14, and 15 of the Universal Declaration of Human Rights.[87] This was not an incidental move. The representatives to the committee spent many days discussing and debating the preamble and in a broader sense the extent to which host countries should provide civil and economic rights to refugees.[88] Preambles to treaties are important inasmuch as they provide a guide for future interpretation by specifying the original intent of the drafters. They also create a context through which governments and lawyers can view the agreement.

The Convention is one of the most significant documents to emerge from within an international protection regime. It recognizes that refugees are an ongoing international actor requiring protection from the comity of nations, and designates them as a special class of people requiring particular human rights guarantees. It also establishes a universal code of rights and obligations and provides standards for their treatment by domestic political and legal systems. For example, it guarantees to refugees the same treatment as other foreign nationals.[89] Most importantly, it codifies the principle of *nonrefoulement* and bans states from expelling legal refugees except in exceptional circumstances related to national security. Even in this most extreme case, refugees are guaranteed the right to present counter-evidence in an independent, legitimate national court. This "due process" clause is at the heart of a liberal legal system; the United Nations characterized it as a "magna carta for refugees."[90]

Expanding the regime

Although it is beyond the scope of this study to examine how the regime expanded over the next several decades, a few points regarding this expansion are relevant. When the UNHCR and Convention were created, few of the representatives predicted the extent to which the refugee problem would skyrocket over the next twenty years. Yet the United Nations and its member states proved their commitment to refugee protection by

---

[87] Article 6 refers to the right of every individual to be recognized as a legal person before the law. Article 14 provides for the right to seek (although not necessarily be granted) political asylum. Article 15 holds that everyone has a right to a nationality.

[88] Weiss, ed., *Travaux Préparatoires of the Convention Relating to the Status of Refugees*, p. 23.

[89] See Nehemiah Robinson, *Convention Relating to the Status of Refugees: Its History, Significance and Contents* (New York: Institute of Jewish Affairs, 1952), pp. 6–7.

[90] See United Nations Department of Public Information, *Magna Carta for Refugees*, New York (August 1951).

responding each time it became apparent that it would. Over the next two decades, the General Assembly progressively expanded the high commissioner's mandate and functions. Within a decade it removed the requirement that he/she seek approval to raise funds and granted the office the authority to provide protection to all groups within its competence regardless of when they became refugees (in essence, canceling the time limitations imposed by the United States during negotiations).[91] Moreover, both the UNHCR and the General Assembly demonstrated an adeptness for responding to new situations.

The Hungarian Crisis of 1956 was the first major operation for the office and marked a transition from a body dealing with the immediate postwar era to a more general organization. The Soviet invasion of Hungary fueled massive refugee flows (about 200,000 people) into Austria and Yugoslavia. Most were judged to have had a "well founded fear of persecution" if they returned, and the UNHCR resettled them quickly and efficiently.[92] In 1958, the General Assembly authorized the UNHCR to assist refugees from the Algerian war of independence facing persecution, marking the first time it became involved in a non-European situation.

By the 1960s, the Convention did not technically apply to the large majority of refugees being protected by the UNHCR. It was clear that the time and geographic limits had to be removed. In 1963, the Assembly passed a resolution calling on states to treat all new refugee groups "in accordance with the principles and the spirit of the convention," in essence, to ignore the 1951 time limit imposed in the original document.[93] This led to the eventual official removal of both constraints through the 1967 Protocol to the Convention. Not only did every Convention state accede to the Protocol, some states that did not ratify the original treaty (such as the United States) did so by signing the Protocol. The Convention was now universal, applying to all situations regardless of time, location, or political system.

Conclusion

The protection of refugees in the twentieth century occurred within the context of state-building and international order construction. The regimes created after both world wars clearly reflected the priorities and

---

[91] See General Assembly resolutions 1129 (XI) and 2039 (XX).
[92] Loescher, *Beyond Charity*, p. 68.
[93] See General Assembly resolution 1959 (XVIII).

values of those building the postwar order and in both cases the refugee system helped to reinforce the type of order favored by the participating states. In the interwar period, the League of Nations only recognized as refugees those displaced persons who were members of specific national groups. The choice of which groups would qualify was not random but rather represented those who could not integrate into the newly created and reorganized national states of the postwar era. Those who could emigrate to a kin state or remain under the League's minority protection system were not included. On the other hand, during the post-World War II period, ethnic criteria were not even considered. Rather, those creating the regime did so on the basis of human rights and individual choice. Refugees were reconceptualized as those denied the protection of their state and who in fact faced persecution by the very entity that was created to ensure their basic rights and fundamental freedoms.

An examination of process and motivations refutes the realist arguments that the regime reflected the interests of the most powerful state and that it was designed as an ideological weapon to help fight the Cold War. Loescher offers one of the most insightful and compelling accounts of the way the system was used by the United States as part of its conflict with the Soviet Union. It is clear that the differences between the Eastern and Western blocs accounted for their varying views on how the refugee question should be addressed. This, however, is far different from demonstrating that the regime was a Cold War institution. The main problem with Loescher's analysis is that it implicitly imputes American motives to the Europeans. The records of deliberation clearly demonstrate that the United States and Western Europe were far apart on this question. Moreover, the circumstantial evidence is equally strongly stacked against this interpretation in two crucial areas.

First, the basic principles of the regime were created in 1946 and 1947, before the Cold War had begun. During the early deliberations within the Third and Special Committees, it was clear that the West Europeans wished to cooperate with the Soviets and worked to alleviate at least some of their concerns. In fact the first major wave of East European refugees did not emerge until after the 1948 Czechoslovakian coup, and neither the United States nor the West Europeans at the time believed that this would spread to other parts of Eastern Europe. It is therefore not clear how the regime was geared toward facilitating defections from the Soviet camp.

Second, it is difficult to argue that the United States helped to create an international protection regime for refugees as a tool to fight the Cold

War when it refused to support any of the work of the UNHCR until 1956. In fact, in the early years, according to Loescher's own account, the United States actively tried to impede its activities. Moreover, foreshadowing a practice that it would repeat several times in future years, after forcing major changes in the 1951 Convention over the objections of the majority, the United States then refused to sign or ratify the treaty until two decades later.

At the same time, I did not find sufficient evidence to suggest that humanitarian motives were dominant. While the state representatives certainly demonstrated concern for the well-being of the refugees, this did not appear to be a major influence determining the outcome of the deliberations. The refusal of the UN members to extend the protection system to the thousands of "stateless" and "displaced persons" who were languishing in camps or roaming Europe support this contention. Certainly humanitarian-based NGOs played an important role within the IRO and the UNHCR, however in all cases it was a support role, not a policy one. They did exert a moral influence on the UN debate; however the regime was ultimately state inspired and state based.

Finally, the institutionalist account does capture at least some of the dynamics that led to the creation of both refugee regimes. Clearly states had an overlapping interest in addressing the problem of refugees inasmuch as they had to go somewhere and it was more efficient to develop a set of rules and procedures for determining how and where. This explanation would also account for the attitude of the United States; its location far from the shores of Europe and Asia created far less urgency for seeing that the problem be resolved. This, however, does not explain why each regime chose to define refugees the way that it did, nor does it answer the question of why states did not simply close their borders and allow the most vulnerable countries to absorb the potential flood of international homeless. Certainly an island nation like Britain – one of the most enthusiastic supporters of the regime – could have done so.

The concepts of refugee and asylum are both products of the consolidation of the nation-state system and the corresponding notion of territorial sovereignty that dominated the world in the twentieth century. The aftermath of both world wars saw strong efforts by the victorious powers to strengthen the nation-state, and equally staunch efforts to address the problems that arose with those who could not be absorbed into the system. After World War I, the legitimation of the national state required that all nationalities either be given their own state or integrated into an existing one as a designated national minority. This system, however, could not work for those who did not fit within one of these categories, and thus the international community had to protect them. After 1945, the legitimation of citizen-based states – with the accompanying set of inherent rights that was considered to be embedded in citizenship – required that the international community become involved whenever those whose most basic rights were violated fled the country. States thus agreed to extend a guarantee of protection to foreign nationals against the exercise of jurisdiction by another state, when the fear of persecution prevented those individuals from returning home.

While the principles of *nonrefoulement* and protection against retribution by the refugees' home states have become a regular part of contemporary international politics, countries have demonstrated inconsistent dedication to securing the welfare of those displaced by persecution. Thus, the ultimate success of the regime created in 1950 is still an open question. On this issue, Gil Loescher's observation about the plight of many contemporary refugees is particularly sobering:

> Many (refugees) are confined to camps or ramshackle settlements close to the borders of their home countries where, deprived of opportunities to work or farm . . . depend on international charity for survival. Refugees are often separated from members of their families, exposed to the dangers of armed attack, subject to many forms of exploitation and degradation and haunted by the constant fear of expulsion.[94]

[94] Gil Loescher, "Introduction," in Gil Loescher and Laila Monahan, *Refugees and International Relations* (New York: Oxford University Press, 1989), p. 1.

7   Conclusion

The politics of international relations is very complex. While it is the primary responsibility of foreign policy officials to promote the security and prosperity of their own populations and domestic institutions, most political leaders are also aware that under conditions of structural interdependence they must occasionally act to further the interests of the broader international society of which they are a part. This produces a constant tension between parochial interest and international responsibility. All other things being equal, political leaders will favor these interests even at the expense of their allies and partners. Yet all things are often not equal. States create international political orders to institutionalize one set of political values over competing ones, and to secure a particular distribution of resources and authority within a region or system. The principles, institutions, and practices that underlie this order shape the political environment through which they interact. States therefore have a strong interest in its future. When the cohesion of this international order is threatened, many political leaders find that they must act on behalf of the collectivity.

In this study, I examined one particular institutional practice aimed at furthering the interests and progress of international society. The preceding chapters considered how states attempted to maintain cohesive political orders by protecting those population groups whose vulnerability was most likely to threaten the stability of these orders. I argued that this practice of protecting foreign populations represents a definable form of institutional cooperation, which I called International Protection Regimes (IPRs).

As the four cases demonstrate, IPRs are not a new phenomenon in international politics. Political leaders have created at least four such institutions over the past seventy-five years alone. Although the empirical chapters focused on the twentieth century, states have collectively attempted to regulate the internal relations of states by protecting segments of their populations since the Peace of Westphalia in 1648. IRPs have, however, become progressively more complex and more intrusive. This can be attributed to the increasing institutionalization of international politics. Each of the regimes was embedded within a broad international order represented by a large intergovernmental organization. Through these organizations, states have not only attempted to formalize their relationships with one another, but also to develop a common set of political principles and values that would govern these relationships.

Since the end of World War I, the organization of international life has increased dramatically, symbolized in the dramatic rise in the number and complexity of international organizations and the number of multilateral treaties states have chosen to sign.[1] Whether this growth signals a new level of international responsibility and obligation for states largely depends on whether there is indeed a correlation between the depth of institutional commitment and the willingness of states to act on behalf of the collectivity. In answering this question, the findings of this study could be illustrative.

This chapter has three goals. First, it will revisit the theoretical claims I advanced in the Introduction in light of the empirical evidence presented in the four case studies. Second, I will discuss the broader theoretical implications suggested by the results of the project. In particular, I will develop the concept of "institutions for the common good" by building from the study of one such institution, international protection regimes. Finally, I will discuss how the theoretical and empirical findings of this study can help us to better understand contemporary international politics.

Evaluating the evidence: the creation of the regimes

In the introductory chapters I argued that political leaders create international protection regimes in the aftermath of a major systemic change

---

[1] The number of intergovernmental organizations has increased from 37 in 1909 to almost 300 in 2000. This does not include the thousands of nongovernmental organizations. See A. LeRoy Bennett, *International Organizations: Principles and Issues* (Englewood Cliffs, NJ: Prentice Hall, 2000), p. 2. Moreover, during the fifty-year period between 1899 and 1950, states signed approximately forty legally binding multilateral treaties. During that same period after 1951, the number is closer to 200. See the Multilaterals Project, The Fletcher School, Tufts University, http://fletcher.tufts.edu/multilaterals.html.

when they believe them to be necessary for the stability of a highly valued regional or global political order. During this "solidarist moment," political leaders seek to reorganize the foundation of international relations in part by requiring new states to adopt principles of governance that are compatible with the principles of the new order. This requires that they protect vulnerable segments of the population from threat by the newly emerging dominant segments because a dissatisfied population or ruling elite may be prone to revolt, secede, or annex themselves to a neighboring state. Depending on the type of states that are created, this could mean protecting the population from the government, the government from the population, or one segment of the population from another. The leading states will thus establish mechanisms to protect populations within states that could potentially disrupt the political order. These mechanisms are the heart of the international protection regime.

In contrasting this approach with several alternative explanations, I argued that IPRs are not primarily designed to secure a favorable balance of power, further some type of parochial state interest, resolve cooperation problems, benefit powerful domestic constituencies, or promote humanitarian goals. Rather, they are institutions designed primarily to further the progress of international society by promoting its principles. The empirical evidence supports these arguments in at least three ways: the process through which the regimes were created, the choice of target population, and the degree to which there was a correlation between support for the regime and level of commitment to the international order.

Process

In each of the four cases, the regimes were created by a core group of states as part of a broader process aimed at building a new political order. None of the IPRs were imposed on the system by a hegemonic power seeking to enhance its parochial interest. Nor did they emerge as an extension of alliance politics or an effort to resolve some type of cooperation problem aimed at achieving some type of material benefit. Rather, the regimes were the outcome of considerable deliberation and discussion by states seeking to develop generalized principles of order. In examining the substance of these discussions, it was clear that the participants sought to reach a broad consensus rather than prevail in a competitive negotiation. While there was considerable debate and some political maneuvering, there was little evidence that strategic calculation, power balancing, or attempts to gain economic or military advantage were significant motivations in the creation of any of the regimes. Moreover, with the exception of the post-World War I case, the regimes were created through broad-based multi-issue organizations where all states had an equal vote.

The creation of the national minority protection regime after World War I occurred at the Paris Peace Conference, and was part of a broader political settlement that focused on the political reorganization of Central and Eastern Europe. The allies created the regime in the process of trying to reconcile the national state with the existence of national minorities in Central and Eastern Europe. It was based on a general consensus among the key allies that the principle of national self-determination would provide the most stable, peaceful, and just foundation for the new European order. In this sense, the protection of national minorities was not incidental to the creation of a new European order, but was in fact one of its most important aspects. Significantly, the issue was separated from the military settlement (or example, imposing limits on Germany's armed forces), and did not reflect geopolitical considerations.

The regime to protect European citizens was created primarily by former Resistance leaders as part of an effort to build a cohesive regional order based on the liberal state. The idea of creating a European human rights charter and a mechanism for enforcement emerged during the early meetings of the Council of Europe, a purely political organization that was not involved in any of the security discussions that would lead to the creation of NATO. The members of the Council believed that since the autonomous citizen was the foundation of the liberal state, the supranational protection of individuals was the best method for preventing the rise of authoritarianism in Western Europe. At the same time, these discussions occurred independently of those aimed at facilitating economic cooperation and trade liberalization. The motives were therefore not primarily economic but political.

Similarly, the protection of ethnic communities after the end of the Cold War was a direct outgrowth of the OSCE's efforts to integrate the eastern and western regions of Europe and build a new political order based on democratic governance and institutionalized cultural pluralism. The regime was created as part of a wholesale reorganization of the OSCE aimed at building a stable political community among its fifty-five members. The representatives thus decided to create an office of high commissioner on national minorities (HCNM) after they determined that an integrated Europe could not remain coherent if a two-tiered system developed between a pluralistic, cosmopolitan West and a exclusionary, intolerant East. The goal of the office was to undermine the political foundation of the national state in favor of a multicultural one. Significantly, the OSCE built the regime as part of its "Third Basket," which dealt with issues of democratic governance and human rights, rather than its "First Basket," which addressed security questions.

Concern with building a new postwar political order was also evident in the construction of the protection regime for refugees after World War II. The issue of refugee protection was one of the first items on the agenda of the newly formed United Nations, however the question was deliberately separated from that of general security. For that reason, the resolution of the refugee problem was not placed on the Security Council agenda, but rather was sent to the Economic and Social Council and the General Assembly's Third Committee, which dealt with humanitarian and social issues. The purpose of the regime was to place those forced to flee persecution under the protection of the international community.

At the same time, the influence of nongovernmental organizations and norm entrepreneurs was limited in all of the cases, suggesting that governmental interests, rather than those of civil society, were dominant. While NGO pressure and activity was present in all four cases, the organizations themselves were not involved in any of the discussions that led to the creation of the regimes. Moreover, I did not find any evidence to indicate that the state representatives were promoting NGO causes or interests.

Choice of population

In all four cases, the creators of the regimes chose to protect only those populations that they believed could destabilize the newly created and reorganized states. Those who did not fit within these categories were excluded, even if their protection could have provided some benefit to the creators. In seeking to stabilize certain types of states, the protectors made general commitments that applied to all those who fell within the definition of protected population, without knowing in advance who might benefit from the system in the future. I did not find any correlation between the identity of these populations and the promotion of a favorable balance of power or the achievement of some material benefit by the protectors. At the same time, since other equally vulnerable populations were excluded from each of the regimes, humanitarian concerns do not appear to be a significant factor in the choice of target populations.

For example, after World War I, the allies chose to protect only national/ethnic minorities within the successor states to the Hapsburg, Russian, and Ottoman empires. The historical record demonstrates that their primary concern lay with the potential of these groups to undermine the foundation of the new national states. Thus, the allies sought to facilitate the assimilation of ethnic minorities into the majority cultures as a means toward creating a stable system of national states in Eastern and Central Europe. Those abused by their governments who did not fall into one of these ethnic categories were ignored.

These priorities changed dramatically after World War II. During this period, the Council of Europe was most concerned with protecting the "human rights" of individual citizens (who in republican theory were considered to be the foundation of the liberal state) even though large numbers of national minorities remained "trapped" in a dozen East and Central European states. The members of the Council did not grant ethnic minorities any special consideration, and their status as a political community was not recognized. Rather, the historical record reveals a belief that protecting the rights of individual citizens was the best guarantee against liberal states descending into authoritarianism.

While the OSCE was also concerned with promoting human rights and democratic governance in the New Europe after the end of the Cold War, the organization did not initiate a protection regime for individual citizens within the OSCE area. Rather, it chose to protect, empower, and recognize ethnic communities, who the OSCE members regarded as foundational groups in the definition of the newly created and reorganized states in Central and Eastern Europe. Unlike in the interwar period, however, the purpose was not to facilitate assimilation into national states, but to transform national states into multicultural ones. The state representatives believed that only by conferring a special external status on such communities could multicultural states remain stable.

The protection of refugees provides perhaps the strongest link between the identity of the protected population and the principles of international order. In both the interwar and post-World War II regimes, only those who fit the narrow definition of refugee were permitted to benefit from the protection system. In the interwar period, the League of Nations recognized only those members of specific national groups who could not integrate into the newly created and reorganized national states of the postwar era. Refugee status was thus tied directly to membership in a recognized ethnic group. After World War II, refugees were reconceptualized as those who were forced to flee states that abrogated

190

their responsibilities to provide for the protection of their basic human rights. The criterion for refugee status was fear of persecution regardless of nationality or the type of political system from which they were fleeing. At the same time, in both regimes, thousands, if not millions, of other displaced and stateless persons were excluded.

Level of commitment

In all four cases, there was a positive correlation between the depth of support for the regime and the depth of support for the new political order. After World War I, the United States and Britain were the strongest advocates of both a European order based on the principle of nationality and an intrusive regime to protect national minorities within them. France was consistently the most skeptical of both. Similarly, those states that were most committed to greater regional integration and the progress of a liberal West European order after World War II also advocated the most intrusive enforcement provisions in the Human Rights Convention and Human Rights Court. In this case, Britain proved to be the most aloof on the question of integration and was also the state which advocated the weakest possible human rights regime.

This connection was also evident in the construction of the refugee regime. The strongest supporters of a United Nations based international order were also those promoting the broadest and most liberal protection system for refugees. Specifically, France, Belgium, the Netherlands, and Britain all fought for an open-ended regime that would protect refugees from anywhere in the world at any time. On the other hand, after the United States shifted its support from a UN-based international order toward regional alliances and *ad hoc* institutions in 1950, it became the primary advocate of a highly restricted protection system with a short life and a limited mandate.

Evaluating the success of international protection regimes

While the extent to which IPRs are successful in practice has not been a central focus of this study, this question can provide some evidence about the motivations and commitment of those creating protection systems. That is, in most cases the success of a regime is at least partly a function of its design, and this in turn reflects the creators' expectations concerning its utility. In examining this question, there are at least four standards that can help us to ascertain whether the regimes reflected parochial state interest, overlapping self-interest, humanitarian concern, or a commitment toward the progress of an international society: first, did the creators *expect* the regimes to succeed when they constructed them or did they build them with the expectation that they would have no significant impact on international politics? Second, did the creators accept the responsibilities stipulated in the regimes as political or legal obligations? Third, did the creators *act* as if they were obligations, that is, did the practice follow the rhetoric? Fourth, *why* did the regimes succeed or fail?

In answering these questions, a realist could argue that political leaders generally assume that IPRs are unlikely to have any significant effect on international politics and require few legal obligations, and therefore the costs of participation are low. Moreover, under these conditions it would be relatively easy to withdraw if the institution threatened some state interest in the future. In this line of analysis, failure is likely to occur as a result of predictable collective action problems and when there is change in the relative power and interests of the participants.

An institutionalist could argue that IPRs will remain robust as long as they continue to provide some benefit to their members.[2] States will accept their responsibilities as long as the other states are meeting their commitments as well. From this perspective, political leaders would likely assume that the regime would be successful, however their expectations would be limited to the well-specified narrow issue areas stipulated by the rules and principles of the institution. The regime will fail when it no longer provides the expected benefits even if the distribution of power remains constant.

A cosmopolitan/humanitarian approach would assume a relatively high degree of sincerity on the part of the creators, the internalization of a moral obligation by the leadership and relative consistency in practice. The success or failure of the regime would be determined by the ability of domestic and transnational actors to maintain political pressure on state officials.

An international society approach should also expect a high degree of sincerity by the founders, however it would view state obligation as being political or legal rather than moral or humanitarian. Similarly, it would predict that the success or failure of the regime be directly related to the success or failure of the international order rather than changes

---

[2] See, for example, Keohane, *After Hegemony.*

in the distribution of power or the benefits accrued by individual states.

Using these standards, I found a moderate degree of correspondence to the IS approach. In all four cases it was clear that the creators of IPRs fully expected them to succeed and considered the institutions to be an important component in the postwar political order. The discussions and deliberations that led to the creation of each institution were robust, often divisive, and continued over an extended period of time, indicating that the participants viewed the outcome as serious and significant. In addition, all of the negotiations involved moderate to high-level state officials, for example, heads of state, top diplomats, and foreign affairs ministers. This suggests that the participating governments considered these institutions to be more than incidental "talk shops."

The expectations were highest within the human rights regime created by the Council of Europe. The transcripts of the meetings where the European Convention was drafted clearly indicate that the participants knew that the regime would be highly intrusive and expected it to help maintain the democratic nature of government in Western Europe. My interviews with the staff of the HCNM also revealed high expectations for success on the part of the OSCE, largely because the target states were strongly committed to becoming part of the New Europe and joining its Western-created institutions. The lowest expectations surrounded the establishment of the minority rights regime after World War I. While the Supreme Council did assume that the regime would succeed in facilitating the assimilation of the minorities into the national culture, they greatly underestimated the potential problems that would arise in this process. In other words, they were sincere in their commitments, but did not assume that the costs of enforcement would be significant. Similarly, in examining the deliberations and debates within the United Nations Third Committee and ECOSOC special committees, it was clear that the participants believed that the protection of refugees would be a successful and significant part of the postwar reconstruction effort; however, they also did not foresee the extent to which the refugee problem would explode over the next several decades.

In all four cases the empirical evidence strongly suggests that the creators accepted their responsibilities as political and legal obligations. This is most strongly demonstrated in the two cases where these obligations were codified into legally binding treaties (the European Convention on Human Rights and the Refugee Convention). The debates surrounding the details of the agreements suggested that the representatives clearly understood that their governments were assuming significant legal obligations in signing these documents. The League of Nations and OSCE regimes were not based on binding treaties (at least not binding on the protectors), however the substance of the discussions that led to the creation of these regimes also suggests a clear acceptance of political obligation. This sense of obligation was much stronger among the OSCE states than within the League. In creating the office of the HCNM, the members accepted that they might be called upon to collectively enforce its provisions at some future date. This was also true of the interwar minority protection regime, which is why the Supreme Council transferred responsibility for enforcement to the League of Nations.[3]

At the same time, in all four cases the substance of the deliberations suggests that the political leaders clearly viewed their obligations as being directed toward other states – and to a lesser extent toward the international organizations to which they belonged – rather than to the individuals and groups who were the beneficiaries of the protection efforts. This suggests that they believed that they were assuming political rather than moral obligations.

The congruence between obligation and practice was more complicated. While the Council of Europe, the OSCE, and UN clearly acted on their responsibilities (at least in the early years of the regimes), the commitment by individual members of these organizations varied. The empirical chapters suggest that the best predictor of states' compliance with their obligations is (once again) the strength of their commitment to the political order. The European human rights system has been highly robust for more than half a century, with states accepting even negative judgments from regional human rights courts. Both individually and collectively, Council members have acted against other states (even those with which they have a close relationship) when they believed such states to be violating their obligations.

Similarly, the members of the OSCE have acted collectively in trying to enforce the multicultural principles of New Europe by strongly supporting the work of the high commissioner on national minorities and putting strong political pressure on those who violate their commitments. In some cases, the OSCE took direct action to coerce compliance

---

[3] Despite the ultimate failure of the League, in 1919 the leaders of the great powers believed that their membership in the organization entailed significant political and legal obligations. See Gary B. Stroller, *The League of Nations, 1919–1929* (Garden City Park, NY: Avery Publishing Group, 1995).

by reluctant states (including, for example, diplomatic, economic, and occasionally military sanctions). At the same time, the organization has also demonstrated significant limits to this action, particularly when a powerful state was accused of violations. Thus, for example, the OSCE has been far more likely to pressure an East European state than Russia. In this sense, the politics of realism has been ever present.

State support for the refugee regime has varied wildly over time, however most states have complied with the letter of their obligations under the refugee convention, even if some have attempted to circumvent its spirit. In fact, even the United States – the most reluctant of the creator states – found it necessary to devise a legal mechanism to keep Haitian refugees out of the United States for fear of violating the Convention.[4] Moreover, as new refugee and "refugee-like" situations arose over the years, the United Nations responded by dramatically increasing the authority and budget of the UNHCR.[5] Again, realist politics has impeded the work of the regime, but the institution has remained robust for half a century.

The greatest divergence between obligation and practice can be found in the League's national minority protection system. The organization established an elaborate system for receiving and investigating complaints, however by the end of the 1920s it was clear that states were no longer willing to risk diplomatic or political conflicts with violating states. While there were some attempts to strengthen compliance and enforcement, few states honored their commitments after its initial success.

Finally, the success/failure issue suggests a positive correlation between the durability of IPRs and the coherence of the international order. Of the four cases, only the League's minority protection system was a complete failure. While it did help thousands of national minorities to assimilate into the major culture of their states, ultimately it could not prevent large-scale discrimination, repression, and ultimately genocide of said minorities. As indicated in chapter 3, the regime rose and fell with the League itself. A realist would be correct in pointing out that states proved to be unwilling to sacrifice their own resources and that state commitments became worthless in the face of economic depression and

[4] See David G. Savage, "Haitian Intercept Policy Backed by High Court," *Los Angeles Times*, June 22, 1993, p. 1.

[5] The UNHCR currently assists almost 20 million refugees, a twenty-fold increase from its 1950 client base. In addition, its staff has increased many hundredfold to 5000. See UNHCR, *The State of the World's Refugees*.

regional insecurity. As I suggested in the Introduction, much of global politics reflects the realist world of conflict and competition. Yet it is also true that the entire system of international relations broke down during this period (including trade relations and security alliances), and that in the absence of a strong commitment to the progress of international society, there is no foundation upon which to maintain an international protection regime.

The other regimes fared better. The continued strength of the Council of Europe's human rights regime was maintained even during the darkest days of the Cold War when security concerns were presumably paramount. Similarly, the Office of the High Commissioner on National Minorities remained robust even during and after ethnic conflicts in the Balkans and the former Soviet republics. In both cases, state commitments toward the principles of the European political orders remained firm.

As suggested above, the international protection system for refugees remains the longest-standing global IPR in history. Even when conflicts within the United Nations prevented the organization from fulfilling its collective security functions during the Cold War, the protection of refugees expanded as new situations arose. Whether this regime has been "successful" of course depends upon definitions of success, however the basic principles of *nonrefoulement* and international responsibility for the plight of refugees have remained firm.

At the same time, the cases do not demonstrate any direct correlation between the degree of humanitarian concern and/or cosmopolitan ideology and the success or failure of the regimes. In other words, I do not find any evidence that the failure of the regimes is in any way related to a decrease in humanitarian impulses nor success to a "moral awakening" on the part of either the global population or political leaders.

Theoretical implications

Although this book has focused specifically on one form of institutional cooperation – the protection of foreign populations – the results suggest broader theoretical implications for the study of international relations. I argued in the introductory chapter that some practices in international relations are best understood within the context of an international society of states. Such an approach shifts the focus from the parochial interests of individual states toward the broader political and social structures of which states are a part. The concept of international society highlights the relationships that states form with each other and examines the political values and social norms that underlie them. The implicit assumption is that states are as concerned with maintaining these relationships as they are with prevailing in a competitive environment.

Some relationships are purely functional and can best be explained by institutionalist theories of expected utility and overlapping self-interest. States do not need a well-developed international society in order to conclude bilateral trade agreements, for example. Other relationships, such as alliances, are primarily opportunistic.[6] They are created through strategic calculation, and we can account for them with theories based on the balance of power and state interest. Yet these forms of interaction and cooperation can produce only limited benefits. In order to pursue longer-term goals and create greater predictability in their relationships with one another, under certain conditions states will agree to recognize the authority of legal rules and institutions that bind each other to follow a set of common practices. It is the recognition by states that these rules and institutions constitute a fundamental foundation of their relationships that differentiates an international society approach from that of realism or institutionalism. As Andrew Hurrell points out, rationalist (or what I term individualist) models of cooperation miss the crucial link between the costs and benefits of specific legal rules and the role of international law as constitutive of the structure of the state system itself.[7]

This study was based on the premise that international protection regimes can develop only within an international society of states. The empirical chapters supported this claim by demonstrating that the creators were indeed conscious of certain common values and conceived themselves to be bound by a common set of rules in their relations with each other.[8] Moreover, through counterfactual inference, each chapter also suggested that these regimes would not have arisen had the conditions for an international society been lacking.

Yet the implications from this study are greater than a simple confirmation of the existence of an international society. Such a finding in and

---

[6] As Lord Palmerston remarked in a 1948 speech to the House of Commons, "We have no eternal allies and we have no perpetual enemies. Our interests are eternal and perpetual, and those interests it is our duty to follow."

[7] Andrew Hurrell, "International Society and the Study of Regimes: A Reflective Approach," in Volker Rittberger, ed., *Regime Theory and International Relations* (New York: Oxford University Press, 1993), p. 59.

[8] This is Hedley Bull's minimal condition for the existence of an international society. See his *Anarchical Society*, p. 13.

of itself would be somewhat banal. There is already a wealth of literature on the theoretical and historical foundations of international society, although most of it is generated solely by European scholars.[9] The more interesting and ultimately more significant questions concern *how* international societies form and the degree to which theories based on them yield different expectations than more traditional systems theories. This study touched on these issues by examining how and why states create institutions whose primary aim is to promote the progress and stability of international society. In doing so, I tried to specify the conditions under which a self-selected community of states will define and defend the norms and institutions of international society as opposed to domestic or cosmopolitan concerns.

Building on the theories developed in chapters 1 and 2, the findings can contribute to the debate in two important areas in international relations theory. First, it can offer some suggestions for resolving the tension between the "solidarist" and "pluralist" conceptions of international society, an issue that is currently part of an ongoing conversation within the English School.[10] Second, it can advance the broader debates within the discipline of International Relations by suggesting how the conceptualization of the international environment as a complex interaction among realist, functionalist, pluralist, cosmopolitan, and solidarist elements can help us to better understand contemporary politics. In this area, I hope to help to bridge the gap between American social science and the communitarian approach of the English school. I will address these questions separately, turning first to the solidarist/pluralist issue.

[9] See, for example, C. A. W. Manning, *The Nature of International Society* (London: London School of Economics, 1962); Herbert Butterfield and Martin Wight, eds., *Diplomatic Investigations* (London: Allen and Unwin, 1955); Martin Wight, *Systems of States* and Hedley Bull, *The Anarchical Society*. For more recent treatments see Adam Watson, *The Evolution of International Society* (London: Routledge, 1992); Armstrong, *Revolution and World Order*; and Timothy Dunne, *Inventing International Society: A History of the English School* (London: Macmillan, 1998). There are, of course, also hundreds of articles that draw from an international society perspective.

[10] This tension between pluralist and solidarist conceptions of international society is particularly prominent in much of the literature on human rights and humanitarian intervention within the English School. See, *inter alia*, Nicholas Wheeler, *Saving Strangers: Humanitarian Intervention in International Society* (Oxford: Oxford University Press, 2000); Robert Jackson, "Pluralism and International Political Theory," *Review of International Studies*, vol. 18, no. 3 (1992); R. J. Vincent, *Human Rights and International Relations* (Cambridge: Cambridge University Press, 1986); and Nicholas Wheeler and Tim Dunne, "Hedley Bull's Pluralism of the Intellect and Solidarism of the Will," *International Affairs*, vol. 72 (1996).

Since the early days of the British Committee on the Theory of International Politics (from which most theories of international society are derived) there has been a tension between "pluralist" and "solidarist" (or Grotian) conceptions of international society.[11] The former presents a minimalist version, arguing that international society is primarily composed of a disparate group of states, many of which represent wildly different belief systems and conceptions of justice and the good. This makes it very difficult to develop an international consensus around a single set of goals and values beyond the fundamental rules of coexistence. Thus, the primary function of international law is to maintain this plurality by ensuring that each state is able to pursue its own ends without compromising the independence and autonomy of other states. For this reason, Hedley Bull argues that the collective goals of states in an international society are limited to the preservation of the nation-state system, the stability of territorial possession, the mutual recognition of sovereignty, the regulation of violence, and the sanctity of agreements.[12] Any attempt to move beyond these goals could endanger the foundation of international order by threatening its fundamental principles of sovereignty and nonintervention. This has been the dominant conception within the international society literature over the past few decades.

A solidarist approach, on the other hand, views international society as reflecting or at least potentially reflecting greater social cohesion among states with respect to the development and enforcement of common standards of international conduct.[13] In a solidarist international society, relationships between the constitutive units are regulated by a broader scope of common values and principles than simple self-preservation and order within the society of states. Nicholas Wheeler and R. J. Vincent, for example, argue that there is often a mutual compatibility between protecting the national interest, promoting international order, and enforcing commonly held values, in their cases humanitarian concerns and human rights.[14] In particular, Wheeler's study of humanitarian intervention convincingly demonstrates a willingness by states to move beyond norms of coexistence to address the concerns of individuals who are threatened by gross and consistent abuses by their

[11] See Dunne, *Inventing International Society*, pp. 100–04.
[12] See Bull, *Anarchical Society*, pp. 16–19. Bull's body of work, however, reveals a tension between this view and a more solidarist approach to international society. See, for example, his *Justice in International Relations*. This publication is also known as the "Hagey Lectures."
[13] See Bull, "The Grotian Conception of International Society."
[14] Nicholas Wheeler, *Saving Strangers*; Vincent, *Human Rights and International Relations*.

governments. Thus, a solidarist conception makes a distinction between just and unjust wars and legitimate and illegitimate treatment of domestic populations, while a pluralist conception does not. From this perspective, states can not only develop a "universal" conception of justice and the good, they can also provide the means for collectively implementing it.

This study found both aspects of international society to be present in the four cases. In each case, political leaders responded to a systemic shock by attempting to establish a basic foundation for a rule-guided international society that would facilitate the peaceful coexistence and independence of its members. Thus the primary goals of three of the organizations studied in this book – the League of Nations, the United Nations, and the Organization for Security and Cooperation in Europe – were to provide new diplomatic mechanisms for conflict management and the peaceful resolution of disputes.[15] For this reason, the first concern of political leaders in drafting the postwar settlements was the establishment and/or legitimation of juridical borders and the provision of security in the new order.

At the same time, the evidence also suggests that in each case political leaders developed deeper conceptions of collective interest that went beyond the minimal goals of mutual survival, territorial sovereignty, and coexistence. While these conceptions did not reflect "universal" values (in the sense that they were ubiquitous and unchanging), they did represent a consensus concerning the nature of security, justice, and order among the core members of an emerging international society. This is evident in the agreement by states to act on the basis of nonminimalist principles such as national self-determination, human rights, democratic governance, cultural plurality, and international responsibility for the persecuted.

This suggests that there are elements of pluralism and solidarism in most international societies. As Wheeler demonstrates in his study of humanitarian intervention, political leaders may be very reluctant to help "strangers" – particularly if there are no tangible benefits but potential risks in doing so – but they often find that they are expected to do exactly that by domestic constituencies, international institutions, nongovernmental organizations, and other states.[16] Clearly, in

---

[15] See for example, Article 1 of the United Nations Charter, the preamble to the Covenant of the League of Nations, and the Ten Principles of the Charter of Paris for a New Europe, respectively.

[16] Wheeler, *Saving Strangers*.

the four cases studied in this book, a wide variety of political actors held extremely high expectations for the creators of the international protection regimes to act in accordance with the principles they had espoused during and after the conflicts that preceded their creation. For example, after promoting the principle of national self-determination as a key war aim for World War I, the allies could not easily retreat on their commitment after the conflict ended. Moreover, it was equally clear that the political leaders could not create the kinds of political orders they sought without taking affirmative action to protect the very principles that underlay these orders.

This suggests that solidarism – unlike cosmopolitanism – does not have to reflect a universal approach to international relations, nor does it need to be based on abstract moral or ethical considerations. It is not a solidarism with humanity that motivates state behavior, but with a self-selected, constructed political community. Within such a community the members hold a collective understanding of what constitutes "justice," "order," "security," "prosperity," and the like. Absent this community of beliefs and interests, there can be no basis for a solidarist international society. Thus, for example, the members of the Council of Europe believed that peace and security were tied to democracy and this in turn was linked to a collective commitment toward the protection of human rights.

Similarly, the allies after World War I believed that stability and order required a congruence between state and nation in the organization of Central and Eastern Europe, and that this required action to protect those who could undermine the national state. At the same time, the members of the OSCE held a radically different set of beliefs about the stability and legitimacy of the national state than did the Council of Five. Learning from the previous decades, but most importantly from the immediate past, the OSCE believed that the principle of cultural plurality was the most just and stable solution to the problem of political integration within the new and reorganized states of Europe. In protecting the corporate integrity of ethnic communities within its member states, they sought to *undermine* the national state. In both cases, states exhibited solidaristic behavior, however their definitions of justice and stability differed considerably.

Another gap in the conversation between pluralists and solidarists has been the question of how a solidarist international society can develop within a state-centric system. If, as realists and pluralists correctly observe, states represent a wide variety of belief-systems and often find themselves pursuing conflicting interests, how do they develop the type of consensus necessary to promote a single set of political values and principles? Or, as a realist may argue, what is to prevent defections from states at the expense of the others when they find the opportunity to do so? This is indeed an important and difficult question. In chapter 2 I argued that the opportunity for creating such a consensus does not often arise, but can usually be found in the wake of a devastating conflict or some other major shock to the international system. I hypothesized that this "solidarist moment" is made possible by a sense of solidarity that often develops among a group of political leaders sharing an experience of high intensity and long duration. During the struggle – and in the process of trying to create a new regional or global order – opportunities for greater consensus arise. This in no way guarantees success, but it does provide a permissive condition.

In the empirical chapters such shocks as world war, genocide, "extraordinary malevolence" against one's citizens, and a rapid and unpredicted end to a generation of Cold War created such conditions. These circumstances were bolstered by an intersubjective consensus among key political leaders concerning the cause of the recent conflicts. Certainly ideology and national values played a role, however in the process of trying to determine the best arrangement of authority, territory, and values in the post-crisis order, the leaders were guided by their beliefs concerning what would provide the most stable and just solution to the dilemmas faced by the reconstructors.

For example, after World War I, the allies saw the denial of nationhood and self-determination as the primary cause of instability and conflict, and therefore agreed that nationalism would be the most stable and just fundamental organizing principle for the new order. West European leaders after World War II came to a different conclusion. A decade of genocide and authoritarianism convinced the new political leaders – many of whom had fought together in the Resistance – that the denial of human rights and democratic governance was the primary cause of insecurity and war. The formation of the Council of Europe reflected a solidarist belief in the ability of West European states to promote a common set of values as the foundation for a new political order. The end of the Cold War saw a rapid swing from great optimism to guarded pessimism, as the new liberal order envisioned in the Charter of Paris was swallowed up by ethnic conflict and intolerance in Eastern Europe. Members of the OSCE became convinced that the problem was the proliferation of nationalizing states in the region.[17] Finally, as we saw in chapter 6, the key members of the United Nations came to a consensus that the primary cause of refugee flows was persecution and gross violations of human rights.

The solidarist element of international society is also suggested by the nature of the organizations states have created as the institutional expression of their common principles. The League of Nations, Council of Europe, United Nations, and Organization for Security and Cooperation in Europe all represent more than a series of attempts to resolve cooperation problems and provide for peaceful coexistence. The charters, organizations, and practice of these institutions suggest a far broader and more ambitious social and political agenda.[18] The League was involved in establishing labor standards and developing international law into a single global legal system; the Council of Europe was concerned with maintaining democracy and human rights in Europe; the OSCE promoted democratization and liberalism among its fifty-five member states; and the United Nations has been involved in a wide variety of social, cultural, and humanitarian issues including alleviating hunger, providing global health care, and prosecuting war criminals. In each case, the organization represented in part the common political principles and values of its founders.

International society and IR theory

The English School approach has had a respectable but limited impact on the field of International Relations in the United States. In part this can be explained by its association with a "traditionalist" methodology during the 1950s and 1960s, at a time when American political science was adopting more rigorous behavioral and social scientific methods.[19] It can also be explained by differences in academic culture

---

[17] Rogers Brubaker defines a nationalizing state as one that is ethnically heterogeneous but whose dominant elites promote the language and culture of the nominally state-bearing nation. See his *Nationalism Reframed*, p. 57.

[18] See, for example, Article 23 of the League Covenant; Article 1 of the Statute of the Council of Europe; and Section VI of the CSCE's *Challenge of Change*; and the preamble and Article 55 of the UN Charter.

[19] See, for example, Hedley Bull, "International Theory: The Case for a Classical Approach," and J. David Singer, "The Incomplete Theorist: Insights Without Evidence," both in Klaus E. Knorr and James N. Rosenau, eds., *Contending Approaches to International Politics* (Princeton: Princeton University Press, 1969).

and, regrettably, a degree of parochialism on the part of some American scholars. During the past decade, however, there have been a number of attempts to bridge the gap between the two academic traditions, as scholars from both continents have begun to publish in each others' journals. More importantly, the adoption of sociological approaches by many American political scientists and the entrance of social constructivism into the mainstream of the International Relations literature has created a greater foundation for commonality.

This study contributes to this conversation by demonstrating how the attributes of an anarchic international *system* can be compatible with those of a rule-governed international *society*. It has not been the purpose of the book to promote an international society analysis at the expense of other frameworks such as realism and institutionalism. As I noted in the introduction, English School theories argue that the global environment contains aspects of a Hobbesian (realist) state of nature, a (Grotian) international society, and a Kantian (cosmopolitan) world community. The interesting question is therefore not which element is the most prominent in world politics – the institution of sovereignty clearly favors parochial interest – but rather the conditions under which states are most likely to act according to the demands presented by one of these conceptions as opposed to the others, at any given time.

I have argued that those states with the greatest stake in the progress of an international society are the most likely to act in support of its fundamental principles and they are most likely to do so when the cohesion and stability of the collectivity are at stake. Under normal circumstances, political leaders tend to take international society for granted. On a day-to-day basis, states engage in routine diplomatic interactions with one another without considering the vital role the institution plays in maintaining communication and facilitating cooperation. They conclude trade agreements, assuming that their partners will adhere to their commitments, without taking into account the role customary treaty law plays in making this assumption possible. And when disagreements escalate into military conflict, most political leaders assume that it will be conducted according to conventions of warfare. That is, they expect that soldiers will wear uniforms, that their armies will make a distinction between combatants and civilians, and that both sides will mostly conform to the limits imposed by the laws of war.

Thus, when diplomats are held as hostages, when states routinely violate their treaty commitments, or when an illegitimate authority randomly attacks a building packed with thousands of civilians, political leaders will act to reaffirm the basic political values of international society. While any of these circumstances could provide an opportunity for rival states to take advantage of the situation and improve their own competitive position, this rarely occurs except when international society has deteriorated to the point of collapse. To do otherwise risks undermining the most fundamental institutions that allow for predictability and stability in international relations. Thus, for example, few states will recognize territorial or border changes created through military aggression, even if such changes could provide them with some type of material benefit. For this reason, Iraq's annexation of Kuwait in 1990 provoked near-unanimous condemnation from states throughout the world, including Iraqi allies and those who believed that Iraq had a legitimate grievance against Kuwait.[20]

This is particularly true for states that have invested considerable political resources in the success of a regional or global political order. Once the states of Western Europe determined that the creation of a liberal community of democratic states would be in their long-term interest, for example, they became intimately tied to the progress of the regional institutions that made its continuation possible. Any threat to these institutions would also be a threat to their own futures. Similarly, the stability of the postwar multilateral global trading system required that states defend and promote the principles of the GATT and WTO, even when doing so would not be in their immediate interest.

I have argued that the values which represent the fundamental goals of a society (and can be considered at the core of its *raison d'être*) constitute the common good of the collectivity. As such, the common good is concerned with the preservation and general welfare of the collectivity itself. This "good" is manifested in institutions, many of which are created in the midst of threatening disorder to the collectivity. Thus, the Western powers created the GATT largely out of their concern with the total breakdown of international trade that occurred prior to World War II and the Europeans formed the Council of Europe in the wake of decades of authoritarianism and horrendous human rights abuses. One could argue, then, that states are most likely to create institutions that support the fundamental goals of an international society when their preferred political values are threatened.

---

[20] For example, Security Resolution 660 (which condemned the Iraqi invasion of Kuwait and demanded an immediate and unconditional withdrawal) was approved 14–0. See United Nations Resolutions, 2932nd meeting of the Security Council, August 2, 1990.

In the Introduction, I argued that any institution that is created primarily to promote, preserve, and/or extend the principles of a regional or global political order or collectivity is an "institution for the common good." In this book I examined one type of institution that primarily reflects the element of international society. The case studies confirm IPRs to be an institution for the common good, in the sense that they were designed to further the progress and welfare of international society or at least the international order. That is, their fundamental purpose was not to protect populations but to protect the international order. Thus, for example, the protection of national minorities was designed primarily to promote the stability of a European society of national states based on the principle of self-determination.

If this theory is indeed generalizable, we should be able to extend this analysis to other institutions addressing different issues but generally serving international society. One such example is the war crimes tribunal. Traditionally the prosecution of war crimes has been initiated by the winning states against the losing parties in a conflict, a practice known as "victor's justice."[21] However, since the early 1990s, states who were neither parties to the conflicts nor allies with any of the belligerents have collectively established international tribunals to investigate and prosecute war crimes in the Balkans, Rwanda, and East Timor. Like the international protection regimes studied in this book, these institutions did not enhance the power or economic advantage of the creators, nor were they the result of alliance politics or strategic calculation. Rather, their purpose has been to promote the rule of law in international relations, by enforcing multilateral treaties that prohibit the most egregious forms of state abuses during wartime.[22] While no single country has accrued any military or economic benefit from these tribunals, they have served to reinforce an important political value of international society – limitations on the use of violence by states – and thus were initiated on behalf of the common good.

[21] See, for example, the London Agreement of August 8, 1945 (officially known as the Agreement by the Government of the United States of America, the Provisional Government of the French Republic, the Government of the United Kingdom of Great Britain and Northern Ireland and the Government of the Union of Soviet Socialist Republics for the Prosecution and Punishment of the Major War Criminals of the European Axis).
[22] See, for example, the Convention on the Prevention and Punishment of the Crime of Genocide, adopted by the UN General Assembly on December 9, 1948 and the Convention (IV) Relative to the Protection of Civilian Persons in Time of War, adopted by the Diplomatic Conference held in Geneva, August 12, 1949.

Consistent with the theories discussed above, states established these institutions when they perceived the cohesion and stability of the collectivity to be at stake. Following the end of the Cold War, all of the major powers committed themselves to building a new international order based on the rule of law, democratic governance, human rights, and collective responsibility for enforcing fundamental international norms.[23] Yet this vision was threatened by Serbia's policy of ethnic cleansing, Indonesia's widespread atrocities against East Timorese civilians, Rwanda's genocide against the Tutsi population, and other practices that states have considered to be unacceptable. Expanding its powers under Article VII of the UN Charter, the Security Council declared these and other similar practices to be a "breach of the peace," and agreed to prosecute the most egregious violators regardless of on which side of the conflict they stood.[24]

The United Nations took a further step toward ensuring the durability of this institution by creating an International Criminal Court. The purpose of the Court, as stated by its creators and within the documents leading to its adoption, is to promote the principles of human rights, the rule of law, nonaggression, and individual accountability, all liberal values in a liberal international society.[25] The Court is unlike any other judicial institution in the history of international relations. For the first time, individual leaders, commanders, and soldiers can be held responsible for genocide and other types of war crimes by the international community. The Court is a universal legal body that has jurisdiction within any state that has signed the treaty (139 signatories and 78 parties as of July 2002). Since the tribunal is composed of judges who do not represent any state, political considerations are greatly muted, although not totally eliminated. Thus, it does not serve the interests of any particular state, nor can any single state use it for its own purpose. It is an institution of international society, designed to further the political values of that society.

---

[23] See Conference on Security and Cooperation in Europe, Charter of Paris for a New Europe, Paris, November 19–21, 1990, "A New Era of Democracy, Peace and Unity."

[24] On Serbia, see United Nations Security Council resolution 827 (1993), adopted by the Council at its 3217th meeting, on May 25, 1993. On East Timor, see Security Council Resolution 1264 (1999), adopted by the Council at its 4045th meeting on September 15, 1999. On Rwanda, see United Nations Security Council Resolution 955, adopted by the Council on 8 November 1994.

[25] The jurisdiction of the court includes crimes of genocide, crimes against humanity and war crimes. See Rome Statute of the International Criminal Court, adopted by the UN Diplomatic Conference of Plenipotentiaries on July 17, 1998, Article 5.

On another level, international law itself can be considered an institution for the common good. While governments certainly stand to gain materially from the general regulation of state behavior and the broad articulation of legitimate norms and practices, the legalization of international relations promotes the progress and general welfare of international society and thus acts on behalf of the common good. Since by its very nature international law applies equally to all sovereign states, its scope is universal extending to unforeseen circumstances. There are some who argue that international law is the law of the strong and that its purpose is to maintain a status quo that benefits the most powerful states.[26] Even if true, once constituted, international law provides for generalized principles of conduct that apply in all circumstances regardless of the parties involved. As the United States has discovered, its own government has to follow international law when it works against the American interest, even when its representatives had largely written the rules.

This analysis can also be applied to the institution of peacekeeping, a practice that requires many states to place their own military forces in danger in regions where they may not have any strategic or economic interest. The institution of peacekeeping evolved as a form of noncoercive conflict control when Cold War constraints prevented the Security Council from taking steps permitted in the Charter.[27] It is a clear institutional expression of international society's principle of limiting violence and providing for the peaceful resolution of disputes. Both of these principles became fundamental goals of contemporary international society with the development and expansion of the United Nations after World War II. The creation of this institution was not a result of strategic interaction among states but rather an innovative program initiated by the secretary-general and approved by the members. Over the past decade, the Security Council has expanded the role of the peacekeepers to include statebuilding, civil administration, facilitating democratization, promoting human rights, disarming militias, protecting populations from attack, caring for displaced persons, and even

---

[26] This approach is known as Critical Law Theory, although this would also be consistent with some types of realism. See, for example, David Kennedy, "The New Stream," in Robert Beck, Anthony Arend and Robert Vander Lugt, eds., *International Rules: Approaches from International Law and International Relations* (New York: Oxford University Press, 1996).

[27] See Boutros Boutros-Ghali, "Empowering the United Nations," *Foreign Affairs*, vol. 71, no. 5 (Winter 1992/93), p. 90.

enforcing Security Council resolutions.[28] While the decision to send or withhold peacekeepers in a particular situation is highly political (subject to the interests of the permanent members of the Security Council), the institution itself serves the broader function of promoting the peaceful resolution of disputes.

Understanding a complex world

Although this book has focused on institutions for international society, the English School approach promotes a broader conception of international relations that includes competition and conflict as well as cooperation; humanitarian concerns as well as state centrism. This conceptualization of the international environment as a complex interaction between realist, pluralist, cosmopolitan, and solidarist elements can help us to better understand contemporary politics. In particular, it can help us to better explain the crucial components of world politics that individualist-based theories leave out, and highlight the obligations that states assume as members of international society.

By the end of World War II, one could argue that a global international society based on territorial sovereignty, international law, multilateral cooperation, and diplomatic communication had penetrated all parts of the world. This was not necessarily the result of a "new enlightenment" by idealistic leaders or norm entrepreneurs. Rather, it reflected the domination of the globe by the nation-state system and the development of a highly institutionalized world polity in which such states organized themselves in terms of universalistic models such as sovereignty, territoriality, citizenship, socioeconomic development, and rationalized justice.[29] This did not eliminate conflict and competition (as some early idealist and functionalist theories predicted), however it provided a common framework through which political leaders could interpret behavior, make judgments, and identify cooperation and defection.

One way of understanding how this international society has developed is to examine the complex nature of the United Nations. Over the past generation, the United Nations has been the principal institutional

---

[28] See, for example, Olara Otunnu and Michael Doyle, *Peacemaking and Peacekeeping for the New Century* (New York: Roman and Littlefield, 1998).

[29] See John W. Meyer *et al.*, "World Society and the Nation-State," *American Journal of Sociology*, vol. 103 (1997), p. 148.

manifestation of this global international society (in both its positive and negative forms), and as such embodies its contradictions and complexities.

The United Nations was originally conceived primarily as a collective security organization, yet its goals, practices, and institutional structure suggest a far broader and more ambitious social and political agenda.[30] It is an organization of, by, and for sovereign states, yet it is also a semi-independent actor staffed with a semi-autonomous civil service.[31] Its constituency is the states that comprise the membership, yet it also serves a wide range of nonstate actors, regional organizations, and even individuals without regard to their nationality or to the internal boundaries that separate them. As such it reflects the complex interaction between the various elements that comprise an international society: the realist emphasis on security and state interest, the institutionalist focus on functional cooperation, the cosmopolitan concern with human welfare, and the solidarist interest in promoting common values and principles among states.

Consistent with the realist element in international society, the United Nations largely reflects the distribution of power and capabilities among its members. It was created after World War II by the winning coalition, and substantive authority rests with the great powers through the Security Council. Despite the idealistic conception of the Council as the trustee for world peace and security, in practice this body represents the interests of its permanent members, who dominate the organization's enforcement mechanisms.[32] The primary intergovernmental function of the organization – the coercive control of state conduct – represents the conventional wisdom of balance of power and conflict management theory: that order in a multistate system is dependent upon the ability of states to check and control each other's behavior.[33] During the Cold War, the organization's security policies largely reflected the dynamics

---

[30] Both the preamble and Article 55 of the UN Charter list such cosmopolitan goals as securing social justice, human rights, social progress, better standards of living, and solutions to problems in health, education, and welfare.

[31] See, for example, Thomas Weiss, David Forsythe, and Roger Coate, *The United Nations and Changing World Politics*, 2nd edition (Boulder: Westview Press, 1997), p. 93.

[32] See, for example, N. D. White, *Keeping the Peace: the United Nations and the Maintenance of International Peace and Security* (Manchester: Manchester University Press, 1997), chs. 3–6.

[33] See Inis Claude, "Reflections on the Role of the UN Secretary-General," in Benjamin Rivlin and Leon Gordenker, eds., *The Challenging Role of the UN Secretary-General: Making "The Most Impossible Job in the World" Possible* (Westport, CT: Praeger), p. 257.

of bipolarity, and subsequently the interests of the only remaining superpower, the United States.[34]

The United Nations also reflects the element of functional cooperation found in the pluralist and institutionalist conceptions of international relations. While much of the organization's focus is on promoting security and resolving interstate conflicts, many of its activities and programs are geared toward overcoming cooperation and collaboration problems on issues that are of mutual concern to the member states. For example, the Universal Postal Union provides a forum for cooperation between postal services and fulfills an advisory, mediating, and liaison role that allows for the smooth exchange of mail across borders. The Office for Drug Control and Crime Prevention works to strengthen international action against drug production, trafficking, and drug-related crime and formulates international policies and cooperative practices to fight crime on a global level. In both cases, they provide the type of coordination functions discussed in institutional theories of cooperation. More ambitiously, the World Bank helps to resolve a difficult collective action problem by providing the world's largest sources of development assistance to poor countries.

The organization also has a strong cosmopolitan element, initiating humanitarian projects to help individuals regardless of their nationality. The decision to create an Economic and Social Council reflects this. For example, the United Nations Children's Fund helps children living in poverty in developing countries, works to reduce childhood death and illness, and to tries to protect children in the midst of war and natural disaster. Similarly, the World Food Program works to eliminate or at least greatly reduce global hunger, and the World Health Organization tries to eradicate epidemic, endemic, and other diseases. While these programs cooperate with governments, their clients are individuals and they tend to work most closely with nongovernmental organizations (see Table 1).

The political implications of this analysis and the theories discussed in this book are clear. States have obligations toward international society that they must be willing to meet or lose the predictability and stability that allows them to act on the international stage. If institutions for the common good are indeed aimed at furthering the welfare and progress of this society, then it is incumbent on all governments to

[34] See John Stoessinger, *The UN and the Superpowers* (New York: Random House, 1966), p. 178.

Table I *Elements of contemporary international politics*

Element of international politics	Types of institutions	Primary goal	Contemporary organizations
Realist	Alliances, security regimes, arms control agencies	Promote state interests, provide for regional or global security	NATO, Organization for the Prohibition of Chemical Weapons
Functionalist	Trade associations; economic and environmental regimes; functional agencies	Resolve specific types of cooperation problems; promote overlapping self-interests among states	World Trade Organization, World Bank, Universal Postal Union, Office for Drug Control and Crime Prevention
Pluralist	Diplomacy, international law	Facilitate the independence and peaceful coexistence among a disparate group of states	UN Security Council, regional and global peacekeeping forces, OAS, OAU, ASEAN
Solidarist	Institutions for the common good	Promote and preserve the principles and values of an international society	International protection regimes, International Criminal Court, International Labor Organization
Cosmopolitan	UN specialized agencies	Provide for the well-being of individuals in international civil society	UNICEF, World Food Program, World Health Organization

support them, particularly when their principles are threatened. Thus, for example, the US refusal to support the International Criminal Court has undermined its attempt to prosecute war criminals in the Balkans and Rwanda. This in turn threatens the liberal notion of holding individual leaders responsible for acts of genocide and crimes against humanity. Similarly, American failure to adequately support the very peacekeeping operations it helped to create threatens the core concept of collective conflict management. While there may be some immediate domestic or parochial gains from this type of behavior, the long-term effects on the international order could be devastating for a state that has long sought to be a leader in the international society of states.

Bibliography

Adler, Emanuel. Seeds of Peaceful Change: the OSCE's Security Community-Building Model. In *Security Communities*, ed. Emanuel Adler and Michael Barnett. Cambridge: Cambridge University Press, 1998

Arendt, Hannah. Concerning Minorities. *Contemporary Jewish Record* 8 (3) 1945: 357–78

Origins of Totalitarianism. New York: Harcourt BraceJovanovich, 1951

Aristotle. *Politics*. Book III. Oxford: Oxford University Press, 1995

Armstrong, David. *Revolution and World Order: The Revolutionary State in International Society*. Oxford: Oxford University Press, 1996

Art, Robert and Robert Jervis. The Meaning of Anarchy. In *International Politics: Anarchy. Force. Political Economy and Decisionmaking*, 2nd edition, ed. Robert Art and Robert Jervis. Boston: Little. Brown and Company, 1985

Bagley, T. H. *International Protection of National Minorities*. Geneva: Georg, 1950

Barber, Benjamin. *Jihad vs. McWorld*. New York: Times Books, 1996

Barkin, J. Samuel and Bruce Cronin. The State and the Nation: Changing Norms in the Rules of Sovereignty in International Relations. *International Organization* 48 (1) 1994: 107–30

Barnett, Michael. Sovereignty, Nationalism and Regional Order in the Arab States System. *International Organization* 49 (3) 1995: 479–510

Bauer, Otto. *The Question of Nationalities and Social Democracy*, trans. Joseph O'Donnell. Minneapolis: University of Minnesota Press, 2000

Beddard, Ralph. *Human Rights and Europe: A Study of the Machinery of Human Rights Protection of the Council of Europe*. London: Sweet and Maxwell, 1973

Bendix, Reinhard. *Kings or Peoples: Power and the Mandate to Rule*. Berkeley: University of California Press, 1978

Bennett, A. LeRoy. *International Organizations: Principles and Issues*. Englewood Cliffs, NJ: Prentice Hall, 2000

Bérenger, Jean. *A History of the Habsburg Empire. 1700–1918*, translated C. A. Simpson. London: Longman, 1997

Betts, Richard K. Systems of Peace or Causes of War? *International Security* 17 (1) 1992: 5–43

Bloed, Arie. ed. *The Conference on Security and Cooperation in Europe: Analysis and Basic Documents, 1972–1993*. London: Kluwer Academic Publishers, 1993

Two Decades of the CSCE Process: From Confrontation to Co-operation. In *The Conference on Security and Cooperation in Europe: Analysis and Basic Documents, 1972–1993*, ed. Arie Bloed. London: Kluwer Academic Publishers, 1993

Boutros-Ghali, Boutros. Empowering the United Nations. *Foreign Affairs* 71 (5) 1992/93: 89–102

Boyd, A. and F. Boyd. *European Movement and the Council of Europe*. London: Hutchinson and Company, 1950

Breuilly, John. *Nationalism and the State*. Chicago: University of Chicago Press, 1994

Brinkley, Douglas and David Facey-Crowther. *The Atlantic Charter*. New York: St. Martin's Press, 1994

British Foreign Office. The Settlement. Memorandum by the Political Intelligence Department, 18 November 1918, FO 608/435

Brubaker, Rogers. *Nationalism Reframed: Nationhood and the National Question in the New Europe*. Cambridge: Cambridge University Press, 1996

Bull, Hedley. The Grotian Conception of International Society. In *Diplomatic Investigations*, ed. Herbert Butterfield and Martin Wight. London: Allen and Unwin, 1966

International Theory: The Case for a Classical Approach. In *Contending Approaches to International Politics*, ed. Klaus E. Knorr and James N. Rosenau. Princeton: Princeton University Press, 1969

The Anarchical Society: A Study of Order in World Politics. New York: Columbia University Press, 1977

Justice in International Relations. The 1983–84 Hagey Lectures. Waterloo, Ont.: University of Waterloo, 1984

Burley, Anne-Marie. Toward an Age of Liberal Nations. *Harvard International Law Journal* 33 (2) 1992: 393–406

Butterfield, Herbert and Martin Wight. eds. *Diplomatic Investigations*. London: Allen and Unwin, 1955

From International System to International Society: Structural Realism and Regime Theory Meet the English School. *International Organization* 47 (3) 1993: 327–52

Buzan, Barry. International Society and International Security. In *International Society After the Cold War: Anarchy and Order Reconsidered*, ed. Rick Fawn and Jeremy Larkins. New York: St. Martin's Press, 1996

Buzan, Barry, Charles Jones and Richard Little. *The Logic of Anarchy: Neorealism to Structural Realism*. New York: Columbia University Press, 1993

Callahan, David. *Between Two Worlds: Realism. Idealism. and American Foreign Policy After the Cold War*. New York: HarperCollins Publishers, 1994

Caporaso, James. International Relations Theory and Multilateralism: The Search for Foundations. *International Organization* 46 (3) 1992: 599–632

Carr, E. H. *The Twenty Years' Crisis. 1919–1939: An Introduction to the Study of International Relations*. New York: Harper and Row, 1939

Chandler, David. *Bosnia: Faking Democracy After Dayton*. London: Pluto Press, 1999

Checkel, Jeffrey. Why Comply? Social Learning and European Identity Change. *International Organization* 55 (3) 2001: 553–88

Chigas, Diana. Bridging the Gap Between Theory and Practice: The CSCE High Commissioner on National Minorities. *Helsinki Monitor* 3 (4) 1993: 27–41

Churchill, Winston. *His Complete Speeches. VII. 1943–1949*, ed. Robert Rhodes James. London: Chelsea House Publishers, 1974

Claude, Inis. *National Minorities: An International Problem*. New York: Greenwood Press, 1955

   Power and International Relations. New York: Random House, 1962

   Collective Legitimation as a Political Function of the United Nations. *International Organization* 20 (3) 1966: 367–79

Cobban, Alfred. *The Nation State and National Self-Determination*. New York: Crowell, 1970

Connor, Walker. *Ethnonationalism: The Quest for Understanding*. Princeton: Princeton University Press, 1994

Cooper, Richard. *The Economics of Interdependence: Economic Policy in the Atlantic Community*. New York: McGraw-Hill, 1968

Council of Europe. *Consultative Assembly Official Reports*. August. Strasbourg, 1949

   Consultative Assembly. First Session. 10 August–8 September 1949. Strasbourg, 1949

   Collected Edition of the "Travaux Préparatoires" of the European Convention of Human Rights, vol. I, May 11 – September 8, 1949. The Hague, 1975

   Consultative Assembly. Ordinary Session. 1950. Documents. Strasbourg, 1950

   Collected Edition of the "Travaux Préparatoires", vols. I–V. The Hague: Martinus Nijhoff, 1975

Cox, Robert with Timothy Sinclair. *Approaches to World Order*. Cambridge: Cambridge University Press, 1996

Craig, Gordon and Alexander George. *Force and Statecraft: Diplomatic Problems of our Time*. New York: Oxford University Press, 1995

Cronin, Bruce. *Community Under Anarchy: Transnational Identity and the Evolution of Cooperation*. New York: Columbia University Press, 1999

Dahl, Robert. *Dilemmas of Pluralist Democracy: Autonomy vs. Control*. New Haven: Yale University Press, 1982

Davies, Norman. *Europe: A History*. New York: Oxford University Press, 1996

De Port, A. W. *Europe Between the Superpowers: The Enduring Balance*. New Haven: Yale University Press, 1979

Deudney, Daniel. Binding Sovereigns: Authorities, Structures, and Geopolitics in Philadelphian Systems. In *State Sovereignty as Social Construct*, ed. Thomas Biersteker and Cynthia Weber. Cambridge: Cambridge University Press, 1996

Diamond, Larry. Rethinking Civil Society: Toward Democratic Consolidation. *Journal of Democracy* 5 (3) 1984: 5–17

Dinan, Desmond. *Ever Closer Union? An Introduction to the European Community.* Boulder: Lynne Rienner Publishers, 1994

Dockrill, Michael and J. Douglas Gould. *Peace Without Promise: Britain and the Peace Conferences, 1919–1923.* Hamden, CT: Archon Books, 1980

Donnelly, Jack. International Human Rights: A Regime Analysis. *International Organization* 40 (3) 1984: 599–642

International Human Rights. Boulder: Westview Press, 1998

Dunne, Timothy. *Inventing International Society: a History of the English School.* London: Macmillan, 1998

Elliot, T. A. *Us and Them: A Study in Group Consciousness.* Aberdeen, Australia: Aberdeen University Press, 1986

Estebanez, Maria Amor Martin. The High Commissioner on National Minorities: Development of the Mandate. In *The OSCE in the Maintenance of Peace and Security,* ed. Michal Bothe, Natalino Ronzitu and Allan Rosas. The Hague: Kluwer Law International, 1997

Eyck, Frank. *The Revolutions of 1848–49.* New York: Barnes and Noble Books, 1972

Falk, Richard. Contending Approaches to World Order. *Journal of International Affairs* 31 (Fall/Winter) 1977: 171–98

Fejtö, François. *Requiem Pour un Empire Défunt: Histoire de la Destruction de l'Autriche-Hongrie.* Paris: Lieu commun, 1992

Ferrero, Guglielmo. *The Reconstruction of Europe: Tallyrand and the Congress of Vienna. 1814–1815.* New York: G. P. Putnam and Sons, 1941

Finnemore, Martha. *National Interests in International Society.* Ithaca: Cornell University Press, 1996

Finnemore, Martha and Kathryn Sikkink. International Norm Dynamics and Political Change. *International Organization* 52 (4) 1998: 887–917

Flynn, Gregory and Henry Farrell. Piecing Together the Democratic Peace: The CSCE. Norms and the Construction of Security in Post-Cold War Europe. *International Organization* 53 (3) 1993: 505–35

Franck, Thomas. Legitimacy in the International System. *The American Journal of International Law* 82. 1988: 705–59

The Power of Legitimacy Among Nations. New York: Oxford University Press, 1990

Franklin, Julian. *John Locke and the Theory of Sovereignty: Mixed Monarchy and the Right of Resistance in the Political Thought of the English Revolution.* Cambridge: Cambridge University Press, 1991

Fried, Albert. ed. *A Day of Dedication: the Essential Writings and Speeches of Woodrow Wilson.* New York: Macmillan Press, 1965

Friedrich, Carl. The Political Theory of the New Democratic Constitutions. In *Constitutions and Constitutional Trends Since World War II,* ed. Arnold Zurcher. New York: New York University Press, 1955

Garvey, Jack. Toward a Reformulation of International Refugee Law. *Harvard International Law Journal* 26 (2) 1985: 483–500

Gellner, Ernest. *Nations and Nationalism.* Ithaca: Cornell University Press, 1983

Ghils, Paul. International Civil Society: International Non-Governmental Organizations in the International System. *International Social Science Journal* 44 (133) 1992: 417–32

Gilpin, Robert. *War and Change in World Politics*. Princeton: Princeton University Press, 1981

Gisch, H. The European Parliamentary Union (EPU). In *Documents on the History of European Integration*, vol. IV, ed. W. Lopgens and W. Loth. New York: De Bruyter, 1991

Glenny, Misha. *The Fall of Yugoslavia: The Third Balkan War*. London: Penguin, 1992

Goldstein, Erik. *Winning the Peace: British Diplomatic Strategy, Peace Planning, and the Paris Peace Conference, 1916–1920*. Oxford: Clarendon Press, 1991

Gong, Gerrit. *The Standard of Civilization in International Society*. Oxford: Oxford University Press, 1984

Goodwin-Gill, Guy. *The Refugee in International Law*. Oxford: Oxford University Press, 1996

Gordenker, Leon. *Refugees in International Politics*. New York: Columbia University Press, 1987

Gregg, Robert W. *About Face?: The United States and the United Nations*. Boulder: Lynne Rienner Publishers, 1993

Grenville, J. A. S. *Europe Reshaped: 1848–1878*. Sussex: Harvester Press, 1976

Grieco, Joseph. Anarchy and the Limits of Cooperation: A Realist Critique of the Newest Liberal Institutionalism. *International Organization* 42 (3) 1988: 485–508

Griffiths, Stephen Iwan. *Nationalism and Ethnic Conflict: Threats to European Security*. SIPRI Research Report 5. Oxford: Oxford University Press, 1993

Haas, Ernst. The Balance of Power: Prescription, Concept, or Propaganda. *World Politics* 5 1953: 442–77

Hall, John. *International Orders*. Cambridge: Polity Press, 1996

Halliday, Fred. International Society as Homogeneity: Burke, Marx, Fukuyama, *Millennium* 21 (3) 1992: 435–61

Hay, Denys. 1968. *Europe: The Emergence of an Idea*. Edinburgh. Edinburgh University Press

Heater, Derek. *National Self-Determination: Woodrow Wilson and his Legacy*. New York: St. Martin's Press. 1994

Hegel, Georg Wilhelm Friedrich. *The Science of Logic*, vol. I. London: George Allen and Unwin, 1929

Henkin, Louis. *How Nations Behave: Law and Foreign Policy*. New York: Columbia University Press, 1979

Heraclides, Alexis. *Helsinki II and its Aftermath: The Making of the CSCE into an International Organization*. New York: Pinter Publishers, 1993

Hobbes, Thomas. *Leviathan*. Baltimore: Penguin, 1968

Hobsbawm, E. J. *Nations and Nationalism Since 1780: Programme. Myth. Reality*. Cambridge: Cambridge University Press, 1992

Holborn, Louise. ed. *War and Peace Aims of the United Nations, January 1, 1943–September 1, 1945*, vol. II. Boston: World Peace Foundation, 1948

The International Refugee Organization: its History and Work, 1946–52. Oxford: Oxford University Press, 1956

Refugees: A Problem of Our Time. The Work of the United Nations High Commissioner on Refugees, 1951–1972, 2 vols. Netuchen, NJ: The Scarecrow Press, 1975

Holsti, Kalevi. *Peace and War: Armed Conflicts and International Order, 1648–1989*. Cambridge: Cambridge University Press, 1991

House, Edward Mandell. *The Intimate Papers of Colonel House*, vol. III, ed. Charles Seymour. New York: Houghton Mifflin Company, 1928

Huber, Konrad. The CSCE HCNM. In *Minorities: the New Europe's Old Issue*, ed. Ian Cuthberton and Jane Leibowitz. New York: Institute for East–West Studies, 1993

Averting Inter-Ethnic Conflict: An Analysis of the CSCE High Commissioner on National Minorities in Estonia, January–July 1993. Working Paper Series of the Conflict Resolution Program of the Carter Center of Emory University, 1994

Hudson, Manley Ottmer. The Protection of Minorities and Natives in Transferred Territories. In *What Really Happened at Paris: The Story of the Peace Conference, 1918–1919 by American Delegates*, ed. Edward Mandell House and Charles Seymour. New York: Charles Scribner's Sons, 1921

Huntington, Samuel. *The Clash of Civilizations and the Remaking of World Order*. New York: Simon & Schuster, 1996

Hurrell, Andrew. International Society and the Study of Regimes: A Reflective Approach. In *Regime Theory and International Relations*, edited by Volker Rittberger. New York: Oxford University Press, 1993

Society and Anarchy in International Relations. In *International Society and the Development of International Relations Theory*, ed. B. A. Roberson. London: Continuum, 2002

Hyde-Price, Adrian. *The International Politics of East Central Europe*. Manchester: Manchester University Press, 1996

Íjgyártó, István. Codification of Minority Rights. In *Minorities: The New Europe's Old Issue*, ed. Ian Cuthbertson and Jane Leibowitz. New York: Institute for East–West Studies, 1993

Ikenberry, G. John. Liberal Hegemony. In *International Order and the Future of World Politics*, ed. T. V. Paul and John Hall. Cambridge: Cambridge University Press, 1999

After Victory: Institutions, Strategic Restraint, and the Rebuilding of Order After Major Wars. Princeton: Princeton University Press, 2001

Israel, Fred. ed. *Major Peace Treaties of Modern History, 1648–1967*, vol. II. New York: Chelsea House Publishers, 1967

Jackson, Robert. Pluralism and International Political Theory. *Review of International Studies* 18 (3) 1992: 271–81

International Community Beyond the Cold War. In *Beyond Westphalia: State Sovereignty and International Intervention*, ed. Gene Lyons and Michael Mastanduno. Baltimore: The Johns Hopkins University Press, 1995

Boundaries and International Society. In *International Society and the Development of International Relations Theory*, ed. B. A. Roberson. London: Continuum, 2002

James, Alan. International Society. *British Journal of International Studies* 4 (2) 1978: 91–106

Janowsky, Oscar. *Nationalities and National Minorities*. New York: Macmillan Press, 1945

Jaworsky, John. Nationalities Policy and Potential for Inter-Ethnic Conflict in Ukraine. In *Managing Diversity in Plural Societies: Minorities, Migration and Nation-Building in Post-Communist Europe*, ed. Magda Opalski. Ontario: Forum Eastern Europe, 1998

Jervis, Robert. Security Regimes. In *International Regimes*, ed. Stephen Krasner. Ithaca: Cornell University Press, 1983

Joll, James. *The Origins of the First World War*. New York: Longman, 1984

Kaplan, Robert. *The Coming Anarchy: Shattering the Dreams of the Post Cold War*. New York: Random House, 2000

Kavinoky, Edward H. and Julian Park. eds. *My Friends: Twenty-Eight History Making Speeches*. Buffalo, NY: Foster & Stewart, 1945

Keck, Margaret and Kathryn Sikkink. *Activists Beyond Borders: Advocacy Networks in International Politics*. Ithaca: Cornell University Press, 1998

Kemp, Walter. ed. *Quiet Diplomacy in Action: The OSCE High Commissioner on National Minorities*. The Hague: Kluwer Law International, 2001

Kennedy, David. The New Stream. In *International Rules: Approaches from International Law and International Relations*, ed. Robert Beck, Anthony Arend and Robert Vander Lugt. New York: Oxford University Press, 1996

Kent, Marian. ed. *The Great Powers and the end of the Ottoman Empire*. London: Frank Cass, 1996

Keohane, Robert. A Functional Theory of Regimes. In *International Regimes*, ed. Stephen Krasner. Ithaca: Cornell University Press, 1982

After Hegemony: Cooperation and Discord in the World Political Economy. Princeton: Princeton University Press, 1984

Multilateralism: An Agenda for Research. *International Journal* 45 (4) 1990: 731–64

Sovereignty, Interdependence, and International Institutions. In *Ideas and Ideals: Essays on Politics in Honor of Stanley Hoffman*, ed. Linda B. Miller and Michael Joseph Smith. Boulder: Westview Press, 1993

Keohane, Robert O. and Stanley Hoffmann. Institutional Change in Europe in the 1980s. In *The New European Community: Decisionmaking and Institutional Change*, ed. Robert O. Keohane and Stanley Hoffmann. Boulder: Westview Press, 1991

Keohane, Robert and Joseph Nye. *Power and Interdependence: World Politics in Transition*. Boston: Little, Brown, and Co. 1977

Keylor, William. *The Twentieth Century World: An International History*. Oxford: Oxford University Press, 2001

Kissinger, Henry. *A World Restored: Metternich, Castlereagh and the Problems of Peace, 1812–1822*. Boston: Houghton Mifflin, 1959

Knock, Thomas. *To End All Wars: Woodrow Wilson and the Quest for a New World Order*. New York: Oxford University Press, 1992

Krasner, Stephen. State Power and the Structure of International Trade. *World Politics* 28 (3) 1976: 317–47

Sovereignty, Regimes and Human Rights. In *Regime Theory and International Relations*, ed. Volker Rittberger. New York: Oxford University Press, 1993

Sovereignty and Intervention. In *Beyond Westphalia? State Sovereignty and International Intervention*, ed. Gene M. Lyons and Michael Mastanduno. Baltimore: The Johns Hopkins University Press, 1995

Globalization and Sovereignty. In *States and Sovereignty in the Global Economy*, ed. David Smith, Dorothy Solinger and Steven Topik. New York: Routledge, 1999

Sovereignty: Organized Hypocrisy. Princeton: Princeton University Press, 1999

Kratochwil, Friedrich. Of Systems, Boundaries, and Territoriality. *World Politics* 39 (1) 1986: 27–52

Krol, M. Where East Meets West. *Journal of Democracy* 6 (1) 1985: 37–43

Kymlicka, Wil. Ethnic Relations and Western Political Theory. In *Managing Diversity in Plural Societies: Minorities, Migration and Nation-Building in Post-Communist Europe*, ed. Magda Opalski. Ontario: Forum Eastern Europe, 1998

Ladas, Stephen. *The Exchange of Minorities: Bulgaria, Greece, Turkey*. New York, 1932

Lamborn, Alan. Theory and the Politics in World Politics. *International Studies Quarterly* 41 (2) 1997: 187–214

Larrabee, F. Stephen. *Eastern European Security After the Cold War*. Santa Monica: RAND, 1993

League of Nations. *Protection of Linguistic, Racial, or Religious Minorities by the League of Nations*. Geneva: League of Nations, 1921

League of Nations Resolutions and Extracts. Minutes of the 37th Council, February, 1926

League of Nations Official Journal. Geneva: League of Nations, 1929

Lehne, Stefan. *The CSCE in the 1990s: Common European House or Potemkin Village?* Laxenburg. Austria: Austrian Institute for International Affairs, 1991

Link, Arthur. *Woodrow Wilson: Revolution, War and Peace*. Arlington Heights: Harlan Davidson, 1979

Lipgens, Walter. *A History of European Integration, vol. 1. 1945–1947*. Oxford: Clarendon Press, 1982

Lipschutz, Ronnie. Reconstructing World Politics: The Emergence of Global Civil Society. In *International Society After the Cold War: Anarchy and Order Reconsidered*, ed. Rick Fawn and Jeremy Larkins. New York: St. Martin's Press, 1996

Lloyd George, David. *British War Aims Statement on January 5, 1918* (Authorized version as issued by the British government.) London: R. Clay and Sons, 1918

War Memoirs, vol. II. London: Adhams, 1938

Loescher, Gil. *Beyond Charity: International Cooperation and the Global Refugee Crisis*. Oxford: Oxford University Press, 1993

The UNHCR and World Politics: A Perilous Path. Oxford: Oxford University Press, 2001

Loescher, Gil and John A. Scanlan. *Calculated Kindness: Refugees and America's Half-Open Door, 1945 to the Present*. New York: Free Press, 1986

Macartney, C. A. *National States and National Minorities*. New York: Russell & Russell, 1968 [1934]

MacIntyre, Alasdair. *After Virtue*. Notre Dame, IN: University of Notre Dame Press, 1984

Mandelbaum, Michael. Foreign Policy as Social Work. *Foreign Affairs*. January/February, 1996

Manning, C. A. W. *The Nature of International Society*. London: London School of Economics, 1962

March, James G. and Johan P. Olsen. The Institutional Dynamics of International Political Orders. In *Exploration and Contestation in the Study of World Politics*, ed. Peter Katzenstein *et al*. Cambridge, MA: MIT Press, 2000

Marrus, Michael. *The Unwanted: European Refugees in the Twentieth Century*. New York: Oxford University Press, 1985

Martin, Lawrence. *Peace Without Victory: Woodrow Wilson and the British Liberals*. New Haven: Yale University Press, 1958

Martin, Lisa. The Rational State Choice of Multilateralism. In *Multilateralism Matters: The Theory and Practice of an Institutional Form*, ed. John G. Ruggie. New York: Columbia University Press, 1993

An Institutionalist View: International Institutions and State Strategies. In *International Order and the Future of World Politics*, ed. T. V. Paul and John Hall. Cambridge: Cambridge University Press, 1999

Mason, John. *The Dissolution of the Austro-Hungarian Empire, 1867–1918*. London: Longman, 1985

Mayer, Arno. *Political Origins of the New Diplomacy, 1917–1918*, New York: Random House, 1970

McDougal, Walter. *France's Rhineland Diplomacy, 1914–1924: The Last Bid for a Balance of Power in Europe*. Princeton: Princeton University Press, 1978

McNeely, Connie. *Constructing the Nation-State: International Organization and Prescriptive Action*. Westport, CT: Greenwood Press, 1995

Mearsheimer, John. The False Promise of International Institutions. In *Theories of War and Peace*, ed. Michael Brown *et al*. Cambridge, MA: MIT Press, 1998

Meyer, John. The World Polity and the Authority of the Nation-State. In *Institutional Structure: Constituting the State, Society and the Individual*, ed. George Thomas *et al*. Newbury Park: Sage Publications, 1987

222

Meyer, John W. *et al.* World Society and the Nation-State, *American Journal of Sociology* 103 (1) 1997: 144–81

Mill, John Stuart. *Three Essays: Consideration on Representative Government, on Liberty, and the Subjugation of Women.* Oxford: Oxford University Press, 1975

Miller, David Hunter. *My Diary of the Peace Conference.* New York: Appeal Printing Company, 1924

Miller, Marion. The Approaches to European Institution-Building of Carlo Sforza, Italian Foreign Minister, 1947–1951. In *Building Postwar Europe: National Decisionmaking and European Institutions, 1948–1963*, ed. Ann Deighton. New York: St. Martins Press, 1995

Milward, Alan. *The European Rescue of the Nation State.* London: Routledge, 2000

Moore, Sara. *Peace Without Victory for the Allies, 1918–1932.* Oxford: Berg Publishers, 1994

Moravcsik, Andrew. Preferences and Power in the European Community: A Liberal Intergovernmentalist Approach. *Journal of Common Market Studies* 31 (4) 1993: 473–524

 Explaining International Human Rights Regimes: Liberal Theory and Western Europe. *European Journal of International Relations* 1 1995: 157–89

 Taking Preferences Seriously: A Liberal Theory of International Politics. *International Organization* 51 (4) 1997: 513–53

 The Choice for Europe: Social Purpose and State Power from Messina to Maastricht. Ithaca: Cornell University Press, 1998

 The Origins of Human Rights Regimes: Democratic Delegation in Postwar Europe. *International Organization* 54 (2) 2000: 217–52

Morgenthau, Hans. *Politics Among Nations: The Struggle for Power and Peace*, brief edition. New York: Knofp, 1973 [1948]

Möttöla, Kari. The OSCE: Institutional and Functional Developments in an Evolving European Security Order. In *The OSCE in the Maintenance of Peace and Security: Conflict Prevention, Crisis Management and Peaceful Settlement of Disputes*, ed. Michal Bothe, Natalino Ronzitu, and Allan Rosas. The Hague: Kluwer Law International, 1997

Müller, Harold. The Internationalization of Principles, Norms, and Rules by Governments: The Case of Security Regimes. In *Regime Theory and International Relations*, ed. Volker Rittberger. New York: Oxford University Press, 1993

Multilaterals Project, The Fletcher School, Tufts University. http://fletcher.tufts.edu/multilaterals.html.

Musgrave, Thomas. *Self Determination and National Minorities.* Oxford: Clarendon Press, 1997

Nardin, Terry. *Law, Morality, and the Relations of States.* Princeton: Princeton University Press, 1983

Neumann, William. *Making the Peace, 1941–1945: The Diplomacy of the Wartime Conferences.* Washington, DC: Foundation for Foreign Affairs, 1950

Nicholson, Harold. *The Congress of Vienna: A Study in Allied Unity, 1812–1822.* New York: Harcourt, Brace, 1946

223

Peacemaking 1919. London: Methuen, 1964

Olson, Mancur. *The Logic of Collective Action: Public Goods and the Theory of Groups*. Cambridge, MA: Harvard University Press, 1965

Organization for Security and Cooperation in Europe, www.osce.org/hcnm/documents/recommendations.

Osiander, Andreas. *The States System of Europe 1640–1990: Peacemaking and the Conditions of International Stability*. Oxford: Clarendon Press, 1994

Otunnu, Olara and Michael Doyle. *Peacemaking and Peacekeeping for the New Century*. New York: Roman and Littlefield, 1998

Owen, John M. IV. If Regime Type Doesn't Matter, Why Do States Act Like it Does? Paper presented at the annual meeting of the International Studies Association. Washington, DC, February 19, 1995

Packer, John. 2000. Making International Law Matter in Preventing Ethnic Conflict: A Practitioner's Perspective. *NYU Journal of International Law and Politics* 32 (3): 715–24

Parrott, Bruce. Perspectives on Postcommunist Democratization. In *Politics, Power, and the Struggle for Democracy in South-East Europe*, ed. Karen Dawisha and Bruce Parrott. Cambridge: Cambridge University Press, 1997

Parry, Clive. ed. Treaty of Osnabrück. In *The Consolidated Treaty Series*, vol. I, *1648–1649*. Dobbs Ferry, NY: Oceana, 1969

Pearson, Raymond. *National Minorities in Eastern Europe, 1848–1945*. New York: St. Martin's Press, 1983

Peterson, M. J. Transnational Activity, International Society and World Polity. *Millennium* 21 (3) 1992: 371–88

Pettai, Vello. Emerging Ethnic Democracy in Estonia and Latvia. In *Managing Diversity in Plural Societies: Minorities, Migration and Nation Building in Post-Communist Europe*, ed. Magda Opalski. Ontario: Forum Eastern Europe, 1998

Pevehouse, Jon. Democracy from the Outside-In? International Organizations and Democratization. *International Organization* 56 (3) 2002: 515–49

Pinder, John. *European Community: The Building of a Union*. Oxford: Oxford University Press, 1991

Posen, Barry R. *The Sources of Military Doctrine: France, Britain, and Germany Between the World Wars*. Ithaca: Cornell University Press, 1984

Preece, Jennifer Jackson. *National Minorities and the European Nation-States System*. Oxford: Oxford University Press, 1998

Puchala, Donald and Raymond Hopkins. International Regimes: Lessons from Inductive Analysis. In *International Regimes*, ed. Stephen D. Krasner. Ithaca: Cornell University Press, 1983

Putnam, Robert. Diplomacy and Domestic Politics: The Logic of Two-Level Games. *International Organization* 42 (3) 1988: 427–61

Ratner, Stephen. Does International Law Matter in Preventing Ethnic Conflict? *NYU Journal of International Law and Politics* 32 (3) 2000: 591–698

Rawls, John. *A Theory of Justice*. Cambridge, MA: Harvard University Press, 1999

Reus, Christian. The Constitutional Structure of International Society and the Nature of Fundamental Institutions. *International Organization* 51 (4) 1997: 555–89

Rich, Roland. Recognition of States: The Collapse of Yugoslavia and the Soviet Union. *European Journal of International Relations* 4 (1) 1993: 36–65

Riordan, Patrick. *The Politics of the Common Good.* Dublin, Ireland: Institute of Public Administration, 1996

Risse, Thomas and Kathryn Sikkink. The Socialization of International Human Rights Norms into Domestic Practices: Introduction. In *The Power of Human Rights: International Norms and Domestic Change,* ed. Thomas Risse, Stephen Ropp, and Kathryn Sikkink. Cambridge: Cambridge University Press, 1999

Risse-Kappan, Thomas. *Bringing Transnational Relations Back In: Non-State Actors, Domestic Structures and International Institutions.* Cambridge: Cambridge University Press, 1995

   Cooperation among Democracies: The European Influence on U.S. Foreign Policy. Princeton: Princeton University Press, 1997

Roberts, Priscilla. *Revolutions of 1848: A Social History.* Princeton: Princeton University Press, 1971

Robertson, A. H. *The Council of Europe: Its Structure, Functions and Achievements.* London: Stevens and Sons, 1961

Robertson, A. H. and J. G. Merrills. *Human Rights in Europe: A Study of the European Convention on Human Rights.* Manchester: Manchester University Press, 1993

Robinson, Nehemiah. *Convention Relating to the Status of Refugees: Its History, Significance and Contents.* New York: Institute of Jewish Affairs, 1952

Rosenau, James N. Governance, Order, and Change in World Politics. In *Governance Without Government: Order and Change in World Politics,* ed. James N. Rosenau and Ernst-Otto Czempiel. Cambridge: Cambridge University Press, 1992

Rousseau, Jean-Jacques. *Rousseau's Political Writings,* ed. Alan Ritter and Julia Conaway. Bondanella, NY: W. W. Norton and Co., 1988

Royal Institute of International Affairs. *Nationalism: A Report.* New York: Oxford University Press, 1939

Ruggie, John. International Regimes, Transactions, and Change: Embedded Liberalism in the Postwar Economic Order. In *International Regimes,* ed. Stephen Krasner. Ithaca: Cornell University Press, 1983

   Continuity and Transformation in the World Polity. In *Neorealism and its Critics,* ed. Robert O. Keohane. New York: Columbia University Press, 1986

   Multilateralism: The Anatomy of an Institution. *International Organization* 46 (2) 1992: 561–98

   Territoriality and Beyond: Problematizing Modernity in International Relations. *International Organization* 47 (1) 1993: 139–74

   Consolidating the European Pillar: The Key to NATO's Future. *Washington Quarterly* 20 1997: 109–4

Salomon, Kim. *Refugees in the Cold War: Toward a New International Refugee Regime in the Early Postwar*. Lund: Lund University Press, 1991

Sandholtz, Wayne and John Zysman. Recasting the European Bargain. *World Politics* 42 (1) 1989: 95–128

Savage, David G. Haitian Intercept Policy Backed by High Court, *Los Angeles Times*, June 22 1993

Scheinman, Ronald. Refugees: Goodbye to the Good Old Days. *Annals of the American Academy of Political and Social Science* Special Issue. *The Global Refugee Problem: U.S. and World Response*. Beverly Hills: Sage Publications, 1983

Schimmelfennig, Frank. The Community Trap: Liberal Norms, Rhetorical Action, and the Eastern Enlargement of the European Union. *International Organization* 55 (1) 2001: 47–80

Schöpflin, George. 1996. Nationalism and Ethnic Minorities in Post-Communist Europe. In *Europe's New Nationalism: States and Minorities in Conflict*, ed. Richard Caplan and John Feffer. Oxford: Oxford University Press, 1996

Schroeder, Paul. The Transformation of Political Thinking, 1787–1848. In *Coping With Complexity in the International System*, ed. Jack Snyder and Robert Jervis. Boulder: Westview Press, 1993

Schuman, Frederick L. *The Nazi Dictatorship: a Study in Social Pathology and the Politics of Fascism*. New York: Knopf, 1937

Schweller, Randall. Bandwagoning for Profit: Bringing the Revisionist State Back In. *International Security* 19 (1), 1994: 72–107

Seton-Watson, Hugh. *Nations and States: An Enquiry into the Origins of Nations and The Politics of Nationalism*. Boulder: Westview Press, 1977

Sharp, Alan. *The Versailles Settlement: Peacemaking in Paris, 1919*. New York: St. Martin's Press, 1991

Shields, Mark. Hungary Backs its Exiles. *The Independent*. August 20, 1992

Sikkink, Kathryn. The Power of Principled Ideas: Human Rights Policies in the United States and Western Europe. In *Ideas and Foreign Policy: Beliefs, Institutions, and Political Change*, ed. Judith Goldstein and Robert Keohane. Ithaca: Cornell University Press, 1993

Simpson, A. W. Brian. *Human Rights and the End of Empire*. Oxford: Oxford University Press, 2001

Simpson, John H. *The Refugee Problem: Report of a Survey*. London, 1939

Singer, J. David. The Incomplete Theorist: Insights Without Evidence. In *Contending Approaches to International Politics*, ed. Klaus E. Knorr and James N. Rosenau. Princeton: Princeton University Press, 1969

Singer, Max and Aaron Wildavsky. *The Real World Order: Zones of Peace, Zones of Turmoil*. Chatham, NJ: Chatham House Publishers, 1996

Skocpol, Theda. Bringing the State Back In: Strategies of Analysis in Current Research. In *Bringing the State Back In*, ed. Peter Evans, Dietrich Rueschemeyer, and Theda Skocpol. Cambridge: Cambridge University Press, 1985

Skran, Claudena. *Refugees in Inter-War Europe*. New York: Oxford University Press, 1995

Snyder, Jack. Averting Anarchy in the New Europe. *International Security* 14 (4) 1990: 5–41

Sobel, Richard. U.S. and European Attitudes Toward Intervention in the Former Yugoslavia: *Mourir pour la Bosnie?*. In *The World and Yugoslavia's Wars*, ed. Richard Ullman. Washington, DC: Council on Foreign Relations, 1996

Stein, Arthur. Coordination and Collaboration: Regimes in an Anarchic World. *International Organization* 36 (2) 1982: 299–324

Steinberg, James B. International Involvement in the Yugoslav Conflict. In *Enforcing Restraint: Collective Intervention in Internal Conflicts*, ed. Lori Fisler Damrosch. New York: Council on Foreign Relations Press, 1993

Steiner, Henry and Phillip Alston. *International Human Rights in Context: Law, Politics, Morals*. Oxford: Clarendon Press, 1996

Stirk, Peter. *A History of European Integration Since 1914*. London: Pinter, 1986

Stoessinger, John. *The Refugee and the World Community*. Minneapolis: University of Minnesota Press, 1956

The UN and the Superpowers. New York: Random House, 1966

Stroller, Gary B. *The League of Nations, 1919–1929*. Garden City Park, NY: Avery Publishing Group, 1995

Szasz, Paul. Current Developments: The Protection of Human Rights Through the Dayton/Paris Agreement on Bosnia. *American Journal of International Law* 90 1996: 304–13

Protecting Human and Minority Rights in Bosnia: A Documentary Survey of International Proposals. *California Western International Law Journal* 25 (2) 1994: 259–88

Tapié, Victor. *The Rise and Fall of the Hapsburg Monarchy*. New York: Praeger, 1971

Taylor, A. J. P. *The Struggle for Mastery in Europe, 1848–1918*. Oxford: Oxford University Press, 1986 [1954]

Temperley, Harold. *A History of the Peace Conference*, 5 vols., London: Oxford University Press, 1969 [1920]

The Foreign Policy of Canning, 1822–1827: England, the Neo-Holy Alliance and the New World. London: G. Bell and Sons, 1925

Ullman, Richard H. ed. *The World and Yugoslavia's Wars*. Washington, DC: Council on Foreign Relations, 1996

United Nations Department of Public Information. *Magna Carta for Refugees*. New York, 1951

United Nations, Documents A/C.3/529; A/C.3/SR; A/C.3/SR.230–269; A/C.3/SR.323; A/C.3/SR.323 and 325; A/C.3/SR.325; A/C.3/SR.329; A/C.3/SR.334; A/C.3/VR 28, June 28, 1946; A/C.3/VR. February 4, 1946; Document E/600, paragraph 46; E/AC.32/SR.3; E/AC.32/SR.33; E/AC.32/SR.5; E/REF/60. May 2, 1946; E/REF/73; E/SR.283–343; E/SR.283–343; E/SR.283–343

United Nations General Assembly. *Official Records*, 1st session. Part II, 1946

United Nations High Commissioner on Refugees. *The State of the World's Refugees: Fifty Years of Humanitarian Action*. Oxford: Oxford University Press, 2000

Van der Steol, Max. The Protection of Minorities in the OSCE Region. Speech given at a meeting of the OSCE Parliamentary Assembly. Antalya. 12 April, 2000

Vernant, Jacques. *The Refugee In the Post-War World*. New Haven: Yale University Press, 1953

Vincent, R. J. *Human Rights and International Relations*. Cambridge: Cambridge University Press, 1986

   Western Conceptions of a Universal Moral Order, *British Journal of International Studies* 4 (1) 1978: 20–46.

von Glahn, Gerhard. *Law Among Nations: An Introduction to Public International Law*. Boston: Allyn and Bacon, 1996

Walker, Lee. Nationalism and Ethnic Conflict in the Post-Soviet Transition. In *Ethnic Conflict in the Post-Soviet World: Case Studies and Analysis*, ed. Leokadia Drobizheva *et al*. London: M.E. Sharpe, 1996

Wallace, William. *The Transformation of Western Europe*. London: Royal Institute of International Affairs, 1990

Waltz, Kenneth. *Theory of International Politics*. New York: Random House, 1979

Walworth, Arthur. *Wilson and His Peacemakers: American Diplomacy at the Paris Peace Conference, 1919*. New York: Norton, 1986

Ward, David. *1848: The Fall of Metternich and the Year of Revolution*. New York: Weybright and Talley, 1970

Watson, Alan. Hedley Bull, *States Systems and International Societies*. Review of *International Studies* 13: April 1987: 147–53

   The Evolution of International Society. London: Routledge, 1992

Webster, Charles. *The Congress of Vienna, 1814–1815*. London: Thames and Hudson, 1934

Weiss, Paul. ed. *Travaux Préparatoires of the Convention Relating to the Status of Refugees*, 1951

Weiss, Thomas, David Forsythe, and Roger Coate. *The United Nations and Changing World Politics*, 2nd edition. Boulder: Westview Press, 1997

Weston, Burns, Human Rights. In *Human Rights in the World Community*, ed. R. P. Claude and B. J. Weston. Philadelphia: University of Pennsylvania Press, 1990

Wheeler, Nicholas. *Saving Strangers: Humanitarian Intervention in International Society*. Oxford: Oxford University Press, 2000

Wheeler, Nicholas and Tim Dunne. Hedley Bull's Pluralism of the Intellect and Solidarism of the Will. *International Affairs* 72 (1) 1996: 91–107

Wheeler-Bennett, John. *The Semblance of Peace: The Political Settlement After the Second World War*. New York: St. Martin's Press, 1972

White, N. D. *Keeping the Peace: The United Nations and the Maintenance of International Peace and Security*. Manchester: Manchester University Press, 1997

Wight, Martin. *Systems of States*. Leicester: Leicester University Press, 1977
  International Theory: Three Traditions, ed. Gabrielle Wight and Brian Porter.
  Leicester: Leicester University Press, 1991
Wolfers, Arnold. *Discord and Collaboration: Essays on International Politics.*
  Baltimore: The Johns Hopkins University Press, 1962
Woodward, Susan. *Balkan Tragedy: Chaos and Dissolution After the Cold War.*
  Washington, DC: The Brookings Institution, 1995
  Diaspora, or the Dangers of Disunification? Putting the "Serbian Model" into
  Perspective. In *The New European Diasporas: National Minorities and Conflict
  in Eastern Europe*, ed. Michael Mandelbaum. New York: Council on Foreign
  Relations Press, 2000
  Compromised Sovereignty to Create Sovereignty: Is Dayton Bosnia a Futile
  Exercise or an Emerging Model? In *Problematic Sovereignty: Contested Rules
  and Political Possibilities*, ed. Stephen Krasner. New York: Columbia Univer-
  sity Press, 2001
Young, Oran. International Regimes: Toward a New Theory of Institutions.
  World Politics 39 (1) 1986: 104–22
Zaagman, Rob and Hannie Zaal. The CSCE High Commissioner on National
  Minorities: Prehistory and Negotiations. In *The Challenges of Change: The
  Helsinki Summit of the CSCE and its Aftermath*, ed. Arie Bloed. Dordrecht:
  Martinus Nijhoff, 1994
Zaal, Hannie. The CSCE High Commissioner. *Helsinki Monitor* 4 1992: 33–37
Zeman, Z. A. B. *The Break-Up of the Habsburg Empire, 1914–1918*. Oxford: Oxford
  University Press, 1961
Zolberg, Aristide. The Formation of New States as a Refugee-Generating Pro-
  cess. In *Annals of the American Academy of Political and Social Science*. Special
  Issue. *The Global Refugee Problem: U.S. and World Response*. Beverly Hills:
  Sage Publications, 1983

Index

CAMBRIDGE STUDIES IN INTERNATIONAL RELATIONS